Law as Process

Law as Process

An Anthropological Approach

Sally Falk Moore

Professor of Anthropology
University of California, Los Angeles

Routledge & Kegan Paul
London, Henley and Boston

First published in 1978
by Routledge & Kegan Paul Ltd
39 Store Street,
London WC1E 7DD,
Broadway House,
Newtown Road,
Henley-on-Thames,
Oxon RG9 1EN and
9 Park Street,
Boston, Mass. 02108, USA
Set in 10 on 12 pt Baskerville by
Computacomp (UK) Ltd., Fort William, Scotland
and printed in Great Britain by
Redwood Burn Ltd
Trowbridge and Esher
copyright Sally Falk Moore 1978

British Library Cataloguing in Publication Data

Moore, Sally Falk
Law as process.
1. Ethnological jurisprudence
I. Title
340.1'15   GN493   77-30241

ISBN 0-7100-8758-6

Contents

Acknowledgments

The author wishes to thank Professors John Middleton and M. G. Smith for encouraging her to publish this book, and the Yale Department of Anthropology for affording a hospitable setting in which to write the Introduction.

Introduction

To sum up, we can therefore say that the State is a special organ whose responsibility it is to work out certain representations which hold good for the collectivity. These representations are distinguished from the other collective representations by their higher degree of consciousness and reflection.

Emile Durkheim, *Professional Ethics and Civic Morals* (tr. C. Brookfield)
(London, Routledge & Kegan Paul, 1957:50)

The central theme that links the essays in this book is that the same social processes that prevent the total regulation of a society also reshape and transform efforts at partial regulation. The making of rules and social and symbolic order is a human industry matched only by the manipulation, circumvention, remaking, replacing, and unmaking of rules and symbols in which people seem almost equally engaged. There is a basic tension between the idea that law epitomizes manmade, intentional action, and constitutes the means by which a conscious and rational attempt to direct society can be undertaken, and most thought in the social sciences, that there are underlying causes of social behavior which are not fully in the conscious control of the actors, yet which are the core of what the social scientist studies.

A conventional self-image of law in the American legal profession is that law constitutes the intentionally constructed framework of social order. Yet everyone in the profession knows that the practice of law by lawyers is by and large an exercise in the manipulation of 'the system.' A recent handbook for law students (Kinyon 1971:9) says,

'The Law' in the broad sense of our whole legal system with its institutions, rules, procedures, remedies, etc., is society's attempt, through government, to control human behavior and prevent anarchy, violence, oppression and injustice by providing and enforcing orderly, rational, fair and workable alternatives to the indiscriminate use of force by individuals or groups in advancing or protecting their interests and resolving their controversies. 'Law' seeks to achieve both social order and individual protection, freedom and justice.

Certainly this is a fair statement of the ideology of law in America as taught in the law schools and repeated in a variety of legal and political institutions. It is not surprising that a professional should depict law as a conscious 'attempt' by 'society' to be rational and fair, orderly and just, and a bulwark against anarchy. This logic puts legal institutions and the state at the core of all social discipline. And, since the description was written by a word-careful lawyer, one also can infer that the word 'attempt' is introduced for a purpose and not by chance. It acknowledges the possibility of irrationality in the system or unfairness in the practice, without conceding anything of the nobility of purpose and unity of the whole. Manmade government/law is deemed responsible for social order. An active Hobbesian war of every man against every man is hinted at darkly as the violent alternative. Conscious goals move an anthropomorphized society.

But a moment's reflection pops the rhetorical balloon. Ordinary experience indicates that law and legal institutions can only effect a degree of intentional control of society, greater at some times and less at others, or more with regard to some matters than others. That limited degree of control and predictability is daily inflated in the folk models of lawyers and politicians all over the world. No week passes in America without extensive public claims being made by political figures for the beneficial effects to be expected from new legislation they sponsor, as if there were no possible uncertainties in the results. Off the record, they are often far less sanguine about the likelihood of success.

The contradiction between the notion of an intentionally directed society, and the sociology of causality is nowhere more evident than in the fieldwork study of what I call 'the reglementary processes,' all those attempts to organize and control behavior through the use of explicit rules. To study rule-orders in action, it is necessary to deal simultaneously with the explicit rules, the occasions on which they are communicated and invoked, and with actual behavior addressed by the rules, the contexts in which it takes place, and the ideas and assumptions that accompany it. The social reality is a peculiar mix of action congruent with rules (and there may be numerous conflicting or competing rule-orders) and other action that is choice-making, discretionary, manipulative, sometimes inconsistent, and sometimes conflictual. Since 'systems' of normative rules are 'used' in social life, they have to be such as to accommodate that action complex. Hence it is inherent in the nature of legal systems that they can never become fully coherent, consistent wholes which successfully regulate all of social life. One formal, logical manifestation of this has often been commented on, namely that legal rule-systems include general principles of application and interpretation which can themselves be interpreted in a variety of ways. Such rule-systems invariably include ambiguities, inconsistencies, gaps, conflicts and the like. But more important from·the point of view of sociological analysis are two inherent characteristics of law in society which substantially prevent the full systematic rationalization of any legal system. One is the piecemeal historical process by which legal systems are constructed (see Transformation I, below). The other is the not fully controllable aggregate effect of the multiplicity of reglementary sources and arenas of action (see Transformation II, below). These multiple sites are particularly visible in complex societies. The impossibility of durable full systematization has implications for the analysis of reglementation and for applied planning and administration.

The analytic import is that if one is dealing with *partial* order and *partial* control of social life by rules, then any analysis which focuses entirely on the orderly and the rule-bound is limited indeed, and does not place the normative in the context of the whole complex of action, which certainly includes much more than conformity to or deviance from normative rules. A rule-focused compliance/deviance approach reduces the colorful hurlyburly of social life and the dynamic logic it has for the actors to so arid a pair of pre-selected and pre-interpreted obedience categories, that understanding of what is actually going on on the ground may be blocked. To recognize fully that legal rules are

3

merely elements of a cultural part-order implies that any attempt to reduce a whole legal 'system' to a few simple key propositions tells very little about how the 'system' worked, and may even be quite misleading.

If partial rule by rules is all that can ever be managed, the fact has considerable import for planning and regulation. Awareness of the limitations on regulation should affect the research objective of those responsible for drawing up rules, predicting their effects, and monitoring their application. A central concern of any rule-maker should be the identification of those social processes which operate outside the rules, or which cause people to use rules, or abandon them, bend them, reinterpret them, side-step them, or replace them. To recognize that such processes are inescapable aspects of the use of rule-systems and to try to understand as much as possible about the conditions of their operation would probably be far more effective than taking the view that such activities might be fully controlled simply by tighter drafting of 'loophole-less' legislation. Social transactions usually take place in the service of objectives to which legal rules are merely ancillary shapers, enablers, or impediments. Conformity to the rules is seldom in itself the central objective.

This introduction will enlarge on some of these points to show the general approach that lies behind the essays in this book and to suggest some of the directions for further study to which such a point of view might lead. The issues are classical ones which are continually recast and reseen as the preoccupations of social science shift. Two related propositions which have appeared and reappeared in the scholarly literature on law and their analysis by earlier writers will serve as illustrations of these issues: one is that legal systems are logical systems, thus their basic character can be reduced to a few fundamental jural postulates. The other is that while tradition and culture shape the law of primitive societies, intellect and intention shape the law of modern societies.

Has modern legal thought evolved from an earlier phase of 'magically conditioned formalism and irrationality ... to increasingly specialized juridical and logical rationality and systematization?' (Weber 1954:304). Weber thought so when he described his 'theoretically constructed stages' of legal development. In his *Theory of Social and Economic Organization* Weber attributed a pivotal place to rational rules, legal and bureaucratic (1964:329–41). He made the development of systematic norms and procedures the central technical achievement of modern organizations, and also saw such rules as a necessity to modern transactions.

Weber's formula was essentially that the more the administrative machinery of government became rational and bureaucratic, the more logical and systematic would the legal system become, both procedurally and substantively. Legal rationality for him meant: (1) that law-making or law-finding be 'controlled by the intellect' and that it involve (2) the application of 'general norms' (1954:63). But he also argued that the development of the particular systems of law that appeared in the West was closely tied both to political history and to the requirements of capitalistic enterprise (1954:224,267,304–5).

After reviewing the diversity of lines of legal development in the Occident, making the point that the evolution of the phenomenon of 'rationalization' was multilinear, even in the West, Weber argues (1954:304–5) that,

> All these events have to a very large extent been caused by concrete political factors which have only the remotest analogies elsewhere in the world.... Economic conditions have, as we have seen, everywhere played an important role, but they have nowhere been decisive alone and by themselves. To the extent that they contributed to the formation of the specifically modern features of present-day occidental law, the direction in which they worked has been by and large the following: To those who had interests in the commodity market, the rationalization and systematization of the law in general and, with certain reservations to be stated later, the increasing calculability of the functioning of the legal process in particular, constituted one of the most important conditions for the existence of economic enterprise intended to function with stability and, especially of capitalistic enterprise, which cannot do without legal security.

Thus Weber emphasizes the simultaneous proliferation of rational rules in several nexus of relations: in the centralized state and its administrative bureaucracy, in other corporate groups, and in the arena of economic transactions. His use of the term 'rational' stresses that particular laws or juridical decisions were in the immediate sense of the actors' awareness a conscious product of the intellect. Yet his concurrent political/economic/historical interpretation suggests that the cumulative development of the legal system as a whole was ancillary to the long-term development of complex large-scale political and economic organization.

The paradox implied by Weber's reasoning is that the most self-conscious, intentional, goal-directed, professionally-wrought piece of rule-making is part of a much larger socio-economic development that is not in anyone's conscious control, and, for that matter, may not even be fully perceived by the actors. This paradox is inherent in the social anthropological analysis of law. It manifests itself in the discrepancy between the study of the logical-technical side of the rules and legal institutions, and the study of the actual part that reglementary activity plays in the social whole, in social life in-the-round, in which a great many other things are going on besides rule-declaring, rule-enforcing and dispute settlement.

The first essay in this book takes up an aspect of that theme, but not in evolutionary terms. It proposes a framework for social/cultural analysis which identifies 'processes of regularization' as a major category of ongoing activity in society. 'Processes of regularization' include all the ways in which conscious efforts are made to build and/or reproduce durable social and symbolic orders. Law is, of course, one product of these activities. Other countervailing activities are also ubiquitously at work which operate to reinterpret, replace, or alter these supposedly durable cultural forms whenever it is situationally advantageous to someone to do so. The continuous making and reiterating of social and symbolic order is seen as an active process, not as something which, once achieved, is fixed. The view is taken that existing orders are endlessly vulnerable to being unmade, remade, and transformed, and that even maintaining and reproducing themselves, staying as they are, should be seen as a process. To try to understand something about law and society in these terms is to address the question how such processes and counterprocesses operate together, and what the preconditions are for reproduction or transformation. It is far more than the study of a set of enforceable rules and the logical principles which may be inferred to lie behind them.

The study of law thus approached raises directly several critical, and thus far unresolvable, theoretical issues in anthropology. They have to do with norms, with time and with context. The exploration of these matters in particular ethnographies has provided us with much of what is known, and with a great residue of puzzles. The first of these issues is that of the relation of explicit rules, plans, symbols, and ideologies to social behavior. A second is the problem of analyzing the historical process, assessing which events matter sociologically and which subsequent occurrences are the consequence of which prior ones. The third is the problem of context, the kind and degree of systematic connection (if any) among the parts of some contemporaneous social/cultural whole. All of these are facets of one basic question, that of causality.

Since legislation is based on folk notions of social causality, on ideas of how to make things happen through the use of the power of government, these anthropological issues are not merely of academic interest. Much legislation today either does not achieve what it purports to set out to do, or when it does achieve specified goals, also spins off many side-effects that were not anticipated. Conventional explanations of failures or unexpected side-effects tend to attribute particular instances to inadequate information, or bad judgment, or political deception. That is as it may be in particular cases. But it is possible that there are also deeper causes of transformation that operate pervasively even under the best conditions of information, expertise, and relative political honesty.

In Western legal theory the sovereign power, the ultimate legal authority in a polity, can legislate on any matter, and can exercise control over any behavior within the state. But it must be clear to everyone that on this point legal theory and practical affairs are far apart. In legal theory, the power of law to control behavior can be infinite. In practical fact it is highly circumscribed. Yet the precise form that the socially determined limitations will take is not always clear in prospect. Neither politicians nor social scientists can fully, nor, often, even satisfactorily predict the consequences of legislation.

Legislation is intrusive. It is a tinkering with an ongoing social field that has areas of relatively autonomous activity and self-regulation. The intervenors, the personnel of the state itself, also constitute a social field which is impelled in part by ongoing internal processes of its own, most notably that of political competition. The appropriateness and efficacy of a specific policy measure for declared public ends may be quite different from its appropriateness or efficacy in a variety of political arena . Both the social field of the intervenors and the social fields tinkered with by legislation (or administrative regulation) are moving all the time, partly connected, partly autonomous. The second paper in this book proposes the 'semi-autonomous social field' as a perspective from which to study law and social change. It argues that the cumulative effect of legislative tinkering is a compound of preconditions in the regulated social field itself, direct effects of the legislation, secondary effects, and, also, the direct and secondary effects of many other simultaneous events and processes which were not necessarily legislated into being. Given this complex of contingent variables, it is not surprising that prediction is often difficult, nor that consistently successful regulation of the whole of social life is utterly impossible.

The field study of law in rapidly changing contemporary societies puts before the anthropologist, with an immediacy from which he cannot turn away, the spectacle of attempts at intentional control and planning, and publicly rationalized imperative decision-making. These are subjects which have not occupied most anthropologists (with a few exceptions) in the past. As a discipline, anthropology has more historical examples than useful theories about these matters. Law seen being made, or seen being 'used' in the world today confronts anthropology with a kind of situational datum for which past techniques of cultural or structural study are more than helpful, necessary, but not sufficient. Social anthropology has been turning away from a heavily normative-descriptive orientation for many decades. Though such an approach continues to serve some as a convenient whipping boy, it is far less used as an ethnographic style. An interest in history, in social change, and in choice-making has given the traditional and the customary (whether ideological or behavioral) a different place in ethnography from the dominant position it once enjoyed. But it is of interest, that, for example, though choice-making in economic matters, and percentages of conformity to norms of kinship are now ordinary parts of ethnographic reportage, choice-making and strategy (other than judicial decision in dispute or choice of tribunal) is much less discussed in connection with law. And it is not only from the point of view of individuals 'working the system' for individual ends that more needs to be known, but more comparative anthropological data and analysis would be useful on the current use by governments and organizations of law and other rule-making in the intentional formation of collective and categorical social, political, and economic relations, and their consequences.

Transformation I Piecemeal alterations over time, accretion and doctrinal synthesis

The redesigning of legal systems in the newly independent countries has been inspired by the idea of making a fresh start. The hope has been that it would be possible to use law, among other instruments, to put the negative aspects of the colonial period behind. The looking backward in order to look forward is often one of the characteristics of reform (D. C. Moore 1976). The piecemeal quality of intentional legal intervention, whether legislative, executive or judicial, is due to its construction as a response to particular circumstances at particular moments. The accretion of many such responses over time makes for a composite, unplanned total result. Even though, at various times and places, there have been attempts to codify everything once and for all, in the long term all legal 'systems' are built by accretion, not by total systematic planning. Incrementalism is not always an avowed policy, but is certainly one of the most commonplace of social processes (Lindblom 1959).

Harding (1966:8) goes so far as to say,

the historical approach introduces the element of irreverence ... for it shows by what absurd shifts and accidents much of the law has been arrived at; that a small part of it may be essential, but most of it is contingent.

Making the bits and pieces 'systematic' is the after-the-fact work of professional specialists, or the before-the-fact work of political ideologues in complex societies. In simpler societies, without writing or full-time jurists, there seems to be less reason to try to construct an apparently consistent and coherent order out of an aggregation of legal norms. Tribal peoples have rules of law, and categories of such, and may hold hearings, but nevertheless seem to have far less need of a unitary rationale than modern states. Where there is no legal profession, and/or no central political authority which legitimates itself through a synthesized ideology of legal principles and rules, there seems little technical capacity or reason to rationalize a supposed connection among all

9

enforceable norms with any degree of elaboration. Even at the state level of social organization, the deep connection is procedural, not substantive, and not necessarily 'logical' or 'moral.' The pervasive unifying element is the theoretical monopoly of the state on the use of force. Any particular substantive rule can be changed, but not that monopoly on ultimate control of procedure.

It is when societies develop full-time specialists whose stock-in-trade it is to compile and master the great variety of legal rules, that there is reason to generate overall modes of classification, and integrating theories. Grand overarching taxonomies and orderly explanations are composed for the purpose by scholars. Pospisil (1971:275) has remarked that,

> The law of Western society traditionally is analysed as an autonomous logically consistent legal system in which the various rules are derived from more abstract norms. These norms, arranged in a sort of pyramid are derived from a basic norm or a sovereign's will. Such analyses present a legal system as a logically consistent whole, devoid of internal contradictions, whose individual norms gain validity from their logical relationship to the more abstract legal principles implied ultimately in the sovereign's will and in a basic norm.

The kind of John Austin, Hans Kelsen rationale Pospisil has described (but does not advocate) implies that even though legal systems evolve over time in a piecemeal fashion, all new rules are somehow logically related to old ones, either consciously or unconsciously playing out certain themes throughout. According to this juristic logic, the underlying normative principles which govern the piecemeal aggregation are discoverable and can be made explicit. The whole then becomes as apparently logical as if it had been intentional. Legal scholars have devoted a great deal of time to defining such principles. For example, Pound enumerated the postulates on which he considered that American private law was based (1942:112–16). Yet an inspection of his principles alone would not give one the slightest idea of the substantive content of any part of the American legal system, nor for that matter the slightest inkling as to for what specific kinds of activities that law actually was pertinent. All of that was an assumed part of the cultural understanding of the reader.

The notion that underlying principles propel legal systems

forward in particular directions of development is extremely difficult to prove. Yet, ideologically, the notion that there are durable fundamental legal postulates may provide a sense of political continuity in the presence of many visible changes. As a useful piece of political ideology, the idea of core principles may help to preserve some of the aura of unquestionability and authority that surrounds a legal system and a legal profession without sacrificing an iota of actual flexibility. The idea of a durable normative core is real enough. But spelling out the content of such a nucleus is another matter.

The concept of law as a 'system,' as a consistent body of rules, is a professional product of some anthropologists as well as of lawyers. As Turner (1975:146) has said,

> Complex, urbanized societies have generated classes of literate specialists, intellectuals of various kinds, including cultural anthropologists, whose paid business, under the division of labor, is to devise logical plans, order concepts into related series, establish taxonomic hierarchies, denature ritual by theologizing it, freeze thought into philosophy, and impose the grid of law on custom.

As lawyers have postulated legal 'systems,' so, too, have some anthropologists been committed to looking at the societies they studied as socio/cultural 'systems,' as relatively consistent cohesive wholes. In such approaches, epitomized thirty years ago in England by the dicta of Malinowski (his field materials belied his theoretical position) and in America by Ruth Benedict, ethnographic evidence was selectively inspected and interpreted to show as much as possible the existence of interconnected institutions (Malinowski) and integrated cultural patterns (Benedict).

It was in this functional and culture-pattern tradition, and also influenced by the same thrust in jurisprudence (Kohler, Pound, Stone) that Hoebel analyzed *The Law of Primitive Man*. For each society he describes, he abstracts certain underlying cultural values and lists the 'basic social postulates' on which he contends the law of the society is based. The reasoning is that law is the practical working out of the values of a society. The assumption seems to be of the causal priority (and temporal?) of ideas and values of which culture and society are an expression. Yet where the actual history of legal systems is known, it is evident that the institutions and the rule-complexes and principles of which they are composed were not generated at one moment in time, nor in response to one set of values, nor one set of political, social, or economic conditions. The antecedents of American law include doctrines developed in medieval law regarding control over land, labor, and military service, the relations of conqueror and conquered, rulers and nobles, lords and serfs, in a setting entirely different from our own. Piece by piece, instance by instance, common law developed. As Holmes is so often quoted as saying, 'The life of the law has not been logic, it has been experience' (1881:1). Even where attempts have been made at complete codification, as in civil law, the code is continually modified, not only by legislation, but by judicial application and juristic interpretation (Lloyd 1965:371). Can such piecemeal aggregations, put together over centuries, be said to express a core of key ideas and values?

Revolutionaries sometimes postulate a new beginning, with new laws as the frame. In revolutionary situations radical political ideologues make claims for the overwhelming improvements to be brought about by a complete and rational reorganization, disdaining partial reforms as inadequate. They are skeptical of limited innovations introduced in the midst of what they consider to be irreparably distorted social and economic relations. They, too, postulate an integrated whole. But over time, they also must face the fact that all legal systems are piecemeal aggregates. Much as they oppose superficial solutions before the revolution, they are, of course, committed to just such repairs and limited changes afterwards. Circumstances shift. New conditions must be met with new measures. The flow of unplanned change is unceasing, and the fallout from the competition for power is ineluctable. New plans ever must succeed old ones. No government can do away with ongoing social processes that reform and deform the best plans they can devise, and set new riddles for the most determined and powerful of planners.

It must be assumed that, for the most part, the legal rules of·pre-industrial societies also developed situation by situation, perhaps with occasional deep and pervasive alterations. All the evidence suggests that the societies whose history is not known cannot have been different in this respect from the societies about which there is a historical record.

What may have been quite different, however, is the rate of

change. If the normative orders of pre-industrial peoples were very durable and change slow, even as archeology shows their economies were durable, and economic change slow, then there is a major difference between their law and ours: the proportion of newly constructed rules to received rules is much greater in modern societies. If it has been correctly assumed that law in pre-industrial societies is relatively more stable, how and why has frequent change been resisted? One possible reason (and there are undoubtedly others, *if* the assumption is right in the first place) may be that in pre-industrial circumstances the maintenance of relationships of social exchange between social units depends heavily on the existence of replicated units with like normative orders. This may act as a brake on significant normative changes within individual subunits since innovations might cut off important relationships. The commitment to maintaining connections among units might account for some of the putative stability of 'customary law.'

Transformation II   Custom, law, and the multiple sources of reglementation

In the nineteenth and early twentieth centuries the origins of law and the course of legal development were the subject of much evolutionary speculation. Among the conceptual categorizations which used to be dear to the hearts of scholars of historical jurisprudence was the dichotomy between law and custom. The premises that shaped that classification differ from those that inform current approaches to anthropology and law.

Custom used to be treated as the precursor of law, its evolutionary source. Customary laws were not thought of as having been imposed from above, but rather as having emerged from popular practice. For the most part, the peoples whose cultures were considered to exemplify an earlier stage of social life were without written records. Therefore, more often than not, the specific beginnings of particular rules of their law were lost from sight. Lacking historical evidence, it was comfortable for observers to take the view that such law was part of an immemorial traditional order, largely immutable and closely linked to the rest of the cultural 'system.' In exotic places, indigenous informants confronted with questions about the origin of particular legal rules often answered, 'We have always done it that way.' Or sometimes myths were adduced regarding the general origin of all custom. It is no wonder that travelers, historians and anthropologists were encouraged to take literally such statements about tradition. Moreover, to the people who practice them, customs, even as laws, often seem part of a coherent logical whole. As a consequence, customs also may seem integrated and consistent to sufficiently empathic observers. But, as implied earlier by the discussion of the piecemeal nature of legal history, this is more easily asserted than proved. It is no simple sociological question to ask to what extent the assortment of customs in a culture constitute a connected system in some sociologically necessary sense, or to what extent they have been assembled by historical accident.

The vision of simpler societies dominated by integrated traditions of ancient origin gave scholars license to differentiate with exaggerated sharpness between the customs of such 'early' societies and the statutes of self-conscious modern states. In modern polities, they asserted, statutory and judicially declared rules of law were arrived at deliberately, reflectively and rationally by professional specialists. Not so in less advanced cultures. The idea seems to have been that, by contrast, in traditional society customs somehow arose from the opinions and practices of 'the people' like mists from a marsh:

> We are accustomed nowadays to the enactment of laws by the State; and we regard legislation – the deliberate elaboration of legal rules – as one of the principal functions of the State. It does not, however, require much learning in order to perceive that such conscious and direct legislation is of comparatively recent growth; it is the attribute of a definitely organized State, the result of a fairly advanced political civilization. In rudimentary unions, in so-called barbaric tribes, even in feudal societies, rules of conduct are usually established, not by direct and general commands, but by the gradual consolidation of opinions and habits. The historical development of law starts with custom. Rules are not imposed from above by legislative authorities but rise from below, from the society which comes to recognize them. The best opportunities for observing the formation and application of custom are presented when primitive societies are living their life before the eyes and under the control of more advanced nations.

The quotation from Vinogradoff (1925:ch.2) is revealing in its emphasis on certain ordinary meanings that lie behind the law/custom duality. Not only is there weight put on the association of law with the historical development of the state, but there is the attribution of custom and customary law both to early European peoples and to colonial subjects. In both settings the notion of custom had distinct political significance. In the colonies, the laws of indigenous populations were of major importance to the administering powers. Order had to be maintained with a small staff, limited funds, and little equipment. Colonial administrators could not possible hope to revamp completely the indigenous legal/political system, and for that matter, in many places, did not aspire to do so. Like it or not, they had to acknowledge the local legal order. It is from just such colonial settings that most of the earliest detailed ethnographic accounts of the legal systems of non-European peoples come (Nader, Koch, and Cox 1966). But European ideas about customary law in this sense date from a much earlier period than the nineteenth-century era of colonial expansion. From the Roman Empire to medieval times, and thereafter, governments and the church were concerned administratively with the great diversity of European ethnic communities and regions, and the variety of their local laws. From the earliest beginnings, European states were obliged to devise ways of dealing with the problematic relation between the centralization and standardization of control over some matters and diversity and local autonomy over others.

In these two settings, colonial and European, the difference between local customary law and the law of the supravening polity was a difference between the kind and level of political unit within which the rule was legitimate. This was as true of medieval Welsh villagers conquered by the English as it was of the Wachagga of Kilimanjaro under German and British colonial régimes. 'Laws' in these settings were the rules of the dominant and geographically widest régime, 'custom' its term for the binding practices of localized subordinate peoples.

Vinogradoff's emphasis on the 'deliberateness' of legislation implies by contrast that spontaneity and the unthinkingness of habit attached to custom. It reminds one of Weber's use of the idea of rationality, and of his notions about 'the application of intellect' in modern legal systems (1954:63). Both emphasize the conscious, logical decision-making of modern men and postulate less rational predecessors. But it has long been known that by no means is all law a matter of voluntary, unthinking habit in pre-state systems, nor is logic in any way absent once one understands the premises (Malinowski 1926). Vinogradoff's statement about an absence of deliberate legislation at the 'tribal' end of his continuum is an exaggeration.

There can be authorities with rule-making power in many forms of organized society less complex than the state. Discussing the most rudimentary levels of political organization, Pospisil argues on the basis of his work in New Guinea, that there certain Big Men (*tonowi*) among the Kapauku, make rules and rulings that bind their followers (1971:65–72). Pospisil makes a similar argument regarding Eskimo leaders (1971:72–8). Working in a more rank-oriented milieu, Schapera has given a detailed account of legislation decreed by Tswana chiefs (1970). While the bulk of Schapera's Tswana evidence deals with the period of colonial administration, there is every reason to believe that some of the legislative and administrative authority he describes had an indigenous foundation. Nor can one have much doubt in the matter of the legislative capacities of other southern Bantu chiefs (Schapera:1956). There is no need to extend the examples. They are not hard to come by, and those cited suffice to suggest that Vinogradoff misjudged the non-authoritative sources of tribal law. On the basis of much more ethnographic data than was available to Vinogradoff, and newer interpretations, it is now clear that to the extent that law is ultimately a potentially coercive order (and not just popular practice, jolly folk custom universally accepted) the regular capacity of some to make rules that bind others has existed at many levels of social complexity. As Dennis Lloyd has commented, the historical school completely confused the fact that the law of a society is related to its social and economic system with the almost mystical notion of a popular consciousness of which the law was supposedly the expression (1965:330). In its stead a social anthropological emphasis on organization, on the ordering of social relationships, rather than on folk ideology by itself, precludes falling into this cultural simplification. By definition, any corporate group has the capacity to make some rules that bind members, and corporate groups of some kind are present in most societies. This circumstance makes corporate groups one of the most useful sites for the comparative study of reglementation.

Should the enforceable and binding rules of all durable, organized social units be considered 'laws,' or should the term be confined to the binding rules enforced by government or the state? Max Rheinstein said, 'the sociologist ... has to concern himself with any kind of organizationally coercive order' (1954:lvi). He goes on to criticize the narrowness of Austin's definition of law, and commends Weber's, saying that the sociologist must consider 'such phenomena as ecclesiastical law, gang law, the law merchant of the Middle Ages, or tribal, international, or other forms of primitive law' (1954:lix). They were all law for Rheinstein. Along the same lines, Pospisil has argued recently that every society has a multiplicity of legal systems and legal levels, and that 'law' as a category of social phenomena, rather than as a professional lawyer's term, exists in all of them (1971:97–126).

It is my view that when one is talking about complex societies, there is an advantage in preserving the conventional distinction between rules potentially enforceable by the government, and rules enforceable by other organizations or agencies. 'Law' is a convenient, succinct way of referring to that distinction, and it conforms to conventional usage, which is no small consideration. In those simpler societies where no political units are of the state level, other tests can be applied to discover the effective political units, the legitimate enforceable norms, and the processes that surround their use.

The conventional category 'law' (meaning rules enforceable by government) is a category of our own culture. When it is applied by anthropologists to societies that are very different in structure, what is being sought are analogous phenomena. Where there is no government, obviously the conventional procedural criterion used to identify law in our society does not exist. Other criteria for a definition of law such as the four proposed by Pospisil: authority, the intention of universal application, obligation, and sanction, can be useful, but then, when equally applied to modern society, they cover the whole field of in-group reglementation (1971:11–96). They apply to law and to all other rules of corporate groups. Pospisil does not shy away from this result and emerges calling everything law that meets his four criteria, asserting that there are a multiplicity of 'legal levels' in society, which range from the family to the state. In short, as he fully acknowledges, Pospisil, following Weber's ideas about the multiplicity of coercive orders (1967:17) and Llewellyn and Hoebel's lead regarding 'sublaw-stuff or bylaw-stuff of the lesser working units' (1941:28), applies the term 'law' to virtually every form of rule pertaining to an organized group in any society. I agree with him and with them that the sociological phenomenon should be broadly conceived. Certainly one effect of reading ethnographies is that once sensitized to lawlike phenomena in pre-state societies, the importance becomes evident of similar, non-government, but lawlike phenomena in modern complex societies, but to call it all law, particularly speaking of complex societies, may be to risk confusion. Instead, the term 'reglementation' proposed here, may serve. It is inclusive enough to encompass government law and non-governmental sites of rule-making and/or rule-enforcing. In complex societies 'law' can then be reserved for the government-enforceable.

In most pre-state or non-state societies, as there are political units which can be mobilized to exert physical force in the name of generally applicable norms, these operate for rule-enforcement purposes as government does in more centralized systems. Those rules or rulings made mandatory or potentially enforceable by such units can be considered law without any inconsistency of definition despite the absence of government, if the legitimate use of force is used as a definitional criterion for law. Hoebel's cross-cultural definition of law[1] is cast in these terms. It uses legitimate physical enforceability as its principal test, and is broadly serviceable (1954:28). The dilemma it presents, however, is that effective coercion, or for that matter, effective inducement, can be managed in most social settings without the use of or even the direct threat of physical force, and any definition of law that rests too heavily on violations of norms and on the use of force, diverts attention from the most important processes by which mundane conformity to norms is ordinarily exacted. These definitional problems are not special to law. They beset all attempts at cultural comparison and sociological analysis. (For a recent discussion of some of the problems of comparison, see Needham 1975). The choice of definitional criteria implies that the characteristics chosen are the sociologically significant qualities. Yet if the very purpose of the comparison is to *find out* what are the sociologically significant qualities in some field of action, too tight a pre-definition can preclude any discovery. Some of the consequent problems of comparison that have bedevilled the law field are addressed in the paper in this collection on Comparative Studies.

The terminological problem aside, everyone interested in the sociology of reglementation recognizes that rules are made within organizations other than the state, both in societies without government and in societies having an overarching state organization. Also, just as legal historians thought, customs which ultimately become rules *can* grow out of transactions, but that is not the only, nor even necessarily the most important, source. In social anthropology Barth's stimulating essay on transactions as the font of new customs and new values, for all its modern game theory and interactional trappings, is insufficient as a total 'generative model' of social change, among other things because it does not deal adequately with reglementary phenomena, with the organization of coercive order (Barth 1966; Paine 1974). But Barth's approach nevertheless may have special pertinence to law generated by intergroup transactions in international law and in acephalous societies, as well as in some instances of rule-generating between transacting subgroups in complex societies.

There is a perplexing question, seldom addressed, about the structure of societies without centralized government, such as band societies or segmentary lineage systems. The question is, how did the subunits come to be as much alike as they are and how and why did they stay alike and interconnected to the extent that they did over time? Here, anthropologists, usually lacking specific historical evidence, have tended to treat these units as traditionally replicated forms which somehow sprang up either through parallel responses to social and ecological exigencies and/or through fission and segmentation. Mythological histories often postulate a single original unit from which other replicas hived off. But neither parallel responses nor segmentary multiplication can suffice as a universal explanation, even if there have been many instances of each. Cultural change is as pervasive and continuous a process as genetic mutation, and presumably occurs in different directions in populations that are isolated from one another. Given that change is a continuous force, the puzzling question is this: is there any systematic way in which legal changes could be diffused throughout these societies lacking formal legislative organs? Diffusion must have taken place if change occurred, given the degree of structural uniformity among these peoples when they were studied. Quasi-legislative innovations could have been introduced by one of the units in such a way and regarding such matter that the innovation would be likely to be imitated by any similar unit that wanted to continue political, economic, and kinship relations with the innovative one. The rule-innovation can have been a symbol of alliance, or even a test of alliance in some cases. One wonders about the original development of the *kula* ring, about the forms of the *potlatch* on the Northwest coast of America, about alliance through clanship among the Tallensi of Ghana. It seems plausible to conjecture that this kind of rulebound arrangement could be introduced from group to group, and all but imposed by prestigious, or strategically well-placed groups on lesser ones in the course of their intergroup transactions. This would account for the continuation of certain structural parallelisms in acephalous societies without postulating continuous parallel evolution, nor purely voluntary diffusion without any element of pressure, nor even less likely, complete absence of change. Whether this legislativelike sequence actually often occurred in pre-state societies, I do not know. It seems possible. And certainly the phenomenon exists today within nation-states, in which a powerful corporate subunit may set certain formal requisites for interaction with lesser ones which wish to deal with it. The field of intercorporate group transaction (and corporate group/ individual transaction) can generate enforceable rules in this way. Vinogradoff probably would have called this 'custom.'

Vinogradoff considered that custom was king in primitive societies, but he readily acknowledged the persistence of custom in a lesser role in more advanced polities. He cites many instances from Constantine's Rome to the medieval law merchant in which customary rules eventually were given legal force. Certainly he was right about the continuing importance of customary practices in modern life, and that many 'informal' usages go on being elevated to the status of law. There are many instances in current North American cases in which judges take judicial notice of the practices in a trade or the customs of some other social milieu to fill in the specific referents of vague legal terms. 'Fairness,' 'reasonableness,' and such, have meanings only with reference to specific social contexts. Did the salesman make a fair claim for his product? Did the roofer deliver the tiles in a reasonable time? In this and other forms, there is no doubt such a thing as the customary law of industrial society.

But Vinogradoff also notes the continuing force of 'custom' in quite a different kind of modern milieu, 'In our days the Stock Exchange is regulated by the practices formed within the circle of its members in transacting business' (1925:27). (That was 1925, but its specific reference need not detain us here.) Taking his remarks all together, 'custom' is used by Vinogradoff in at least three senses: it refers to the received 'traditional' law of *a cultural community* (colonial peoples or historical forebears). It alludes to the practices of certain *transacting individuals (or groups)* which gradually become general usage and are ultimately acknowledged as binding rules for those transactions, whether there is a state or not. And last, it seems to cover a somewhat different entity, the rules and usages deliberately generated by non-governmental *formal organizations and arenas* to run their own affairs in the presence of the state. (For a discussion of other scholarly uses of the concept of custom, see Lloyd 1964:226–55.) The distinctions among these three are important to anyone interested in the social sources of reglementation. To lump them all together as custom, blurs important differences. Such an amalgam focuses on the lawlike result at the cost of ignoring the way the binding rule was generated and the milieu in which it operates. 'Custom' used that way is a residual category for what is not law. This fits very well with the perspective that all rule-making agencies other than the state are fully subordinate to it, and hence are analytically of little importance to the study of law itself. Such an approach gives insufficient attention to the degree of autonomy of organizations and arenas outside of government (or subunits in totalitarian systems) and the profound effects of their activities on the operation of government itself.

In capitalist countries the dichotomy between 'law' and the residual category, 'rules that are not law,' is encapsulated in the notion of 'government' as opposed to 'private' regulation. The preservation of the division between the state-regulated sector and the private sector is an ideological point of honor. The boundary is stressed not only in matters relating directly to the economy, but also in connection with the right to found, regulate and manage organizations, and also in matters of individual action. In capitalist countries many a scandal is the consequence of demonstrating overly close connections between the 'government' and 'private' sectors. Yet there is much legitimate interpenetration and contact that is an essential part of the structure.

In communist and socialist countries the unitary nature of the polity and the economy is the only admissible ideological self-representation. Anything that reveals internal divisions is anathema. But it is evident that competing entities within the state, as well as extralegal activities, produce much more division than is admitted to, and generate the exercise of much more autonomy, organizational and individual, than is ideologically acknowledged. The sociological/analytic problem of a multiplicity of reglementary fields is not confined to capitalist countries. Nor is it confined to industrial societies. The analytical focus on multiple areas of autonomy also is essential to the political anthropological study of non-industrial societies. The close connection between political organization and law makes comparative political analysis necessary to the anthropological study of law. Chapter 6 of this book on Politics, Procedures, and Norms in Changing Chagga Law addresses this point.

It is well established that the comparative study of the political systems of non-European peoples cannot be coped with by means of a typology of central authorities, since, as has been mentioned, there are a number of organizational types (including bands and segmentary lineages) which are what Bohannan (1967:51) has called, 'multi-centric.' These systems are without centralized government and are of crucial theoretical interest. Nor does it suffice to sort out societies into centralized and decentralized polities, since that pair of variables is far too crude. There are a great many kinds of centralized system. Balandier has gone so far as to say that the diversity of political organizations has thus far utterly eluded adequate classification in anthropology and sociology. He asks, 'do anthropology and sociology possess models that are adequately adapted to political forms?' and replies, 'The answer for the moment is no' (1970:48). But a good technique exists for the initial sorting that is especially pertinent to the study of reglementation.

The necessary and basic preliminary step is to approach the problem of analysis and comparison with a framework that is neutral to the question how many regulatory fields there may be, and what their relations are. With some modifications and additions, M. G. Smith's approach seems to me to be a most useful point of departure for this purpose (1974:91–105). The essence of his formulation is that the anatomy of a society is to be examined in terms of its corporate groups, as he defines them.[2] The corporate focus provides no more than a framework for the initial organization of the ethnographic facts. But this focus is extremely useful because it addresses the very structural facts that are pertinent to the more formal reglementary processes. The emphasis on putatively permanent, formal organizations, from the state itself to all those less encompassing organizations within it, delineates the social collectivities which are explicitly rule-ordered. As Etzioni (1961:xvii) has said in another context,

> Organizations serve as collectivities within which the general problem of social order may be studied empirically. They constitute a 'strategic site' for such study because social order in modern society is based to a great extent on interaction in and among organizations.

The site is just as strategic for a whole range of non-modern comparisons and social histories. But a morphology of corporate organizations is only the beginning. Smith's formulation of politics is repeatedly criticized as either too static and rigid, or as too elevated and general a vocabulary of key concepts (Balandier 1970:15,25). His style of presentation lends itself to some of these criticisms, but many of the ideas encased in his difficult prose are indeed worth the struggle of decipherment. Any attempt to use his formulation to analyze a particular historical/ethnographic case takes one immediately to the heart of a whole series of critical analytic problems. Smith's definitional criteria of corporateness force one to ask such things as, what are the 'common affairs' of particular groups, or whether their procedures for dealing with these common affairs are 'adequate,' questions which require interpretation as well as description in any answers. The questions are seldom as easy to answer as they are to ask. The formulation loses its rigidity and some of its neatness as soon as it is applied. It raises further and new questions, Smith's categories do not solve the problems addressed. No categories could, as such. But they greatly accelerate entry into complex data by organizing it and focusing it.

Smith's corporate approach goes much further in the analysis of the *sites* of reglementation, in so far as they are groups, than Pospisil's. Of anthropologists writing recently on law, Pospisil has most clearly expressed and repeatedly emphasized the importance of the multiplicity of what he calls 'legal systems.' Pospisil has drawn attention to the fact that subgroups in any society can be significant rule-making units. However, while obviously agreeing with him and with others who have recognized the same phenomenon, there are aspects of his formulation which I find unhelpful. I have already indicated my reservations about calling all subgroup rules 'legal systems.' But that is just a matter of terminology. There are more serious problems with Pospisil's related notion of 'legal levels.' The only principle of relationship among these 'legal systems' to which he gives major significance is that of ranking by degrees of inclusiveness of the groups involved. He says (1971:107), 'Since the legal systems form a hierarchy reflecting the degrees of inclusiveness of the corresponding sub-groups, the total of the legal systems of sub-groups of the same type and inclusiveness (for example, family, lineage, community, political confederacy) I propose to call *legal level*.'

Pospisil recognizes that an individual is thus subject to the rules of several levels simultaneously and that these rules may be in conflict, and that the rules of the subgroups of the same level may differ. What Pospisil has erected as an analytic classification has much in common with the jurisdictional hierarchies and divisions of our court system. To my mind this formulation does not sufficiently address the question of the differences in *kind* between organizational units, and is overly focused on inclusiveness, as if that were always the most important criterion of hierarchy and difference.

As Durkheim noted long ago, the core of complex societies is the diversity of its organizational base, while one of the characteristics of simpler societies is that they tend to have many replicated units and fewer kinds. The simpler the society, the more useful Pospisil's criterion of inclusion. But any theoretical framework that is supposed to be usable for analyzing complex societies as well as simple ones should address more directly the varied nature of corporate groups, the differences in the subject-matter of their reglementation, the complexity of their inter-relations, and provide criteria that will bring those differences to the fore. Even with regard to simple societies, the criterion of inclusiveness is not enough.

M. G. Smith's inquiring approach to corporations seems to me to supply a much more open, and multidimensional framework, that neither precludes nor presumes neat legal levels. His definitional criteria raise for each corporation examined the question what might be its internal structure, its external relations, its areas of autonomy and common affairs, and the like. Pospisil, focused on rules, has not provided nearly as full a framework for the examination of the nature of organizations, yet groups and subgroups are an essential part of his formulation.

Smith's approach itself needs to be filled out in operation. His model does not address questions about the nature of transactional and competitive arenas, which I see as important sites and sources of reglementation, yet which need not be corporate groups. But his framework does not in any way exclude addressing these questions, and in fact, lends itself to refinement and expansion in this direction. As will be made evident in the essays that follow, I use Smith's framework but modify and extend it, finding it most helpful when employed, (1) as a broad set of questions about degrees and kinds of organizedness and about the kinds of activities in which organizations engage, both internally and in relation to other organizations and social fields (as compared with activities engaged in by individuals and non-corporate aggregations of individuals in the same society), and (2) when the corporate approach is tempered with other analytic techniques such as the study of competitive arenas (economic, political, ideological, etc.) and the study of networks and transactions, in order to discover how much of the aggregate social result is the consequence of formal organizational activity and how much of it is of non-corporate activity.

Corporate analysis, somewhat extended and modified, and always seen in the corrective light of non-corporate activity, provides a practical middle-ground for the study of reglementation. It helps escape the dilemma of seeing law or other reglementation as a phenomenally confusing diversity of single rules, or as a fictitiously coherent 'systematic' cultural whole. It also permits escape from the confines of the conventional Western juristic categories, which though very useful for some purposes, are more often than not narrowly addressed to a particular kind of property, a particular category of transaction, or a particular category of relationship, rather than to a social milieu in the round.

Once a corporate analysis is used to sort out societal data, it serves as an organizing device that keeps the ethnographic facts sufficiently in order to make them intelligible, but not so orderly that they cannot produce information one did not have to begin with. It is an instrument only, a criterion of arrangement, not in itself an answer to anything. But the dimension of formal organization is so important and so visible that it makes a most convenient and informative structural sketch-map with which to proceed to a processual analysis.

This is not the place for extended remarks on Smith's corporate approach, and the various emendations and elaborations of it which I find useful. But it is apposite to indicate a few of the ways in which general processual questions can be fed into the corporate frame to see how it moves in action. For example, it can be postulated that there are certain contradictory principles which must be addressed in all corporate organizations, and in the ordering of higher level relations, the organization of organizations. One such pair of contradictory principles is the tendency toward hierarchy *versus* the tendency toward equivalence, or equality. The handling of these antinomies can be identified as prevalent if not universal organizational concerns. For the individuals involved, these are often high-pressure issues, as there can be much gained or lost in the way structures and events related to these 'oppositions' devolve. Hence these very tensions are usually the subject of enforceable rules. In other words, it is inherent in the reglementation of organized collectivities that they must deal with certain questions, and these can be identified, and the action-pressures to change, work around or maintain such rules are part of the ongoing life of the organization. The assumption can be made that over time these 'opposites,' in this case, hierarchy/equivalence, are permanently in tension. Whichever prevails for a time is nevertheless threatened by tendencies toward its opposite, and someone must work at keeping those under control.

Another pair of 'oppositions' which formal groups (and organizations of organizations) must face is a struggle between elements pushing toward greater and greater rationalization of centralized direction, and elements pulling away toward subunit autonomy. The process of trying to set and keep limits on the centralizing and centrifugal tendencies is often at least in part a consciously rule-ordered or rule-enforcing process, though the rules may manifest themselves in veiled forms.[3] Organizations necessarily make rules about what is settled and what may be competed for, about the terms and conditions of competition and access to resources and the like. Over time, the chances are that if the prizes are important, the pressure in one direction or the other will not be completely contained by the rules. The domination/ autonomy struggle may be waged between groups, or between individuals and groups, or, for that matter, as is apparent in everyday life, between individuals. It may be confined to particular events and issues, or it may be a question of durable relationships and the permanent shape they are to take.

The tension between domination and autonomy, and the tension between hierarchy and equality-equivalence are obviously often related, both ideologically and operationally. They are also closely connected with law, since law involves the potentiality of coercion, and coercion is related both to domination and to hierarchy. In any corporate polity, some of the substantive law will be occupied with these questions. In any corporate groups, some rules will address these matters.

Other important organizational antinomies have to do with numbers of organizational units and their kind, with amalgamating or dividing, proliferating units or reducing their numbers. The diversification of structural forms as against the replication of existing ones is part of the formal question of 'kind' in organizations. But the formal lineaments are only part of the story. The substantive question what activities the organizations undertake, and in what ways the activities of different organizations are linked or divided is central to understanding the operation of the structure. Political strategies are often focused on formal reorganization to achieve substantive ends. The hierarchy/ equivalence, domination/autonomy issues must be met in the external relations of organizations as well as in their internal structures. Organizations can be pyramided on top of one another, or generated to occupy 'adjacent' positions rather than places above or below. The historical paper in this book having to do with the last hundred years of Chagga legal procedures and their connection with Chagga political change, shows a progressive sequence of amalgamating and pyramiding as a means of introducing profound political changes without appearing to disrupt established interests in lower-level units (see chapter 6, Politics, Procedures, and Norms in Changing Chagga Law).

The constitution of a state is, among other things, an organization of organizations. The more complex the society, the more the layers of rule-systems, the more adjacent ones there are, and the more numerous and diverse the separate 'jurisdictions' or autonomous fields, and the more intricate the questions of domination/autonomy, hierarchy/equivalence, proliferation/reduction, amalgamation/division, replication/diversification in the relations within and among the constitutive levels and units. Formal rules or laws notwithstanding, these contradictory possibilities continue to pull against each other from event to event, from situation to situation. If the form of an organization is to continue as it was, persons must work actively to reproduce it in succeeding generations (or cohorts). They must prevent slippage or resist pressure in any transforming direction. The pressure may emanate from inside the organization or from the outside. It may accompany a substantive change in activities, but need not. The possibility of alteration and shift is always there.

Moreover, formal corporate organizations and their reglementary activities are not the only patterers of social relations, nor the only agencies of stability or change. Personal networks, arenas of transaction, and arenas of competition also may be very durable and important fields of action. Though not necessarily corporate, they too, can be subject to, or generate, explicit rules. There often are in a society any number of incompletely corporate aggregations of persons whose collective weight is socially significant. The relation between the formal corporations and these more diffuse aggregates is extremely important in the analysis of the workings of any polity, as are the ways in which corporations form and dissolve.

To postulate the universality of these, or other similarly opposed tendencies in and between organizations, and the necessity of considering them analytically, is to approach the study of organizations with what are presumed to be elementary puzzles with which all such formal structures must deal. Anthropologists have long looked at the sexual and biological building-blocks out of which kinship systems are constructed as the fundamental elements on which cultural variations are elaborated. Universal organizational dilemmas can be identified and approached in the same way, as a limited basic set on which there are variations, permutations, and transformations. The dilemmas mentioned here are not offered as a full set, but rather adduced to show some of the possibilities. Such organizational material is patently useful in the study of the subject-matter of reglementation, as it provides significant sociological criteria for the classification of related rules.

Since, in a society as a whole, reglementation emanates simultaneously from many social fields, including both corporate groups and less formally bounded action-arenas, the aggregate effect is extremely complex. Intricate at any one moment, the aggregate is the more so over any period of time, and cannot be fully planned, predicted or under control. This is, of course, particularly obvious in complex societies in which detailed information about the activities in many contemporaneous social fields is available. In modern nation-states the effectiveness of the hierarchical layering of organizations competes against multiple autonomies and parallel structures of organizations and arenas. Characteristically some of the organizations which are theoretically subordinate engage in activities which spill over into, invade and otherwise penetrate and affect other 'levels' above and below, often in extrareglemented ways. Individuals circulate, associate, manipulate. Wheels turn and deals are made. Official formal relations (or even official non-connections) between corporate groups are mediated and modified by 'informal' arrangements which, though often disavowed, are an integral part of the operation of the whole.

If law in modern societies is theoretically subsumed within the general sociological analysis of reglementation, it is seen as the product of the state and its organs, the theoretically superordinate, most inclusive corporate organization and its sub-branches. Perceived in this way, the law of the central state is but one kind of reglementation emanating from one kind of organization. But I would emphasize that organizations are not all the same because they are all organized. That is only one dimension. Moreover, the state is doing many things besides making and enforcing rules, and its existence in the presence of other reglementary organizations and arenas is affected not only by their reglementation, but by their other activities as well. Within this framework, which includes activities as well as rules, arenas as well as organizations, the way is made for differentiating the ideology of jurisdiction and control from the operative realities in any polity. This approach takes into account that there is a constant struggle between deliberate rule-making` and planning, and other more untameable activities and processes at work in the social aggregate, and argues that these should be inspected together.

It seems incontrovertible that the more complex a society, and the greater the appearance of rational control, the more delegation there will be in government and administration and the more areas of discretion and semi-autonomous activity there will be in the subparts of the society, formal and 'informal.' The sociological study of reglementation is in part the study of such segregated areas of autonomy and their impact on one another. These preserves of autonomy may be explicit, 'rationally' prescribed in the Weberian-bureaucratic manner, with small monopolies of jurisdiction and discretion officially set out. Or they may be hammered out in action, in competition, in transactions within, between and by the side of, formal organizations. Even more likely, both 'rational' prescriptions and negotiating activities are carried on simultaneously.

This view of complex society, or of any society, leads one to a paradox. Formal reglementation can control certain behavior, but not the aggregate of behavior in a society. The more 'rational' a society seems in its parts, and its rules, and its rules about rules, the thicker the layer of formalism and ideological self-representation to be penetrated to find out what is really going on. In the course of events in the past, no society has approached anything near complete planned control, nor any kind of complete reglementation, nor, in my view, could it. That does not mean that particular legislative or executive decisions cannot be made which affect everyone in a given society, nor that for limited times or limited matters, remarkable levels of control cannot be achieved. But over time, reglementary control can be only temporary, incomplete, and its consequences not fully predictable. The study of reglementation is therefore the study of the way partial orders and partial controls operate in social contexts. The essays in this book illustrate this theme in a variety of settings.

Notes

1   Hoebel (1954:28) defines law as follows:
    A social norm is legal if its neglect or infraction is regularly met, in threat or in fact, by the application of physical force by an individual or group possessing the socially recognized privilege of so acting.

2   Smith's definition (1974:94) of a public, or a corporate, group is:
    an enduring, presumably perpetual group with determinate boundaries and membership, having an internal organization and a unitary set of external relations, an exclusive body of common affairs, and autonomy and procedures adequate to regulate them.

3 An example of a veiled way of limiting centralizing tendencies can be found among the Tiv of Nigeria. The Tiv, a society of segmentary lineages without any central government, had the concept of *tsav*, a power that grew on the hearts of community leaders. *Tsav* was usable for good or for evil. Its existence was an ideological/jural device which made it possible to explain how some men rose to leadership, but also made it possible for them to be struck down for misuse of their powers. *Tsav* may have contributed toward the maintenance of Tiv political acephaly. (See Bohannan 1957:163.)

Chapter 1

Uncertainties in situations, indeterminacies in culture

When discrepancies exist between ideology and social reality, what do people do? What happens when a community that idealizes communal harmony is faced with internal conflicts and contradictions? This book has discussed such questions. It is not that there is anything new about recognizing the existence of such inconsistencies. It is that attention to the ways in which they are resolved raises basic theoretical issues. One of these is the question, What is the relationship between ideology and action? In the past, a great deal of work in anthropology and sociology has focused on congruities between ideology and the organization of social life. Much current work is occupied with the lack of complete correspondence between the two, and the ways in which social processes unfold in the face of this lack of consistency. But obviously there are degrees and kinds of congruence and

Reprinted from *Symbol and Politics in Communal Ideology*, edited by Sally Falk Moore and Barbara Myerhoff. Copyright © 1975 by Cornell University. Used by permission of the publisher, Cornell University Press.

Author's note
The author wishes to acknowledge with thanks two opportunities she had to present this material publicly, once to the staff-student seminar at the University of Manchester and once to staff and students at University College, London. Both discussions were very helpful, as were conversations with Professors M. G. Smith, Max Gluckman, and David Lowenthal, my husband Professor Cresap Moore, and my colleagues Professors Barbara Myerhoff and Jay Abarbanel, to whom I first presented these ideas. I also wish to thank Professor Victor Turner for encouragement generously given and much appreciated.

contradiction. This raises the question, What kind of analytic framework can be used to consider the congruities *and* the discrepancies between ideology and action in social situations? Processual analysis raises further questions. How is the time factor to be dealt with? How can the same analysis simultaneously handle continuity and change? How can situations which are small in scale be analyzed in such a way as to keep the larger cultural context in view? It is one of the objectives of this epilogue to propose a simple processual framework which may clarify the analysis of these problems. But first we will review some of the ways in which the relationships between ideology and social structure have been dealt with, and some of the implications of the term 'process' as it has been used in anthropology.

Ideology and social structure: congruent or not?

Seeking or postulating congruence between ideology and social structure has been as attractive to utopian idealists and to social planners as it was to social scientists. Cultural and ideological materials have been as frequently treated as a blueprint for a new society (or some specific part of it) as they have been considered the reflection of an existing structure. Discrepancies have been explained away as the consequence of transition, of lag, of imperfections in planning and the like. Thus where congruence and consistency are the core of the analytic model, the absence of these characteristics in ethnographic fact can be treated not as an inadequacy of the model, but as a historical phase of the society being analyzed.

Quite a variety of conclusions have been generated by models based on congruence. Durkheim, for example, saw in religion a representation of society itself. When the Australian aborigines gathered together to whirl their bull-roarers, or to sing to make the totemic animals multiply, or to mourn the death of one of their number, they were, in Durkheim's eyes, *representing* and *reaffirming* the social group through ritual. Religion as he saw it, was both a focus of social cohesion and a symbolic representation of society (Durkheim 1912; 1961 ed.). This is a mirror-image approach to ideology and structure. One reflects the other. Congruence is absolute.

Weber's view of the matter was more complex. He conceived of ideas and values as directly informing action, as a shaping force in the social order as well as a reflection of it. In his analysis it was the ideology of protestantism combined with economic circumstances that made the bloom of capitalism possible (Weber 1904–5; 1958 ed.). Attached to each of his ideal types of political authority is a set of ideas that legitimates it – congruence again, but with more subtle connections (Weber 1925; 1964 ed.). He specifically warns that 'it is probably seldom if ever that a real phenomenon can be found which corresponds exactly to one of these ideally constructed pure types' (1925; 1964 ed.:110).

Like Durkheim, Radcliffe-Brown saw religion as a correlate of social order. While he said that beliefs and rituals should be studied 'in action,' he does not seem to have doubted for a moment that if one did so one would discover a correspondence with structure. He recognized that the parallelism was sometimes hard to trace. 'In some societies,' he said, 'there is a direct and immediate relation between the religion and the social structure,' and cites ancestor worship and Australian totemism as illustrations. But then he turns to other, more heterogeneous societies, in which there are a multiplicity of churches or sects or groups. In such heterogeneous societies, Radcliffe-Brown says (rather mournfully, one feels), 'the relation of religion to the total social structure is in many respects indirect and not always easy to trace' (Radcliffe-Brown 1952:177). But he seems sure it is *there*.

On secular territory scholars have repeatedly pursued correspondence between kinship ideology and kinship organization, since Morgan explained types of kinship terminology as expressions of particular forms of marriage and groupings of kin (Morgan 1877; 1963 ed.). Causal links have been sought between the actual organization of groups of persons on the ground and their ideas about kinship, such as the matrilineal and patrilineal principles, terminologies that classify kin and such. One general assumption Morgan made (which has been made since, notably by Murdock) is that at some *point in time*, at the apogee of development of a particular system, there is a logical parallelism between kinship ideology and kinship organization (Murdock 1949). It is at this point of maximal logical congruence that ideas about descent and terms that classify relatives are presumed to have adapted completely to fit the pre-existing realities of marriage and local grouping. Morgan's way of dealing with discrepancies, with instances where there was no fit, was to assume that this was simply an indication of a transitional phase.

His underlying postulate was that ideology was more durable than organization, hence that cultural expression would lag behind social reality. According to this view, new forms of social organization would arise first, and these would produce their corresponding systems of classification. Incongruities could be explained as the result of a period of overlap between old ideology and new organization. For Morgan, kinship terminology itself could be used as the medium for a social archeology. Primitive promiscuity, one of the specific historical reconstructions Morgan made on this basis, has been discarded happily. However, the notion that ideology can be more durable than the organization with which it was congruent remains a theme in anthropology.

Such, for example, is the framework of Murdock's *Social Structure* (1949), in which he postulates a sequence in which a stable kinship system is supposed to experience change. It starts with a modification of the 'rule of residence' which eventually results in changes in the form of kin groups and, ultimately, in changes in terminology. Thus change is assumed to begin with alterations in 'on-the-ground' organization, which subsequently produces changes in ideology. Incongruities between kinship ideology and organization are invariably explained by Murdock as examples of change, or intermediate phases. It is not our purpose here to discuss Murdock's results, nor for that matter Morgan's. Rather it is to point out that both of them see the ideological aspects of kinship as a reflection of organizational realities that preceded the ideology in time. Our purpose is to contrast this conception of sequence with the perspective of the socal planner, the political ideologue, the club organizer, and the systems man. These are conscious organizers, people who plan organization. For them the ideology, the model, the plan and purpose, the structure, comes first, and the actual organization is assembled afterward. These are two quite opposite developmental sequences, but both treat *congruence* between ideology and organization as a key concept, as the culmination toward which the process moves.

There is another approach, an instrumental approach, to the problem which also emphasizes congruence, but in quite a different way. Malinowski, Evans-Pritchard, and others have analyzed ideology as a legitimator of current political and economic activity, as a charter for the legal exercise of rights and authority. It was not the foresight of the ancestress of each Trobriand subclan which made her emerge at the very spot where her descendants would establish their village and gardens, but rather the hindsight of her supposed descendants, who justified their land claims by inventing her (Malinowski 1935:341). Malinowski interpreted much of Trobriand myth and belief as an exotic legitimator for quite practical activities. The same can be said for the genealogical rationale of the Nuer political system (Evans-Pritchard 1940).

In all of these interpretations, congruence is stressed. Whether ideology is seen as an expression of social cohesion, or as a symbolic expression of structure, whether it is seen as a design for a new structure or as a rationalization for control of power and property, the analysis is made in terms of fit. Yet on close and less selective inspection, it becomes evident that the fit of certain parts of ideology to organization is frequently on a very high level of generality. The Tiv and the Nuer share a segmentary-lineage ideology, but the composition of the local settlements of each is not at all the same. To read a constitution is not to understand how the political system works.

Today few anthropologists are exclusively occupied with consistency and congruence. Lévi-Strauss has put the question, 'To what extent does the manner in which a society conceives its orders and their ordering correspond to the real situation?' (1958; 1963 ed.:312). Leach has said that, 'When social structures are expressed in cultural form, the representation is imprecise,' and the 'inconsistencies in the logic of ritual expression' thus produced are necessary to the functioning of the social system (1954:4).

Turner has put the problem in processual and situational terms,

> From the point of view of social dynamics a social system is not a harmonious configuration governed by mutually compatible and logically inter-related principles. It is rather a set of loosely integrated processes, with some patterned aspects, some persistencies of form, but controlled by discrepant principles of action expressed in rules of custom that are often situationally incompatible with one another. (1967:196)

Apart from some conspicuous rhetorical exaggerations of the pervasiveness of social structures and cultural patterns, few anthropologists, past or present, have been unaware that there generally are differences between ideal norms and real behavior. In recent decades what has happened in some quarters in anthropology is that there has been a shift of emphasis from the study of normative models to the study of specific situations and specific sequences of events. This shift in ethnographic subject-matter has been accompanied by an intensified awareness, ignored at one's peril, that 'ideological systems' as well as 'social systems' are frequently full of inconsistencies, oppositions, contradictions, and tensions, that there is much individual and situational variation, and that cultural and social change is continuous, though it may take place at a more or less rapid rate and be more or less radical or pervasive. Even the classical British structural-functionalists, who are often accused by their critics of being unaware of all these circumstances of social life, were not by any means all unaware of them. They chose rather to ignore them in order to concentrate on the elements of order. If one reads the pronouncements of some of their representatives, one finds that they say quite explicitly that their models are 'as-if' models, used as heuristic fictions, as selective constructs, that they are not offering a mirror for reality but seeking to understand the regularities in social life (Gluckman 1968; Nadel 1957:147, 154; Firth 1964:12, 59).

But recently among the historically, politically, and situationally minded in British social anthropology as well as elsewhere, there has been discomfort with an exclusive reliance on structural-functional models, a discomfort that goes much deeper than worry over the matter of reification. A model that is artificially timeless and focuses exclusively on regularities and systematic consistencies is useful because it is selective; but being so selective it has severe limitations. The question repeatedly raised in the last two or three decades is, whether a focus on regularity and consistency should not be replaced by a focus on change, on process over time, and on paradox, conflict, inconsistency, contradiction, multiplicity, and manipulability in social life? (see Firth 1964:59; Barth 1966; Mitchell 1964:v–xiv; Leach 1962:133; Turner 1957; van Velsen 1967).

Murphy, who has written one of the most recent of these academic calls to arms, has named his book *The Dialectics of Social Life*. He says, 'Social life is indeed a series of contradictions' (1971:143). He calls on the anthropologist to practice 'the dialectical exercise,' which he asserts to be 'simple in the extreme.' The anthropologist should, according to Murphy (1971:117):

question everything that he sees and hears, examine

phenomena fully and from every angle, seek and evaluate the contradiction of any proposition, and consider every category from the viewpoint of its noncontents as well as its positive attributes. It (the dialectical exercise) requires us to also look for paradox as much as complementarity, for opposition as much as accommodation. It portrays a universe of dissonance underlying apparent order and seeks deeper orders beyond the dissonance.

Essentially, his formula is to seek the opposite of everything that seems obvious, what is hidden behind everything that seems apparent, and what in turn is hidden behind that. Simple indeed! A major objective of the method he proposes is to uncover as much as possible the lack of congruence between conscious models of society and the way it actually works. He sees this lack of congruence as a central fact of social life, and as a central problem of scholarly epistemology.

Murphy's attitude is not unique, though he is somewhat eclectic in his interpretation of the place of these phenomena. His approach is very much in keeping with tendencies in the discipline. This is particularly so of two of his preoccupations: the concentration on 'activity,' that is, on process seen through particular events and situations, on people in action, and the stress on contradiction, inconsistency, and paradox. The cases and questions presented in the present volume embody these concerns. All involve specific situations in which contradictions, inconsistencies, and paradoxes in social life and ideology have had to be dealt with by people committed to a harmonious way of looking at themselves.

Are such contradictions and the lack of perfect fit between conscious models and social actions the dominant feature of social life? Murphy has argued, 'It is the very incongruence of our conscious models, and guides for conduct to the phenomena of social life that makes that life possible' (1971:240). Certainly elements of incongruence are omnipresent, but so are elements of consistency, and elements of order. Order and repetition are not all illusion, nor all 'mere' ideology, nor all fictive scholarly models, but are observable on a behavioral level, as well as in expressed ideas. There is frequently some underlying order even in the contradictions and paradoxes and in the way they affect social life, as Murphy himself suggests.

What Murphy calls 'the dialectical exercise' is a good open-ended technique for scholarly exploration, but it is neither a classificatory nor an explanatory device. It is a lively reaction against the exclusive use of normative models, but since these are *passé* anyway the problem remains what to use instead, particularly as norms are themselves social facts. Models are temporarily useful heuristic devices, the purpose of which is to focus attention on particular features of social life and relationship. All societal and processual models are simplifications. But they help to sort out the complexity of reality into manageable problems.

How can one analyze such order and regularity as there is while fully taking into account the innumerable changes, gaps, and contradictions? I propose that one useful way is to look at social processes in terms of the inter-relationship of three components: the processes of *regularization*, the processes of *situational adjustment*, and the factor of *indeterminacy*.[1] The conditions to which these terms allude are ubiquitous in social life. There seems to be a continuous struggle between the pressure toward establishing and/or maintaining order and regularity, and the underlying circumstance that counteractivities, discontinuities, variety, and complexity make social life inherently unsuited to total ordering. The strategies of individuals are seldom (if ever) consistently committed to reliance on rules and other regularities. For every occasion that a person thinks or says, 'That cannot be done, it is against the rules, or violates the categories,' there is another occasion when the same individual says, 'Those rules or categories do not (or should not) apply to this situation. This is a special case.'

Social life presents an almost endless variety of finely distinguishable situations and quite an array of grossly different ones. It contains arenas of continuous competition. It proceeds in the context of an ever-shifting set of persons, changing moments in time, altering situations, and partially improvised interactions. Established rules, customs, and symbolic frameworks exist, but they operate in the presence of areas of indeterminacy, or ambiguity, of uncertainty and manipulability. Order never fully takes over, nor could it. The cultural, contractual, and technical imperatives always leave gaps, require adjustments and interpretations to be applicable to particular situations, and are themselves full of ambiguities, inconsistencies, and often contradictions.

Every interpersonal encounter, every interaction may contain, on a microcosmic scale, some elements of this kind, some options, some range of alternatives. Even long-term relationships may 'develop' over time. That is, they may be minutely renegotiated, or reaffirmed, or both, with every meeting. The observations of Goffman and the detailed studies of the ethnomethodologists have brought into relief those nuances of interaction out of which there can emerge a mutual construction of social 'reality.' But the options are far from unlimited. To emphasize the potentialities within situations that depend on how the players play them out is an appropriate reaction against the most simplistic and archaic normative models. Yet it would be equally simplistic to yield to a vision of perpetual and total social amorphousness, unbounded innovation, and limitless reinterpretation. An emphasis on the range of manipulability within microsituations does not do away with the fact that larger political and economic contexts exist, that common symbols, customary behaviors, role expectations, rules, categories, ideas and ideologies, rituals and formalities shared by the actors with a larger society are used in these interactions as the framework of mutual communication and action. These place real and sometimes merely apparent limits on what is negotiable. By definition this set of social contexts and cultural artifacts affects the form of the interaction, and usually profoundly affects the content and outcome as well. Every interaction contains within it elements of the regular and elements of the indeterminate, and both are 'used' by individuals. This is true not only of small-scale, face-to-face encounters. It can also be said of plans and actions on a large impersonal scale, as in administrative action and legislation.

The whole matter contains a paradox. Every explicit attempt to fix social relationships or social symbols is by implication a recognition that they are mutable. Yet at the same time such an attempt directly struggles against mutability, attempts to fix the moving thing, to make it hold. Part of the process of trying to fix social reality involves representing it as stable and immutable or at least controllable to this end, at least for a time. Rituals, rigid procedures, regular formalities, symbolic repetitions of all kinds, as well as explicit laws, principles, rules, symbols, and categories are cultural representations of fixed social reality, of continuity. They represent stability and continuity acted out and re-enacted: visible continuity. By dint of repetition they deny the passage of time, the nature of change, and the implicit extent of potential indeterminacy in social relations. They are all a part of what we have called the 'processes of regularization.' Whether rituals, laws, rules, customs, symbols, ideological models, and so on, are old and legitimated by tradition, or newly forged and legitimated by a revolutionary social source, they constitute the explicit cultural framework through which the attempt is made to fix social life, to keep it from slipping into the sea of indeterminacy.

Yet, despite all the attempts to crystallize the rules, there invariably remains a certain range of maneuver, of openness, of choice, of interpretation, of alteration, of tampering, of reversing, of transforming. This is more so for some people than for others, more true of some situations than others. In many circumstances the people involved exploit the rules and indeterminacies as it suits their immediate purposes, sometimes using one resource, sometimes the other within a single situation, emphasizing the fixity of norms for one purpose, exploiting openings, adjustments, reinterpretations and redefinitions for another. As in the *kibbutz* or the *moshav*, sometimes a whole community consciously organizes itself according to a set of explicit principles and rules. Such a community may enthusiastically turn to rule-making processes and orderly symbols as if thereby girding itself against the amorphous uncertainty of indeterminacy, trying to prescribe against it as against a contagion. Other collectivities embrace particular indeterminacies as part of their credo, valuing above all individuality and spontaneity and a certain absence of rules (for example, some anti-planning communes and the 'happenings' of the Woodstock youth and the French students).

Turner has constructed a polarity of these collective ideologies. He considers them based on two fundamentally different kinds of *social relationship* which alternate and oppose each other in the course of history. He calls one 'structure' and the other 'communitas,' characterizing structure as based on 'norm-governed relationships between social personae,' and *communitas* as founded on 'free relationships between individuals' (1969:128, 132). Turner points out that over time, structured communities are subject to change, their rules are reinterpreted and redefined, they face new situations and unforeseen events and must make adjustments. In short, they may become less structured in terms of their original rules, principles, and plans. The opposite can be said of collectivities committed to an absence of structure, committed to indeterminacy. If they succeed in enduring over time, they often become more and more structured. Thus Turner sees society as the product of a dialectical process with successive phases of 'structure' and 'communitas' (1969:112, 203). He also recognizes their simultaneity. Turner's book *The Ritual Process* is subtitled, 'Structure and Anti-structure,' like some sort of social matter and anti-matter, in a dialectical relationship that produces the complex synthesis that is social life.

A number of the cases described in this book appear to fit the conditions of Turner's model, inviting analysis in these terms, for example see the comments of the editors. However, the analytic model proposed in this epilogue is only partly congruent with Turner's. For one thing, Turner is talking about two bases of *social relationship*, seeing them in opposition to each other (1969:131). He looks at the two modalities in many contexts: in ritual, the social organization of lineage-based societies, and in the context of a wide range of anti-establishment social and religious movements. Throughout, Turner is concerned with complementary and contradictory complexes of social relationship and the ideas associated with them. But the complexes of 'structured' and 'anti-structured' relationships and associated philosophies with which Turner is occupied can be seen as special cases of a much wider and more fragmented distribution of regulatory processes, situationally specific adjustments and indeterminacies in social life. The present model thus derives much from his basic concept of a dialectical relationship between structure and anti-structure, but it is not limited to the special circumstances to which he has applied the structure/anti-structure paradigm. There are much more general, in fact, omnipresent processes involved.

Process: changes in individual situations and changes in culture

What is a process? Is a process history, a sequence in time of connected events leading to a particular result? Or is it concerned with repeated types of series? The term is variously used in ethnographies: (1) to describe universal contexts of social contact such as processes of competition, or of co-operation, and the like: (2) to describe series of events that recur again and again in certain institutional contexts, such as, political processes, economic processes, educational processes, and so on; and (3) to describe the kinds of circumstances that lead to certain results, such as the process of industrialization, the process of urbanization, the process of segmentation, the process of stratification, and so on. These are obviously different levels of specificity and range. All have in common the element of observations made over time. All involve movement in the fortunes and relationships of individuals. Some also imply social and cultural change. Thus on the microscale, all processes involve change because they involve alterations in the situations of the individuals involved. But they do not necessarily involve social and cultural change on the macroscale.

When Gluckman calls his book *The Judicial Process*, or Turner calls his *The Ritual Process*, they are indicating that, though they may analyze Barotse or Ndembu material, in the main their purpose is not narrowly ethnographic (Gluckman 1955a; Turner 1969). They are identifying certain kinds of repeated unfoldings of events in an institutional context and in a regular sequence. The implication throughout is that similar types of unfolding series occur in other societies with different cultures. It is also clear that, as Gluckman and Turner conceive them, 'the judicial process' and 'the ritual process' may accommodate considerable change, though they operate within apparently stable formal frameworks.

In many theoretical writings 'process' is contrasted with structure. Partly defined in terms of what it is, it is even more often characterized by what it is not. 'Process' also is often the flag under which attacks are made on studies of 'structure.' A brief review of some of the dichotomies and discussions may provide a clearer picture of the current connotations of 'process' in anthropology. Firth, for example, has long had his own way of dealing with process and its terminological predecessor 'dynamic analysis' (see 1964:7–29 in which he reviews his position in relation to the work of others). His basic theoretical dichotomy is between 'structure' and 'organization.' Organization is processual, 'the working arrangements of society' (see 1964:45, republishing an essay of 1954). It encompasses all the decisions and choices that make up daily life, the nuances, the variations and the changes. 'Social structure,' in Firth's terminology, consists of continuities, the persistent and invariant in social life. 'It will be clear,' he says (1964:45–6):

> that these concepts of social structure and social organization, though complementary, are not parallel.... Social organization

43

... [is] ... a point of view.... The two concepts cross-out each
other.... The relation between form and process may be
difficult to elucidate; it may be easier for us to make
generalizations about form than process. But this does not
absolve us from the necessity of studying process.

In 1955, a year after this was written, Nadel took issue with the
notion that social structure was something different from process.
He saw 'structure' as an abstraction from repetitive events, and
used 'process' to refer to recurrent types of movement *within* social
structures, 'the mechanics of intake and circulation' in social roles
and positions (published 1957:129–30). Nadel had two particular
kinds of process in mind: (1) shifts of persons in roles and positions
that are regularly relinquished, and (2) shifts of persons' positions
resulting from 'all conflict relationships,' including, 'all the forms
of antagonism we normally call competition and rivalry'
(1957:130).

Though he spoke in terms of social structure, Nadel emphasized
that it was an abstraction, that it should not be reified. He quoted
Firth with approval, saying, 'The social structure viewed as
something within the grasp of the ethnographer's account is a
myth' (1957:153). Nadel had no illusion that structure implied
total internal unity or coherence. 'Our ordered arrangement,' he
said, 'far from being a total one, must remain fragmentary. In a
word, it seems impossible to speak of social structure in the
singular' (1957:97). Nadel also acknowledged that there are
necessarily questions about the relative durability and relative
repetitiveness of various elements that are abstracted into the
'ordered arrangement' called 'structure.' He fully recognized that
there may be considerable areas of indeterminacy in a social
system, for example: *indeterminate role relationships* not governed by
established norms (in which options are 'roughly unlimited' and
the incidence of actual choices show a random scatter (1957:138)),
and *zones of indeterminacy* in the 'system' of social positions. (If one
thinks of structure as an ordered arrangement of social positions
and roles, then those that are disconnected, or not equivalent to
others, cannot be fitted into a total order.) Nadel does not connect
these kinds of indeterminacy with the term 'process,' but simply
shows by means of them that his definition of the structural model
is only relatively and imperfectly coherent, determinate, and
durable. As indicated earlier, process for Nadel is essentially 'the

mechanics of intake and circulation' of persons through a fixed set of social roles and positions (1957:129–30).

Ten years later Barth developed a model that used the basic form-process dichotomy that Firth had discussed. Barth added his own elaborations, and these have stimulated a great deal of creative work. Barth treats process as the opposite of structure, using process essentially as a means of understanding social change. He asks how social structures, or, as he calls them, 'social forms' are generated. As core ethnographic datum, he proposes 'transaction [as] a prototype for a processual model of interaction' (1966:5). His argument is that anthropologists should study transactions to identify the basic variables that produce particular social forms. These variables could then be used to construct 'generative models,' rather like Chomsky's 'generative grammar.' The generative models could be manipulated to produce a variety of social forms through the juggling of the variables. The model could be checked and tested by being compared with actual social systems. Barth complains, 'We have been altogether too ready in social anthropology to produce special explanations for everything ... ,' and argues that his models are an attempt to generalize (1966:30). But a page later he acknowledges the difficulties attendant on making processual comparisons. 'Admittedly,' he says, 'it is very difficult to maintain any great rigor in the comparisons.... Each new case introduced in the comparison compels one to introduce new factors as variables' (1966:31–2).

There is no need to deal here with the semantic model-building niceties involved in whether one includes 'process' within the framework of social structure or whether one treats it as something outside; whether like Firth and Nadel one treats 'structure' as a myth, a useful one, or whether one treats 'structure' as a distorting artificial construct, so static that it distracts from the study of dynamic processes. For present purposes these questions should be set aside. They involve an unnecessary either/or polemic. What is useful in these various writings is that taken together they suggest certain gross classifications of processual studies. They seem to divide roughly between the study of regular repetitive events having to do with the circulation of persons, power, goods, and information, and the study of events specifically having to do with processes of changing social and cultural regularities. In abbreviated outline:

A *The movement of individuals through roles and positions*
Repetitive or cyclic events that nevertheless imply shifts and
changes of relations between or among particular persons:

    (a) temporarily occupied roles.

    (b) shifts and adjustments connected with conflict,
competition, exchange, communication, and the exercise of
power.

B *Changes of norms and of social/cultural regularities*
Events that imply shifting and changing social/cultural
frameworks and symbols; the generation of social forms:

    (a) from indeterminacy to determinacy or vice versa (i.e., the
generation of social forms where they did not exist before, or
the degeneration of social forms into indeterminacy).

    (b) the replacement of existing rules or forms with new rules
or forms (i.e., the change from one kind of determinate
arrangement to another).

What is immediately evident is that A and B are not and cannot be
exclusive categories. The mechanisms of circulation and
competition are continuously in operation, and they imply
unending movement of individual circumstances. The persons
they involve are interested persons, who often manipulate their
situations and are not merely automatons passing through
mandatory role shifts. These situations of relative individual
movement may be *par excellence* the parts of social life into which
questions of indeterminacy and change in social regularities are
most immediately introduced. This is why 'transactions,' which
Barth has emphasized, are in fact so often very revelatory.
Through the observation of transactions, many of the detailed
operations of the regular circulatory and redistributive
mechanisms that change the lot of individuals may be understood,
as well as the conditions of interaction that permit the
introduction of or adjustment to certain kinds of change in the
rules of the game. *Changes in the relative positions of individuals and
changes in social regularities are connected though not coextensive phenomena.
It is this connection which certain structural models have deliberately ignored.*

Structural models deliberately discount all that is not regular
and all that is particular. Nadel says, 'in progressively discounting
the particular features of social situations ... we prepare the way
for the discovery of general characteristics and regularities, and
hence of the lawfulness – such lawfulness as obtains – in the realm

of social existence' (1957:154). 'Regular' can be taken in at least two ways. It can refer simply to any repeated behavior, or it can refer to behavior that is dictated by culturally explicit rules. Lévi-Strauss has called models based on these two types of regularity 'statistical models' and 'mechanical models.' They differ in that the former focuses on behavior and the latter on ideas; but they are similar in that both emphasize regularity, repetition, continuity, and consistency (1963:283–9).

The point has been reached in anthropology at which it may be more illuminating to look on repetition and regularization as processes in competition with other processes, rather than as dichotomizing absolutely between structure and process, or the static and the changing, or the consistent and the contradictory. This is certainly the implication of the work of the Manchester school in situational analysis, extended case study, and network analysis. It is the implication of Barth's transactional analysis, or current sociological studies that are heavily ethnographic, and the microsociology of Goffman and the ethnomethodologists. Needham has said, in another connection,

> If our first task as social anthropologists is to discern order and make it intelligible, our no less urgent duty is to make sense of those practically universal usages and beliefs by which people create disorder, i.e., turn their classifications upside down or disintegrate them entirely. (Needham 1963:xl)

Granted that structural models have serious limitations, some of the attacks on structural anthropology place unnecessary limits on the alternatives. Certain critics of structural models assume that 'structural' is equivalent to 'static' and that 'processual' is equivalent to 'changing.' The problem with this view is that it excludes looking at the processes that produce continuities and repetitions, and focuses only on the processes that produce innovations.

In the cruder versions of this critique of structure in which process becomes too exclusively associated with change yet another blind-spot is produced. If the categories of analysis treat *change* as in some sense the opposite of *regularity*, there is not sufficient place given to indeterminacy, to elements in situations which are neither regular nor changing, but are rather matters of open or multiple option. As soon as one inspects real situations supposedly governed by culturally determined rules, one discovers that even within such 'regulated' situations there are invariably elements and levels of indeterminacy. This is very evident in legal studies. Change, as indicated earlier, can be a matter of actually changing the rules, that is, of explicitly replacing one regularity with another. Or change may be a much more subtle thing, a shift from regularity to indeterminacy, or from indeterminacy to regularity, or through the whole series of possibilities occurring in the way Barth (1966) has emphasized, through the cumulative effect of changing individual choice.

It is important to recognize that processes of regularization, processes having to do with rules and regularities, may be used to block change or to produce change. The fixing of rules and regularities are as much tools of revolutionaries as they are of reactionaries. It is disastrous to confuse the analysis of processes of regularization with the construction of static social models. The effect of this confusion is to discard from processual analysis some of the basic techniques of societal organization. Analogously, it is clear that not all transactional interaction produces social change. The negotiations of individuals within situations may themselves be so patterned or repetitive that they can perpetuate a social condition just as effectively as the calculated maintenance of an explicit set of rules. One can analyze the efforts of people to use in different ways and to different ends the regularities and the indeterminacies presented by their situations (or which they introduce into these situations). The presence or absence of social change as an eventual outcome is an independent question. An adequate processual study of change is inextricably bound up with the processual study of continuity and indeterminacy. An adequate study of what is negotiable in situations cannot be made without attention to what is not negotiable in the same situation.

An analytic framework

It was indicated earlier that one of the objectives of this epilogue is to propose a very simple framework to clarify the analysis of situations, a framework to take account of ideology and action, continuity and change, micro- and macroperspectives. The basic postulate proposed is that the underlying quality of social life should be considered to be one of theoretically absolute indeterminacy. To put it simply, in this model social life is presumed to be indeterminate except in so far as culture and organized or patterned social relationships make it determinate. The assumption is that it is useful to conceive an underlying, theoretically absolute cultural and social indeterminacy, which is only partially done away with by culture and organized social life, the patterned aspects of which are temporary, incomplete, and contain elements of inconsistency, ambiguity, discontinuity, contradiction, paradox, and conflict. It is therefore suggested that even within the social and cultural order there is a pervasive quality of partial indeterminacy. Even in matters where there are rules and customs socially and culturally generated, indeterminacy may be produced by the manipulation of existing internal contradictions, inconsistencies, and ambiguities within the universe of relatively determinate elements.

A further qualitative complication arises as soon as one considers the dimensions of symbol and form as opposed to content. Apparent determinacy, in the guise of regularities of classification, symbol, and of form, may veil fundamental instabilities and changes of content. The Constitution of the United States is a good example of historic continuity of a determinate form subjected to continuous reinterpretation of content. Seeming indeterminacy of form may, in turn, veil actual regularity of content. Another example: certain types of meetings and gatherings are carried on in an atmosphere of mandatory informality and apparent openness of options. Yet these amorphous procedures may obscure very firm underlying regularities of power and decision. Thus regularity and indeterminacy may be of form and symbol or of content (or most often of some mixture). This greatly complicates analysis. To recognize this is to recognize that an anthropology exclusively focused on clear regularities of form, symbol, and content, and their presumed congruence (whether 'structural,' 'cultural,' or 'processual' in orientation) is leaving out fundamental dimensions. The negotiable part of many real situations lies not only in the imperfect fit between the symbolic or formal level and the level of content, but also in the multiplicity of alternatives and meaning within each, which may accommodate a range of manipulation, interpretation, and choice. Individuals or groups may exaggerate the degree of order of the quality of indeterminacy in their situations for myriad reasons.

An analysis based on the assumption that there are elements of indeterminacy, potential and present in most if not all situations, makes it possible to interpret behavior in terms of two kinds of processes: the first are of the kind in which people try to control their situations by struggling against indeterminacy, by trying to fix social reality, to harden it, to give it form and order and predictability. These are the kinds of processes that produce 'conscious models,' that produce rules and organizations and customs and symbols and rituals and categories and seek to make them durable. This is done so that the individuals involved can hold constant some of the factors with which they must deal. A fixed framework of rules or understandings has certain significant advantages. It means that every instance and every interaction does not have to be completely renegotiated in a totally open field of possibilities. It means that there is some stability and predictability in people's affairs and that complex projects can be undertaken and suitable strategies planned on the basis of reasonable expectations about the behavior of other persons and/ or their frames of reference. This would seem to be why people 'constructing social reality,' as the ethnomethodologists put it, often try to make their constructs durable and binding on others. We have called these attempts to crystallize and concretize social reality, to make it determinate and firm, 'processes of regularization.' The second, the countervailing processes, are those by means of which people arrange their immediate situations (and/or express their feelings and conceptions) by exploiting the indeterminacies in the situation, or by generating such indeterminacies, or by reinterpreting or redefining the rules or relationships. They use whatever areas there are of inconsistency, contradiction, conflict, ambiguity, or open areas that are normatively indeterminate to achieve immediate situational ends. These strategies continuously reinject elements of indeterminacy into social negotiations, making active use of them and making absolute ordering the more impossible. These processes introduce or maintain the element of plasticity in social arrangements. We have called these 'processes of situational adjustment.'

In the effort to construct, in so far as possible, a social reality that suits their purposes, people may resort to both kinds of techniques, often in the very same situation. What this model provides is a way of looking at what is taking place in terms of its effects, not on individual fortunes alone, but on the solidifying or eroding or transforming or dissolving of cultural and social regularities. The effects selected out for attention by this model are the increase or decrease of the determinate and fixed in social relations and cultural expressions. The model takes it into account that determining and fixing are processes, not states that are ever permanently achieved. The fixed in social reality really means the continuously renewed. And it is clear from the model that the processes of situational adjustment are likely to make what start out as processes of renewal into processes of change.

What is also clear is that strategies used in situational adjustment – adopted, to be sure, in the context of immediate needs – if repeated sufficiently often, by sufficient numbers of people, may become part of the processes of regularization. Analogously, if new rules are made for every situation, the rules cease to be part of the processes of regularization and become elements of situational adjustment. Thus each of these processes contains within itself the possibility of becoming its schematic opposite.

This model, which provides an open-ended way of working with a great variety of materials, including the cases in this book that show a marked discrepancy between expressed ideals of community harmony and a more complex social reality, makes it possible to look at the long history of the theme of congruence between ideology and social life, and the newer tradition that emphasizes lack of fit between the one and the other, and see that both sociological attitudes may contain enough truth to be illuminating. There is no need to *replace* a past preoccupation with systematic regularity by substituting a present preoccupation with systematic contradiction. On the contrary, it is possible to harvest the insights of both. One can see the focus on systematic consistency as an analytic emphasis on the cultural products of the processes of regularization, and the concentration on discontinuity, contradiction, and paradox as a focus on the cultural concomitants of processes of situational adjustment. Neither does justice to indeterminacy.

Ideology may be regarded as a product of what we have called the regularizing processes. Yet its instance-by-instance use permits the kind of reinterpretation, redefinition, and manipulation that is associated with processes of situational adjustment. Sometimes an ideology or part of it can be constructed precisely to cover the complex mess of social reality with an appearance of order, simplicity, harmony, and plan. But sometimes, and at other levels, the ideology of a society, or of some subpart of it, is not more of a harmonious whole than the on-the-ground realities. The fact is that when we speak of the ideology of a group of persons, or of a society or some part of it, we are speaking of it as a whole. But usually, in action, in particular situations, only pieces of ideology are invoked. Since ideology is used this way – piecemeal – inconsistencies are not necessarily apparent, as they might be when put together in an analysis.

It is this imprecision that gives plausible ethnographic support to almost all the various theoretical positions described earlier, even though the positions seem contradictory. The explanatory puzzle that remains tantalizing is that in some instances cultural representations of social relationships seem to be much more closely reflective of social reality than in others. There sometimes appears to be a remarkable degree of fit between ideology, or symbolic system, or organizational plan and on-the-ground realities. At other times and places, or in other parts of the socio-cultural system, the fit is very poor. This chapter has tried to propose an analytic framework that could account for such a range of circumstances. If the assumption is made that in some underlying and basic sense social reality is fluid and indeterminate, and that it is transformed into something more fixed through regularizing processes, yet can never entirely or completely lose all of its indeterminacy, a great range of variability can be accounted for. Regularizing processes can be analyzed as they are tempered by processes of situational adjustment and both may be shown to be operating in a partially indeterminate social medium. All of these elements can be analyzed in terms of symbolic representations as well as on the level of social relationship.

This is a framework usable in the analysis of particular situations and their detailed dénouement, and equally usable in the analysis of larger-scale phenomena such as institutional systems. It is perhaps worth reiterating that this is not a matter of analyzing the forces of systemic maintenance as they are unsettled by forces of change. Whether the processes are unchanging or changing is not the dichotomy proposed. Processes of regularization and processes of situational adjustment may each have the effect of stabilizing *or* changing an existing social situation or order. What is being proposed is that the complex relationship between social life and its cultural representation may be easier to handle analytically if the interlocking of processes of regularization, processes of situational adjustment, and the factor of indeterminacy are taken into account.

Note

1 Lest there be any confusion, it should be made clear that 'determinacy' is not being used here to refer to cause and effect. What is meant by 'determinate' in this chapter is that which is culturally or socially regulated or regularized.

Chapter 2

Law and social change: the semi-autonomous social field as an appropriate subject of study

We must have a look at society and culture at large in order to find the place of law within the total structure.

E. Adamson Hoebel, *The Law of Primitive Man*,
Cambridge, Massachusetts (1954:5)

In our highly centralized political system, with its advanced technology and communications apparatus, it is tempting to think that legal innovation can effect social change. Roscoe Pound perceived the law as a tool for social engineering (1965:247–52). Some version of this idea is the current rationale for most legislation. Underlying the social engineering view is the assumption that social arrangements are susceptible to conscious human control, and that the instrument by means of which this control is to be achieved is law. In such formulations 'the law' is a short term for a very complex aggregation of principles, norms, ideas, rules, practices, and the agencies of legislation, administration, adjudication and enforcement, backed by political power and legitimacy. The complex 'law,' thus

Reprinted from *Law and Society Review* (Summer 1973: 719–46) by permission of the Law and Society Association.

Author's note
I acknowledge with gratitude a grant from the Joint Committee on African Studies of the Social Science Research Council given me in 1968 and 1969 which made this fieldwork possible. I also wish to thank Professor Max Gluckman for his helpful comment on this paper.

condensed into one term, is abstracted from the social context in which it exists, and is spoken of as if it were an entity capable of controlling that context. But the contrary can also be persuasively argued: that 'it is society that controls law and not the reverse' (Cochrane 1971:93–4). This semantic morass is partly the result of the multiplicity of referents of the terms 'law' and 'society.' But both ways of describing the state of affairs have the same implication for the sociological study of law. Law and the social context in which it operates must be inspected together. As Selznick has said, there is no longer any need 'to argue the general interdependence of law and society' (1959:115). Yet although everyone acknowledges that the enforceable rules stated and restated in legal institutions, in legislatures, courts and administrative agencies, also have a place in ordinary social life (Bohannan 1965), that normal locus is where they are least studied. (See, for example, the emphasis on the study of official behavior in the recent Chambliss and Seidman (1971), and on dispute settlement in much of the recent anthropological literature, cf., Moore (1969). A significant exception is the emphasis on 'law-in-society' in Friedman and Macaulay (1969).)

Both the study of official behavior and the study of dispute settlement have been very productive. Schapera, in his study of Tswana chiefs, has produced the only anthropological study of tribal legislation and social change, and a very interesting work it is (Schapera 1970). Thus it is without any critical animus that this paper will suggest that there are other productive approaches as well, that it may be useful for some purposes to return to the broad conceptions of Malinowski who set out to 'analyse all the rules conceived and acted upon as binding obligations, to find out the nature of the binding forces, and to classify the rules according to the manner in which they are made valid' (1926:23). Malinowski looked at ordinary Trobriand behavior to find this material. For reasons I hope to make clear, this breadth of approach applied to a narrow field of observation seems particularly appropriate to the study of law and social change in complex societies.

The approach proposed here is that the small field observable to an anthropologist be chosen and studied in terms of its semi-autonomy – the fact that it can generate rules and customs and symbols internally, but that it is also vulnerable to rules and decisions and other forces emanating from the larger world by which it is surrounded. The semi-autonomous social field has rule-making capacities, and the means to induce or coerce compliance; but it is simultaneously set in a larger social matrix which can, and does, affect and invade it, sometimes at the invitation of persons inside it, sometimes at its own instance. The analytic problem of fields of autonomy exists in tribal society, but it is an even more central analytic issue in the social anthropology of complex societies. All the nation-states of the world, new and old, are complex societies in that sense. The analytic problem is ubiquitous.

Much as we may agree with Professor Hoebel that force, legitimately applied (or the threat of its application), is a useful criterion for distinguishing legal norms from others for certain analytic purposes, an emphasis on the capacity of the modern state to threaten to use physical force should not distract us from the other agencies and modes of inducing compliance (Pospisil 1971:193–232; Weber 1954:15). Though the formal legal institutions may enjoy a near monopoly on the legitimate use of force, they cannot be said to have a monopoly of any kind on the other various forms of effective coercion or effective inducement. It is well established that between the body politic and the individual, there are interposed various smaller organized social fields to which the individual 'belongs.' These social fields have their own customs and rules and the means of coercing or inducing compliance (see Pospisil on 'Legal Levels and Multiplicity of Legal Systems,' 1971:97–126). They have what Weber called a 'legal order.' Weber argued that the typical means of statutory coercion applied by private organizations against refractory members is exclusion from the corporate body and its tangible or intangible advantages, but that they also frequently exert pressure on outsiders as well as insiders (Weber 1954:18–19).

Weber also recognized the difficulties of effectuating successful legislative coercion in the economic sphere. He attributed these difficulties partly to the effects of the complex interdependence of individual economic units in the market, partly to the fact that, 'the inclination to forego economic opportunity simply in order to act legally is obviously slight, unless circumvention of the formal law is strongly disapproved by a powerful convention' (Weber 1954:38). He was also very much aware of the chances of getting away with non-compliance, among other things, because:

it is obvious ... that those who continuously participate in the market intercourse with their own economic interests have a far greater rational knowledge of the market and interest situation than the legislators and enforcement officers whose interest is only ideal. In an economy based on all-embracing interdependence in the market, the possible and unintended repercussions of a legal measure must to a large extent escape the foresight of the legislator simply because they depend upon private interested parties. It is those private interested parties who are in a position to distort the intended meaning of a legal norm to the point of turning it into its very opposite, as has often happened in the past. (Weber, *ibid.*)

This paper will argue that an inspection of semi-autonomous social fields strongly suggests that the various processes that make internally generated rules effective are often also the immediate forces that dictate the mode of compliance or non-compliance to state-made legal rules. It will also argue a methodological point: that the semi-autonomous social field is *par excellence* a suitable way of defining areas for social anthropological study in complex societies. It designates a social locale to which anthropological techniques of inquiry and observation can be applied in urban as well as rural settings. By definition it requires attention to the problem of connection with the larger society. It is an area of study to which a number of current techniques could be fruitfully applied in combination: network analysis (Mitchell, *et al.* 1969), transactional analysis (Barth 1966), the analysis of negotiation (Gulliver 1963, 1969), the politics of corporate groups (Smith 1966), situational analysis and the extended case method (Garbett 1970; van Velsen 1967; Turner 1957) and the analysis of public explanations made in normative terms (Gluckman 1955a, 1965b; Moore 1970).

The semi-autonomous social field is defined and its boundaries identified not by its organization (it may be a corporate group, it may not) but by a processual characteristic, the fact that it can generate rules and coerce or induce compliance to them. Thus an arena in which a number of corporate groups deal with each other may be a semi-autonomous social field. Also the corporate groups themselves may each constitute a semi-autonomous social field. Many such fields may articulate with others in such a way as to form complex chains, rather the way the social networks of individuals, when attached to each other, may be considered as unending chains. The interdependent articulation of many different social fields constitutes one of the basic characteristics of complex societies.

The concept of a semi-autonomous social field puts emphasis on the issues of autonomy and isolation, or rather, the absence of autonomy and isolation, as well as focusing on the capacity to generate rules and induce or coerce conformity. It is the issue of semi-autonomy which principally differentiates this definition of the problem from a purely transactional one. In Barth's model, he has analyzed the ways in which new values and norms can be generated in transactions (1966). But in each of the cases of change he discusses, the chain of change has been initiated outside the transacting field, whether it is technological change in the case of the herring fishermen, or a road and imposed peace in the case of the Swat Pathans, or a demographic change in Iraq. In Barth's examples, it is after the initial change reaches the social field that transactions generate new norms and values. In Barth's model rules 'evolve.' They emerge from many individual transactions and choices which cumulate in new norms and values. There is no doubt that some norms develop in this way and that his model is very useful. But norms are also legislated by governments, or dictated by administrative and judicial decisions, or imposed in other intentional ways by private agencies. These impinge on semi-autonomous social fields which already have rules and customs.

One of the most usual ways in which centralized governments invade the social fields within their boundaries is by means of legislation. But innovative legislation or other attempts to direct change often fail to achieve their intended purposes; and even when they succeed wholly or partially, they frequently carry with them unplanned and unexpected consequences. This is partly because new laws are thrust upon going social arrangements in which there are complexes of binding obligations already in existence. Legislation is often passed with the intention of altering the going social arrangements in specified ways. The social arrangements are often effectively stronger than the new laws. It is not with any optimism about practical consequences that it is suggested that semi-autonomous social fields are of anthropological interest. It is rather because studies in the nature of the autonomy and the quality of their self-regulation may yield valuable information about the processes of social life in complex societies.

To illustrate these points, this paper will sketch the outlines of two quite different social fields – one in the United States and one in Africa today. The first is a small segment of the dress industry in New York. I have not done fieldwork in the garment industry; the information comes from having spoken with some people involved in it and reading some books. No attempt has been made to deal directly with the issue of change in the dress industry example, since the purpose of the illustration is simply to show how a semi-autonomous social field works, some of the internal and external links it has, and how legal, illegal and non-legal norms all intermesh in the annual round of its activities. The African material was gathered in fieldwork among the Chagga of Mount Kilimanjaro in 1968 and 1969.

Mutual obligation, legal and non-legal, in the better dress line

The production of expensive readymade women's dresses in New York is divided between the *jobber*'s establishment where the designing is done, and in whose showroom garments are displayed to retailers, and the *contractor*'s workshop, where the cloth is cut and the dresses are actually made. Some jobbers are themselves designers, some hire a designer. In either case the designing is done at the jobber's end of the arrangement. Sometimes the jobber also maintains a small workshop, an 'inside shop' to produce a few garments, but if he is doing well, the inside shop is never large enough to handle all his manufacturing, so he must use outside contractors in addition. The view from the contractor's shop is the one taken here as this was the part of the industry with which my informant was associated.[1]

The garment trade at this level is very volatile, dependent upon the vagaries of fashion, subject to great seasonal changes. At one moment there may be a great glut of work and not nearly enough machines or workers or time to meet some burst of demand for a particular line of garments. At other times business may be very slack, with barely enough work to keep things moving. It is a piecework industry.

The jobber makes a sizable capital investment in the showroom, in the designer, in other skilled personnel, and in the fabric with which a garment is to be made. The jobber supplies the fabric to the contractor. If the jobber does not have the capital to buy the fabric, he may borrow from a *factor* who lends money for this purpose for interest. The jobber may not get his money back on his investment until the next season, and so the factor may have to wait some months for his repayment. Two key people in the establishment of the jobber are his production man, who works out the details of the arrangements concerning the contractors (how much work is to go to each contractor, which style, what the price paid to the contractor is to be for each style, etc.), and his examiner, who looks over the garments after they have been made by the contractor to see that they meet the designer's specifications and the jobber's standards. She sends garments back for reworking if she does not find them up to the standards of the house.

On his side, the contractor must have a going establishment, a capital investment in workshop and machinery, and a group of skilled workers in his employ, the most important of whom is the 'floor lady.' The 'floor lady' not only supervises much of what goes on in the shop, on the workroom floor, but she also is strategically important in negotiations with the jobber's production man, since she and he are the people who bargain out what the price of any garment shall be. She is also the principal trade-union representative in the shop, and represents the workers *vis-à-vis* the contractor. She leads in deciding what garments they are willing to make and which they are not, since some work is much harder than other work.

There is another figure of importance, on the union side, and that is the union business agent. He is a full-time employee of the union, and it is his job to see that union rules are obeyed both by the boss-contractor and by the union workers. He also collects dues and has other administrative functions. The basic union contract in which these rules are spelled out is a contract between an association of contractors and jobbers and the International Ladies' Garment Workers' Union. This contract specifies such things as wages and hours. However the exigencies of the business are such that it would be impossible to make a profit unless the precise terms of these contracts were regularly broken. For one thing, when the opportunity arises to do a lot of work it has to be done quickly or there is nothing to be gained. A design will sell at one particular moment, and not at any time thereafter. Hence when business is plentiful, workers and contractors must produce dresses in a hurry and put in many more hours than the union contracts permit. On the other hand, when business is slack, workers must be paid even when they are not in fact working. The floor lady, for example, since she is the person in the most favored position in the contractor's shop, may be paid while she cruises around the world on vacation. It is simply understood between the union's business representative and the contractor that he will not enforce the contract to the letter. Presumably any alteration of the labor contract which would make its terms more closely approximate the actual seasonal conditions of the dress business would have undesirable side effects. That part of the bargaining position of the union that depends on overlooking violations would be impaired.

In return for his 'reasonableness,' the union representative receives many favors from the contractor. He may be given such tokens as whiskey in quantity at Christmas. The contractor may make dresses for his wife (which at the rate of $300 retail value per dress means that three dresses constitute a sizable present). He may present gifts on all the occasions of domestic rites – a child's birth, a child's graduation, marriage, or whatever. The contractor may, over the long term, develop a relationship with the union business agent, in which he visits him in the hospital when he is ill and has a general stance of solicitude and concern for his affairs. Like a concerned kinsman, the contractor may put the union man in touch with a doctor he knows, or try to get occupational advice for the union man's son. The person who is in charge of the gift of dresses to the union man's wife is the floor lady, who will either make them in part herself or supervise their production. She also is a significant figure in the making of 'gift' dresses for other persons, most notably for the jobber's production man, whom the contractor must sweeten regularly in order to assure himself that business will come his way. A contractor may develop the same kind of solicitous relationship of giving gifts and performing favors with a few important production men. The examiner is another person who also must be given gifts to insure that everything will go smoothly when she looks over the finished garments produced at the contractor's shop.

All these givings of gifts and doings of favors are done in the form of voluntary acts of friendship, and the occasions when they are given are holidays such as Christmas or other times when this would be in keeping with a relationship of friendship. None of them are legally enforceable obligations. One could not take a man to court who did not produce them. But there is no need for legal sanctions where there are such strong extralegal sanctions available. The contractor has to maintain these relationships or he is out of business.

The union contract with the association is legally binding, and the activities of the union man and the contractor regularly violate these legally enforceable provisions. They both recognize the business necessity of doing so and engage in repeated exchanges that demonstrate mutual trust. The union man closes his eyes, and the contractor makes dresses for the union man's wife. A satisfactory balance is achieved.

The contractor also depends on his workers to keep mum on this subject, to work the extra hours when these are needed in return for other favors at other times. He also may depend on his workers in other ways. As the garment workers, many of them married women, normally put a substantial part of their earnings into savings banks, they represent a source for loans when the contractor needs capital. The contractor himself may be a convenient source for loans to production men. Production men are salaried in the jobber's establishment, but not infrequently have outside deals in which they want to invest to earn extra dollars. They may appeal to the contractor to help them out. The jobber, too, may depend on the contractor for what are virtual loans. He may count on the contractor not to press for payment of what is owed him for the work done. This amounts to many months' extension of credit, and virtually an interest-free loan.

The discussion thus far of the exchanges of favors has not mentioned flattery and sexual attentions which are also used in the relationships between the contractor and the various women, both in his own establishment and in the jobber's place. Not only gifts, but other attentions may well accompany the more concrete evidence of esteem.

All these extralegal givings can be called 'bribery' if one chooses to emphasize their extralegal qualities. One could instead use the classical anthropological opposition of moral to legal obligations and call these 'moral' obligations, since they are obligations of relationship that are not legally enforceable, but which depend for their enforcement on the values of the relationship itself. They are all gifts or attentions calculated to induce or ease the allocation of scarce resources. The inducements and coercions involved in this system of relationships are founded on wanting to stay in the game, and on wanting to do well in it.

What general principles are suggested by this material on the dress industry? What processes can be identified? For one thing, there would appear to be a pervasive tendency to convert limited instrumental relationships into what are, at least in form and symbol, friendships. It may be that just as fictive kinship is associated with societies in which public organization is ideologically conceived as based on criteria of descent and marriage, so, in societies like our own, in which public organization is ideologically conceived as voluntary, many obligatory, public, strongly instrumental relationships take on the forms and symbols of friendship (see Paine 1969, on friendship and its definition). One might call these 'fictive friendships.' These fictive friendships are part of the process by which scarce resources are allocated. The flow of prestations, attention and favors in the direction of persons who have it in their power to allocate labor, capital, or business deals, may be thought of as the 'price of allocation.' The 'price of allocation' is symbolically represented as an unsolicited gift, the fruit of friendship.

Despite the symbolic ambience of choice, there are strong pressures to conform to this system of exchange if one wants to stay in this branch of the garment industry. These pressures are central to the question of autonomy, and the relative place of state-enforceable law as opposed to the binding rules and customs generated in this social field.

This complex, the operation of the social field, is to a significant extent self-regulating, self-enforcing, and self-propelling within a certain legal, political, economic, and social environment. Some of the rules about rights and obligations that govern it emanate from that environment, the government, the marketplace, the relations among the various ethnic groups that work in the industry, and so on. But many other rules are produced within the field of action itself. Some of these rules are produced through the explicit quasi-legislative action of the organized corporate bodies (the union, the association) that regulate some aspects of the industry. But others, as has been indicated, are arrived at through the interplay of the jobbers, contractors, factors, retailers, and skilled workers in the course of doing business with one another. They are the regular reciprocities and exchanges of mutually dependent parties. They are the 'customs of the trade.' (Compare an anthropological account of three garment shops in Manchester, Lupton and Cunnison 1964.)

The law is obviously a part of this picture. Surely were it not for the vast amount of pertinent labor law, the union representative would never have come to have the powerful position he occupies. He would not be an allocator of scarce resources. He may not, in fact, enforce the actual terms defining wages and hours in the contract with the union, but it is his legal ability to do so that gives him something to exchange. Were it not for the legal right of the contractor to collect promptly the bills owed him by the jobber, his restraint in not pressing for collection would not be a favor. It is because he has the legal right to collect and does not do so that he has something to give. Thus legal rights can be used as important counters in these relationships. Stewart Macaulay has called attention to a number of these issues in his paper on 'non-contractual relations in business' (1963).

Many legal rights in this setting can be interpreted as the capacity of persons inside the social field to mobilize the state on their behalf. Just so the capacity to mobilize the union or the association of jobbers and contractors are important counterweights in the business dealings which are carried on in the dress industry. Looked at from the inside, then, the social field is semi-autonomous not only because it can be affected by the direction of outside forces impinging upon it, but because persons inside the social field can mobilize those outside forces, or threaten to do so, in their bargainings with one another.

It would take this discussion far afield to enumerate all the laws that impinge on the individuals in the garment industry, from traffic laws to the rights and obligations of citizenship, but it is useful to emphasize that of the tremendous body of rules that envelop any social field, only some are significant elements in the bargaining, competing, and exchanging processes, while the rest are, so to speak, in the background. Moreover, the moment that one focuses attention on these processes of competition, negotiation, and exchange, one becomes equally aware of the importance of binding rights and obligations that are *not* legally enforceable. The legal rules are only a small piece of the complex.

The penalty for not playing the game according to the rules – legal, non-legal, and illegal – in the dress industry is: economic loss, loss of reputation, loss of goodwill, ultimate exclusion from the avenues that lead to money-making. Compliance is induced by the desire to stay in the game and prosper. It is not unreasonable to infer that at least some of those legal rules that are obeyed, are obeyed as much (if not more) because of the very same kinds of pressures and inducements that produce compliance to the non-legal mores of the social field rather than because of any direct potentiality of enforcement by the state. In fact, many of the pressures to conform to 'the law' probably emanate from the several social milieux in which an individual participates. The potentiality of state action is often far less immediate than other pressures and inducements.

The Chagga of Mount Kilimanjaro

The recent history of the Chagga tribe has been repeatedly looked to as a model of successful 'development.' A hundred years ago the Chagga were divided into many tiny warring chiefdoms, which raided each other for women, cattle, and presumably also for control of the slave and ivory trade routes. Today the Chagga are the most prosperous and worldly tribe in Tanzania. Symbolic of deeper changes are the visible ones; from a time when they were earringed, spear-carrying Kichagga-speaking warriors, they have become trousered, shirt-wearing, Swahili-speaking, farmer-citizens of a socialist state. There is a transistor radio in the village bar. Along with broadcasting government news broadcasts, the radio brings American rock music on the Nairobi hit parade. For eighty years the Chagga have been proselytized by industrious catholic and protestant missionaries who enjoyed being posted to the mountain climate. Today most Chagga are Christians, a few are Moslems, and still fewer continue to adhere exclusively to the Chagga religion. Most have been to school and many are literate in some degree. Chagga prosperity comes in a large measure from the production of coffee which has been cultivated on Kilimanjaro for many decades. Since the 1920s the Chagga have sold into the world markets the coffee grown in their family gardens. It has been auctioned off through their African-owned co-operative, the Kilimanjaro Native Co-operative Union. Hence they have long been involved in a partially cash economy.

The myriad concomitant changes, societal and legal, which have taken place in Chagga life in this century are too numerous to specify here, but it is useful to have a look at certain aspects of the Independent Government's recent attempts to legislate socialism into existence, and to consider in some detail how these impinge on an ongoing social system with deep roots in the past.

Since we live in a period in which the potential effectiveness of central planning and the use of law as the tool of the social engineer are heavily emphasized, it is perhaps worth stressing what is probably obvious, that by no means all, nor even the most important social changes necessarily get their principal impetus from legislated or other legal innovations, even in centrally planned systems. A corollary proposition is probably equally obvious, that the effect of legislative innovations is frequently not what was anticipated, though perhaps with adequate sociological analysis, it might have been predicted.

Legislation consists of conscious attempts at social direction. But clearly societies are in the grip of processes of change quite outside this kind of control. On Kilimanjaro two such unplanned processes have been under way for some time: the changes consequent on the introduction of the cash cropping of coffee, and the changes in the availability of land after the explosion of the Chagga population. These have both profoundly affected the context of operation of Chagga law. On the side of intentional social control is much of the recent legislation of the Independent Government intended to promote a socialist egalitarianism. In Chaggaland, some of this legislation can be shown to have had only very limited effects. Traditional Chagga social relationships are proving to have remarkable durability despite the efforts of hardworking social planners in Dar es Salaam to substitute new arrangements for the old.

For example, in 1963, the Independent Government declared that from then henceforth there would no longer be any private freehold ownership in land, since land as the gift of God can belong to no man but only to all men, whose representative was the government. (The Freehold Title (Conversion and Government Leases) Act (1963). Cf. P. J. Nkambo Mugerwa, 'Land Tenure in East Africa – Some Contrasts,' *East African Law Today* (British Institute of International and Comparative Law, Commonwealth Law Series, no. 5, 1966).) All freehold land was converted into government leaseholds by this act, and improperly used land was to be taken away.

If this 1963 Act is to be taken as a statement of ideology in an agrarian socialist state, it makes sense. The means of production must not be privately held in such a polity. But as an operationalized piece of legislation in the context of Chagga life, it has had very limited and rather specialized results, since though no one 'owns' the land any longer, most people in general have precisely the same rights of occupation and use they had before, to say nothing of contingent rights in the lands of kinsmen, an important element in these days of land shortage. What has been changing drastically over the past few decades in Chaggaland are not the formal legal rules about land rights (these being governed largely by customary law), but the actual ratio of population to land, a change not engineered by any legislation, nor planned by any administrative authorities.

In 1890 land was plentiful on Kilimanjaro. Those were the days when its green slopes were populated by perhaps a hundred thousand Chagga tribesmen who were organized into dozens of small autonomous chiefdoms, each divided from the others by some natural barrier – a deep ravine with a stream, or a wall of high hills. In each chiefdom here and there between the homesteads were some open meadows where fodder could be cut for Chagga cattle and where newcomers could settle. Today there probably are about 400,000 Chagga living on the mountain. The results of this population explosion are being felt at every hand. The shortage of land will soon be severe. More and more huts and houses are built, on ever-shrinking plots. Each house must have a garden around it to support the household. These gardens are crammed with vegetation. At the highest level are the tall banana plants, below them the coffee bushes, and under these the vegetables. The banana is the traditional staple food of the Chagga and the vegetables are also usually for domestic consumption. The coffee is sold for cash.

Each homestead and garden is contiguous to several others. A tangle of such homestead gardens forms a several-mile-wide band, the banana belt, that rings the mountain. The open lands are all but gone. As in the past, there are no villages. Dwellings and gardens lie one right next to another for miles with narrow winding footpaths between them. A single main road, wide enough for cars, but unpaved and intermittently muddy for many months of the year, cuts through the central banana belt and winds around most of the mountain. A few feeder roads lead down from it and give access to the hot, dry lowlands below. Here and there along the main road today one sees a marketplace, a school, a church, a courthouse, a small collection of tiny stores, a butcher shop, and a beer shop. These clusters constitute Kilimanjaro's civic centers. Otherwise the banana belt is a continuous string of households and gardens.

The cultivation of coffee has meant that many goods and services purchasable for cash have become available on the mountain. This has opened secondary, non-farming occupations to some men. Land itself, formerly never bought or sold, can now be had for cash if the would-be buyer can find someone willing to sell. Long ago in the days of plenitude of land, a man wishing to settle in an area could have obtained a plot quite easily from a hospitable lineage not unhappy to increase its local male strength, or from a chief wishing to increase the number of his subjects. Now a man must inherit land, be allocated it by his father in his lifetime, or buy it. The government has recently added to these options the possibility of moving away from the mountain to pioneer in unsettled areas of Tanzania in return for a plot of land. Most men do not want to move away.

The opportunities to accumulate the cash to buy land are few. On the whole they are available either to the educated men who have a salary as a source of income, or to the very lucky and enterprising who find ways to launch themselves in small businesses and manage not to fail. What were once open government lands in the immediate area have long since been individually allocated. Thus, for the vast majority of men, the only way to obtain land is to inherit it or to be given it by one's father. The effect of this has been to tighten rather than loosen the attachment of men to their local lineage groups, to stress and strengthen rather than to weaken the importance of that whole body of law and custom pertinent to the mutual rights and obligations of kinsmen and neighbors. For despite 'modernization' in many other matters, many thousands of families still live in localized clusters of kin. The government declaration of 1963 that no one owns the land could conceivably have had considerable significance in a region in which there were vast stretches of unclaimed unoccupied territory. But the situation on Kilimanjaro is just the reverse.

As far as I was able to tell, the government declaration directly affected only three categories of Chagga landholders: tenants of the church, who were given the land they occupied; persons holding small pieces of unimproved land; and persons holding land that was originally conveyed to their forebears as a loan, not as a total transfer of interest.

Technically the buying and selling of rights to land goes on just as before the 1963 Act, though previously sales would have been in the form of rights to own land, while now they are construed as rights to use land. But most people, court personnel as well as ordinary farmers, make no such distinction, i.e., barely acknowledge that any change has taken place, since it so little affects the relative distribution of ordinary rights. What has happened to loaned land, however, is that if it has been held under these conditions for a long time, the occupier now is emboldened to demand that the loaning lineage redeem the land immediately or relinquish all further claims to it. Redeeming involves reimbursement not for the land, but for the coffee trees and banana plants and buildings. Ordinarily the descendants of the original loaner of land cannot produce the cash on demand and the loan is declared to be at an end. People say, 'We do not pay *masiro* any longer. The land belongs to no one.' *Masiro* is the customary annual payment of beer or produce from the borrowing lineage to the lending lineage. It amounts to public acknowledgment of the 'true ownership,' and there has always been an implication in this that should the owner choose to repay the borrower for all improvements, he could at any time reclaim the land for his own. The 1963 Act has meant a marked improvement in the position of borrowers. Now they have the option of demanding payment or relinquishment of interest. In effect, as locally construed, it has put a time limit on the redeemability of their land holdings (the demand of loanee governs the timing) and once and for all ended these loans.

The other effect the 1963 Act might have had is easy to get around. Theoretically it makes it impossible for someone having unoccupied unused land to sell rights in it, since he does not 'own' the land. But it is simple enough to build a small building of some sort on the plot and sell that. It is difficult to believe that this highminded declaration of socialist principle was ever intended to have the curious effect it has had on Chagga life. It was directed against the exploitation of tenant-farmers by estateholders. It could scarcely have been intended to single out three limited categories of Chagga farmers for a change in their rights.

Among other things, this illustrates that although universality of application is often used as one of the basic elements in any definition of law, universality is often a myth. Most rules of law, in fact, though theoretically universal in application, affect only a limited category of persons in a limited number of situations. And beyond this fairly elementary proposition, the limited effect of the 1963 declaration on Chaggaland indicates something of greater moment. All legal rights and duties are aspects of social relationships (see Hohfeld 1919). They are not essentially rights in things, though they may pertain to things. They are rights to act in certain ways in relation to the rights of other people. The implication of the Chagga reception of the 1963 declaration is clear. It is only in so far as law changes the relationships of people to each other, actually changes their specific mutual rights and obligations, that law effects social change. It is not in terms of declarations, however ideologically founded, about the title to property. Most Chagga are living where they lived before 1963 *as* they lived before 1963. The semi-autonomous social field that dominates rural Chagga life is the local lineage-neighborhood complex; that complex of social relationships having much to do with land rights continues intact and almost unchanged by the 1963 Act.

The most important component of many farmers' lives is the localized patrilineage or patriclan in which men of the regions of older settlement live. These may be comprised of as many as three or four dozen families residing in contiguous plots, but they are usually smaller. In theory all the clansmen are descended either from a common male ancestor or from a group of brothers or patrilateral cousins, but often the precise genealogical ties are lost beyond four or five generations. Some people would doubtless describe these remains of an earlier form of Chagga lineage organization in terms of the survival of often-expressed values, 'Kinsmen should help each other,' or 'Brothers should support each other' (the term 'brothers' being extended to all male kinsmen of the same generation), or 'Land should never be sold without the consent of one's brothers.' However, these values may also be interpreted as the ideological side of a very considerable modern mutual social and economic interest. They are not *merely* a survival from a traditional past.

At one time there would seem to have been a very firm intralineage organization of a corporate nature. Lineages had senior officials who had political, religious, and jural functions, both within the lineage and in relation to chiefs and other lineages. All this is gone and has been gone for fifty years. Most lineages do not meet as a body any longer, but small localized groups of lineal kinsmen do meet very regularly, not only at all life-crisis rituals when large groups assemble, but to slaughter animals and eat meat together in small lineage segments. Landholding is individual. However, since each collateral line is the potential heir of any close collaterals who might die without male offspring, the brothers and brotherly lines (and cousinly lines) look on one another jealously. Even today the illness of children not infrequently brings accusations of witchcraft or sorcery by the wife of one brother against the wife of another.

Moreover, brothers are all very much interested in each other's fortunes in the modern setting. Death without male issue is no longer the only way the land of a collateral may become available. Crushing debts may make a man sell land and he is under obligation to offer it to his brothers first. They want it for themselves and for their sons. The situation of land shortage is such, particularly in the socially desirable areas (those in which the kin clusters still live), that kinsmen are not always sad to see their brothers or other neighbors in financial trouble. It follows from this that though there are no longer common lands held by the lineage as a unit, the residuary and contingent interests of kinsmen in one another's property is considerable and gives the more prosperous and enterprising considerable leverage over those less so. This is a profound bond and one with latent organizational implications.

Though there is usually no formal corporate organization of kinsmen today, agnates nevertheless form a bounded unit of individuals closely connected through their contingent interests in one another's property as well as through ties of tradition, neighborly contiguity, and sometimes affection. In this loosely constituted aggregate, certain men are recognized as leaders, others as far less powerful. The basis is seniority, or education – each is usually found in combination with property (or the control by an old man of sons having education or property).

The potential power of seniors to affect the lives of juniors through the allocation of land and through supernatural effects on their lives permeates all contact between them. The flow of prestations and services and deferential gestures toward these men is continuous. The locus of power is acknowledged ceremonially, not only at the moments of allocation of land. Clear rules about seniority are regularly reiterated in the priorities of distribution of meat every time animals are slaughtered, and in the ways in which beer is given out on those occasions to celebrate a baptism, a circumcision, or a wedding. Certain of the older men have it in their power to seal the fate of many of the younger ones. The seniors still have much to say about who shall be financed in school, or in an apprenticeship, or who shall get which parcel of land. Their disapproval of a son's choice of spouse may lead to serious troubles. It is Chagga custom in the Vunjo region that a young man is given a plot of land by his father or guardian when he marries. Youngest sons ultimately inherit the plot and house of the father on his death, but older sons are provided for at marriage. These are not legal rights in the sense that a son cannot bring a lawsuit in court to oblige his father to provide such a plot: he cannot. The option lies with the father, to provide or not provide. Woe to the son who displeases his father, or the nephew under an uncle's guardianship who does not accept his uncle's allocation of land with grace. There are more than economic sanctions involved. Kinsmen can have certain magical effects on one another. But even more potent, they can have profound social effects on one another. A man must rely on neighbors and kin for security of his person, his reputation, his property, his wife and his children, and for aid in the settlement of any disputes in which he may become involved. Thus the lineage-neighborhood complex is an effective rule-making and sanction-applying social nexus. While it is not part of the official legislative or administrative system, that system often has occasion to acknowledge its existence and importance.

A direct attempt to change these local social relationships was made when a system of ten-house cells was set up throughout Tanzania. These were grafted onto the local branches of lineage and neighborhood. At the end of 1964, TANU (Tanganyika African National Union), the national party, set up this system of cells to be the base unit of the party. These were to link TANU more effectively with the rank and file, largely to enable the party to collect and distribute information. There had been an army mutiny early in 1964, and no doubt one of the considerations in setting up the cells was the collection of information relating to security. Bienen indicates that the work of the cells was outlined under three main headings, 'bringing people's problems and grievances to the party and government, coordinating the work of the cells with the development committees, and ensuring the security of the nation' (Bienen 1967:358). On Kilimanjaro every ten households has a ten-house cell leader, chosen by the member households. I was told that the choice was partially governed by the question whether the man could be in the neighborhood all the time. Chagga with jobs in the town, or salaried jobs in schools and dispensaries on the mountain, or who had shops, were not suitable because they could not be available at all times. Thus there was a systematic selection process which militated against the most educated men, in favor of their neighbors whose only occupation was farming. The ten-house cell leader, called the *balozi* by the Chagga, is supposed to be informed of all events of importance in his cell: births, deaths, marriages, divorces, crimes, altercations of all kinds, and the like. He must be present at any meeting of importance involving cell members. Periodically he meets collectively with other ten-house cell leaders, and is given instructions from central party ideologues and planners, which he then conveys to his member households.

Because ten-house cells are units of neighbors, they inevitably involve people who have old attachments to one another, attachments of kinship, affinity, and neighborhood. The very non-kinsmen who are in a man's ten-house cell are likely to be of such social closeness that he would normally send them a portion of any slaughter share of meat when he got home from a lineage feast. They are persons who would be called on to help in a house-building, or in the cultivation of the *shambas* at the foot of the mountain. They would have been present at any hearing of a law case in the neighborhood that was not strictly an intralineage affair, and might even have attended some of those. They would certainly have been at any beer party of any size given in the vicinity. The members of the ten-house cell are, in short, men whose primary identity for one another is as neighbor, affine, or kinsman. Only secondarily are they members of TANU cells. This does not mean that the secondary identity is never important. It sometimes does matter, particularly with respect to the ten-house cell leader. For example, if there is need of supporting testimony in the Primary Court, it is useful to have the word of the *balozi*. It is sensible not to make an enemy of him, but then it always was wise to have friendly neighbors. The whole ten-house cell apparatus is an addition to pre-existing neighborhood patterns, not a replacement. What has happened is that relationships that were multiplex in the first place have now had a strand added. Not the *balozi*, but the senior man of each minimal lineage branch, the grandfather of the family, or his elder brother, is the person to whom the most important ritual prestations of beer and meat are regularly made. The office of ten-house cell leaders does not, after all, carry with it discretion over the allocation of land, nor any mystical powers at all.

The continuing control exercised by the lineage neighborhood nexus over its members is illustrated by every dispute it settles. No man can hope to keep his head above water if he does not have the approval and support of his neighbors and kinsmen. He may drown in debt, and get no helping loan. He may claim lands that should be his by any normative standards, and find that all local witnesses are against him. He may go to court expecting to get redress there, only to find that his witnesses never turn up. Unless the lineage and neighborhood support him through illnesses, through financial crises, through disputes, he is in deep trouble. The ten-house cell system does not change this a whit, or at least had not in 1969. Only the educated who have salaried employment can escape some of these pressures through their affluence and outside connections. Their partial independence has undermined and altered some of the localized control. They 'know' people in the town, people in local government, people in the school system. They have salaries in addition to coffee money. Their kinsmen must listen to them. They are, by reason of employment, not ten-house cell leaders, and also by reason of employment, enjoy a certain higher status than the *balozi*. But they too are farmers, and are inside the lineage neighborhood nexus as well as having connections outside. Their wives and children are in the neighborhood all day, every day. The ties are still strong. Permeable but dominant, the Chagga lineage-neighborhood complex has never fully surrendered to any government – chiefly, colonial, or independent.

Though the lineage-neighborhood nexus has changed again and again over the decades, it has retained considerable autonomy and considerable control over its members throughout. It enforces non-legal arrangements such as the allocations of land by fathers and uncles to sons and nephews, and the attempts by brothers to block the sale of land to non-kinsmen. It conducts illegal hearings on such matters as witchcraft. It also enforces innumerable legal rules from the respecting of garden boundaries to the support of indigent kin. It is both a maker and keeper of rules, its own and those of the state.

Relationships long established in persisting semi-autonomous social fields are difficult to do away with instantly by legislative measures. This is shown in another Tanzanian attempt to legislate egalitarianism as it affected the Chagga: the abolition of chiefship, an institution that was dispensed with by the Independent Government in 1963. This political change was not unwelcome in many quarters of Chaggaland. It completed a process that had been under way since the end of the Second World War. For some years there had been both pressure and legislation in the direction of cutting down the powers of local chiefs. Their self-enriching prerogatives, accumulated in earlier colonial decades, were eroded after 1946 by laws directly cutting down their powers, and also by legislation establishing a few higher executive offices (superchiefships, so to speak) and perhaps most important of all, by enlarging the powers of various representative legislative bodies and councils. What the abolition of chiefship did in 1963 was effectively to give all formal local bureaucratic powers to a new administrative élite, drawn from commoner lineages, and nominated for office according to the length of their membership in and the degree of their commitment to TANU, the governing party. Thus the legislation reorganized and reallocated certain offices, instituting a new criterion of recruitment to office.

However this legislation did not and could not have abolished completely the informal position of advantage enjoyed by some chiefly families. For one thing, having been better off than many of their subjects for several generations, they were able to afford to pay for the education of more of their children. Their close kinsmen and associates benefited similarly. Educated men, being few and badly needed in an ever more Africanized administration, occupy many key positions of responsibility, and hence are more powerful than most of their less literate farmer brothers. The ex-chiefs themselves, with a few notable exceptions, are not in these posts; but some of their kinsmen and associates and their children are. Shoulder to shoulder with the new élite are a substantial number of relatives and associates of the old élite who are, so to speak, doubly qualified for office, meeting both traditional and new criteria of recruitment.

An important element in the informal positions of advantage of these men is the network of 'connections' that members of chiefly lineages had with persons in positions of power and authority both in businesses and in government. Today such a network is of considerable importance in the chain of relationships that connects rural men to men occupying positions in the cities. Complex links built over many years, ramifying into business, army, church, education, and other posts tie both the old and elements of the newer élite to each other. The chiefs have become ex-chiefs and many are living quietly in welcome political obscurity. But some, and a few of their erstwhile dependants and hangers-on, long ago acquired the skills and connections to swim in the new seas of opportunity. Thus certain kinds of powerful extended networks in which the chiefs were formerly an important link have persisted longer than the offices that were their original starting-point.

This has happened before in Chaggaland, for during the colonial period there was a process of consolidation of smaller chiefdoms into larger ones. The more powerful swallowed the weaker, incorporating them. The chiefs of the smaller entities lost their offices. But it is plain from any detailed study of local officeholding in these areas, that the lineages that lost the chiefship did not entirely lose a generalized position of advantage in the diverse fields of local competition that opened up over the years. Members of such ex-chiefly lineages turn up as small entrepreneurs, such as owners of butcher shops, beer shops, trucks, and as officials of the local Co-operative Society. Often these were the new small capitalists. Though the misfortunes of consolidation had lost these petty chiefs their offices, neither they nor their relatives entirely lost their informal social advantages, and their economic head-start.

This Chagga experience of the abolition of chiefships, twice repeated, first in the period of administrative consolidation, and later in the press for equality connected with Independence, has certain very general implications for the study of law and social change. It suggests that those parts of the social system that are most visible to and are considered most accessible to legislative (or other official action) are often the formal parts of the system. Yet the powerful position that comes from the *informal* accretion of economic, educational advantages, and network contacts may be far less immediately accessible to formal legal action, and may have great durability over time. The strategic position of general advantage would also seem to have great adaptability as to sphere of operations, while the office has a specified scope.

The reasoning involved here is pertinent to attempts to legislate basic changes in social relationships in our own society, e.g., to desegregation and to civil rights legislation. Social positions and networks that involve the accumulation of informal, spin-off advantages over time are difficult if not impossible to legislate into instantaneous existence, though it is clear that formal changes can create the conditions under which such advantages may eventually be accumulated. For this reason newly acquired formal 'equality' of opportunity brought into existence by legislation is often not in fact equal to long-held social position.

Three examples of externally imposed formal laws and rules affecting existing semi-autonomous social fields have been drawn from the recent Chagga experience: the abolition of private property in land, the establishment of ten-house cells and the abolition of chiefship. The first two rules were examined in so far as they affected that local, non-corporate social field which I have called 'the lineage-neighborhood complex.' The third, the abolition of chiefship, was designed to alter a larger-scale, higher-level corporate social field, the 'village.' I have suggested that the spin-off products of the old chiefships, the general social position and networks of ex-chiefs and their families and associates, have had a persistence over several generations of time, despite repeated changes in surrounding formal organization and cultural context. Since such networks and chains of transactional relations may generate fairly durable rules regarding the relative status and mutual obligations of their members, it is useful to analyze them as semi-autonomous social fields. The TANU organization has moved from the status of being a non-legal voluntary organization to being part of the official, formal *de jure* body politic. The chiefly networks have moved in the other direction, from being attached to legal offices to the status of completely informal connections.

In the Chagga situation as in most others, much that is new coexists with and modifies the old, rather than replacing it entirely. For the Chagga, there have been some abrupt changes in the legislated rules of the game and many other rule changes that have been generated more gradually. To understand these rules – legal, non-legal, or illegal – it is essential to know something of the working social context in which they are found. There is a general utility in looking at legal rules in terms of the semi-autonomous social fields on which they impinge. It tempers any tendency to exaggerate the potential effectiveness of legislation as an instrument of social engineering, while demonstrating when and

how and through what processes it actually is effective. It provides
a framework within which to examine the way rules that are
potentially enforceable by the state fit with rules and patterns that
are propelled by other processes and forces.

Conclusions

The concept of the semi-autonomous social field is a way of
defining a research problem. It draws attention to the connection
between the internal workings of an observable social field and its
points of articulation with a larger setting. Bailey (1960) used a
similar set of concepts when dealing with political change.
Theoretically, one could postulate a series of possibilities:
complete autonomy in a social field, semi-autonomy, or a total
absence of autonomy (i.e., complete domination). Obviously,
complete autonomy and complete domination are rare, if they
exist at all in the world today, and semi-autonomy of various
kinds and degrees is an ordinary circumstance. Since the law of
sovereign states is hierarchical in form, no social field within a
modern polity could be absolutely autonomous from a legal point
of view. Absolute domination is also difficult to conceive, for even
in armies and prisons and other rule-run institutions, there is
usually an underlife with some autonomy. The illustrations in this
paper suggest that areas of autonomy and modes of self-
regulation have importance not only inside the social fields in
which they exist, but are useful in showing the way these are
connected with the larger social setting.

The law (in the sense of state-enforceable law) is only one of a
number of factors that affect the decisions people make, the
actions they take and the relationships they have. Consequently
important aspects of the connection between law and social
change emerge only if law is inspected in the context of ordinary
social life. There general processes of competition – inducement,
coercion, and collaboration – are effective regulators of action.
The operative 'rules of the game' include some laws and some
other quite effective norms and practices. Socially significant
legislative enactments frequently are attempts to shift the relative
bargaining positions of persons in their dealings with one another
within these social fields. The subject of the dealing and much else
about the composition and character of the social field and the
transactions in it are not necessarily tampered with. Thus much

legislation is piecemeal, and only partially invades the ongoing arrangements. Hence the interdependence or independence of elements in the social scene may sometimes be revealed by just such piecemeal legislation.

Examples from two very different settings have been briefly described to illustrate these points. Activities in the garment industry analyzed at one point in time show very clearly what is meant by the concept of a self-regulating social field and the important but limited place of law in it. The key figures in this part of the dress industry are the allocators of scarce resources, whether these resources are capital, labor, or the opportunity to make money. To all of those in a position to allocate these resources there is a flow of prestations, favors, and contacts, producing secondary gains for individuals in key positions. A whole series of binding customary rules surrounds the giving and exchange of these favors. The industry can be analyzed as a densely interconnected social nexus having many interdependent relationships and exchanges, governed by rules, some of them legal rules, and others not. The essential difference between the legal rules and the others is not in their effectiveness. Both sets are effective. The difference lies in the agency through which ultimate sanctions might be applied. Both the legal and the non-legal rules have similar immediately effective sanctions for violation attached. Business failures can be brought about without the intervention of legal institutions. Clearly neither effective sanctions nor the capacity to generate binding rules are the monopoly of the state.

The analysis of this illustration also suggests that many laws are made operative when people inside the affected social field are in a position to threaten to press for enforcement. They must be aware of their rights and sufficiently organized and independent to reach and mobilize the coercive force of government in order to have this effect. A court or legislature can make custom law. A semi-autonomous social field can make law its custom.

The second example, that of certain attempts to legislate social change in Tanzania, shows the same principles in a less familiar milieu. Here neighborhood and lineage constitute a partially self-regulating social field that, in many matters, has more effective control over its members and over land allocations than the state, or the 'law.' The limited local effect of legislation abolishing private property in land and establishing a system of ten-house cells demonstrates the persistent importance of this lineage-neighborhood complex. The way in which this legislation has been locally interpreted to require only the most minimal changes suggests something of the strength of local social priorities and relationships. The robustness of the lineage-neighborhood complex, and its resistance to alteration (while nevertheless changing) suggests that one of the tendencies that may be quite general in semi-autonomous social fields is the tendency to fight any encroachment on autonomy previously enjoyed. The advantageous situation enjoyed by some of the kinsmen and associates of ex-chiefs shows that the momentum of such an interlocking set of transactional complexes may not be entirely arrested by legislative alterations of parts of its formal organization.

These examples all involve at least two kinds of rules: rules that were consciously made by legislatures and courts and other formal agencies to produce certain intended effects, and rules that could be said to have evolved 'spontaneously' out of social life. Rules of corporate organizations, whether they are the laws of a polity or the rules of an organization within it, frequently involve attempts to fix certain relationships by design. However, the ongoing competitions, collaborations and exchanges that take place in social life also generate their own regular relationships and rules and effective sanctions, without necessarily involving any such pre-designing. The ways in which state-enforceable law affects these processes are often exaggerated and the way in which law is affected by them is often underestimated. Some semi-autonomous social fields are quite enduring, some exist only briefly. Some are consciously constructed, such as committees, administrative departments, or other groups formed to perform a particular task; while some evolve in the marketplace or the neighborhood or elsewhere out of a history of transactions.

Where there is no state, a wide range of legitimately socially enforceable rules are counted by anthropologists as law. When there is a state, two categories are recognized by lawyers – state-enforceable law, and socially enforced binding rules. Pospisil has argued that it should all be called 'law,' with the qualifier added that it is the law of a particular group. He argues that there are in society a multiplicity of legal levels and a multiplicity of legal systems (1971:ch.4). Pospisil is certainly right about the multiplicity and ubiquity of rule-making and rule-enforcing mechanisms anchored in social groups. In fact he may not even go far enough, since, as this paper suggests, not only corporate groups, but other, looser transactional complexes may have these rule-making and rule-enforcing capacities. But on the point of melting it all together as 'law,' this is a question of what one is trying to emphasize for analysis. If the bindingness of rules is the issue, then the argument can be made for looking at all binding rules together as products of common processes of coercion and inducement. But there are occasions when, though recognizing the existence of and common character of binding rules at all levels, it may be of importance to distinguish the sources of the rules and the sources of effective inducement and coercion. This is the more so in a period when legislation and other formal measures – judicial, administrative, and executive – are regularly used to try to change social arrangements. The place of state-enforceable law in ongoing social affairs, and its relation to other effective rules needs much more scholarly attention. Looking at complex societies in terms of semi-autonomous social fields provides one practical means of doing so.

Note

1 The information on which this account is based was obtained from an informant who has had many years of close contact with the dress industry in New York.

Chapter 3

Legal liability and evolutionary interpretation: some aspects of strict liability, self-help, and collective responsibility

1 Introduction: some sherds of the theoretical pot

When Evans-Pritchard described the Nuer 'tribe' as 'the largest group within which legal obligation is acknowledged,' he was using as one of his principal criteria for the definition of a political unit the potential resolution of disputes within it (Evans-Pritchard 1940:279). The implications of this formulation, that law is to be understood in a socio-political framework, go far beyond the operation of acephalous societies. This paper will have a look at some evolutionary conceptions of the trend of legal development in the light of this idea. There are significant differences in the social and political role of legal disputes in different types of societies, though one would never know it from the content of most legal evolutionary schemes. I shall suggest some of these differences.

The issues are apparent when one examines such modes of allocating and enforcing legal responsibility as strict liability, self-help, and collective responsibility. Self-help, particularly when it involves the mobilization of others in one's cause, and collective responsibility, which by definition involves a social aggregate, are particularly clear illustrations of the social and political context in which legal obligations may be set and enforced. Strict liability, usually dealt with by jurists in terms of a presumed primitive legal

Reprinted from Max Gluckman (ed.), *The Allocation of Responsibility*, 1972, by permission of Manchester University Press.

disregard of motive and intention, is also, as Gluckman has argued, more comprehensible if analyzed in terms of its social setting (1965b:204–41). All three – strict liability, self-help, and collective responsibility – are often thought of as especially characteristic of 'primitive' legal systems. Yet some instances and forms of all three appear in the legal systems of complex societies, and all three appear in quite varied forms in pre-industrial societies.

It is useful to review some of the scholarly contexts in which these ways of dealing with responsibility have been treated as 'primitive.' An inspection of these contexts makes one aware of those assumptions of various prominent writers about the nature of modern law which cause them to paint its antecedents in appropriate colors. If modern law is conceived as essentially comprised of a set of principles, quite separable from any particular social environment, then legal evolution is treated as the sequential and cumulative development of those principles. As is so often the case in other fields, in law the supposedly primitive is frequently alluded to and used to support certain conceptions of contemporary institutions rather than to explain the institutions of pre-industrial societies. A case in point is Roscoe Pound's *The Spirit of the Common Law* (1921).

There is much that is interesting about the rhetoric of the Anglo-American law, particularly as spoken by its saints. Pound approaches the common law tradition as a genealogy of ideas, and, as in most genealogies, this one is adjustable and is presented as a single unbroken tradition which has succeeded in incorporating innumerable alien ideas 'without disturbing its essential unity ... ' (1921; 1963:5). Pound described the stages of legal evolution as four in number. Each was characterized by a different basis for the allocation of liability. Since he put it that 'the staple institutions of primitive society are reprisals, private war and the blood feud,' the first stage of legal evolution was that which developed 'composition for the desire to be avenged' (1921; 1963:85, 139). In the second stage the state superseded self-help in all but exceptional cases and the law was characterized as 'the strict law' (1921; 1963:140–1). By this Pound meant a highly formal, inelastic and inflexible formal system of rules in which

the chief end sought is certainty.... The strict law is indifferent to the moral aspects of conduct or of transactions that satisfy its letters.... But the strict law gives us as permanent contributions the ideas of certainty and uniformity and of rule and form as means thereto (1921; 1963:140–1).

The third stage is the stage of equity, or natural law. The watchwords of this period were morality, equity, and good conscience. At this stage law is identified with morals, and moral duties become legal duties. Liability is allocated only where there is moral fault. Reason rather than strict adherence to the letter of the rules is relied on to administer justice. 'Aside from liberalization of the law, the permanent contributions of this stage are the conception of good faith and moral conduct to be attained through reason, ethical solution of controversies and enforcement of duties' (1921; 1963:141). The fourth stage is a happy marriage of stages three and four with certainty and equity married, 'the watchwords are equality and security' (1921; 1963:142).

Pound also described the modern Anglo-American legal tradition as characterized by 'an extreme individualism' tempered only by 'a tendency ... to look to relations rather than to legal transactions as the basis of legal consequences' (1921; 1963: 13–14). The individualism is on the equity side of the fourth stage (above); 'relations' are the certainty part. What he meant by individualism was 'unlimited valuation of individual liberty and respect for individual property' (1921; 1963:13). What he meant by 'relations' were such categorical role pairs as employer-employee, landlord-tenant, debtor-creditor, and so on. These he understood to be statuses. When Pound said that Maine was quite wrong about the shift from status to contract, Pound meant that the rules pertaining to these relationships (or, as he considered them, statuses) fixed duties and liabilities independently of the will of those bound. He does not seem to have realized that Maine explicitly reserved status for familial status, or, better, status in a kinship group. Pound thought in 1921 that the law was about to enter a new, fifth stage of development, a stage of 'socialization of law' in which the interest and protection of the general public rather than the individual would be paramount (1921; 1963:195).

The terms of this evolutionary sequence were and are clichés, categories in general circulation in Anglo-American law. They have strongly affected the theoretical approach of E. A. Hoebel, doyen of American legal anthropologists, whose training was in this tradition. Doctrines which Pound put in evolutionary sequence and saw as accumulating to form the compound of modern law are commonly found in Anglo-American cases as paired opposites. Strict rules yield certainty but are sometimes unfair. Equity gives attention to fairness and morality, but at the expense of legal certainty. The individual must be free to act, but he must also be bound by law, the rules governing social relations. While individual freedom must be preserved and protected, it must not encroach on the public good. The general march of civilization is from the extremes of selfish individual or kin group self-interest (self-help, feud, war) in the direction of taming and curbing such private self-interest in favor of the general public good. This last, as we shall see, is one of the dominant concepts in Hoebel's approach.

That legal systems are not to be understood exclusively in terms of the value-laden principles they invoke, and that adequate description can scarcely be condensed into one principle at a time, anyone would grant today. The tenets which Pound used to characterize stages of legal evolution, and which are frequently cited as the bases of case decisions, are more illuminating, not when. taken literally, but rather when studied as a system of categories and legitimating classes, or as ideological aphorisms. Yet the attitudes which this kind of material represents have inevitably affected the choice of problem to which some anthropologists have addressed themselves. If one wants to generalize about the law of pre-industrial society in contrast with our own, there is no escaping the fact that Maine and Durkheim and Pound and Malinowski have already had something to say on the subject, and that they have thought of it in terms of the traditional rationalizations of Western law.

The three modes of allocating responsibility with which this paper will deal – strict liability, self-help and collective responsibility – all fit neatly into Pound's evolutionary sequence. Strict liability fits into Pound's stage of 'strict law,' self-help into the prior stage of 'composition for the desire to be avenged,' and collective responsibility is by implication assigned a primitive place when Pound cites the Anglo-American emphasis on 'extreme individualism.' I am not arguing that Pound's scheme itself specifically has affected the work of anthropologists, but rather that it is a good representation of certain ideas in the Western legal tradition which have affected anthropology.

For some of the legal evolutionists, self-help epitomizes the dominance of private interests instead of impartial public justice; strict liability suggests insufficient regard for the question of moral fault, hence it too leads to 'injustice,' and collective responsibility shows inadequate regard for individual culpability, identifying the guilty with the innocent. In this framework historical changes in legal systems can be perceived as some sort of progress toward 'justice.' And a warm air of self-congratulation suffuses the evolutionary sequence.

Two things are wrong with this traditional jurisprudential way of looking at these problems: first, the social-structural setting of the practices is not given sufficient attention, hence the meaning attributed to them is out of context; second, the practices are taken to epitomize legal principles which are assumed not to exist, or to be of no importance, in complex societies. It is one thing to acknowledge that certain practices have changed. It is another to explain what this means. One anthropologist has gone so far as to say that there are two entirely different types of legal systems, and only two basic ones; those which include collective responsibility as well as individual responsibility, and those in which there is individual responsibility only – liability for one's own acts and one's own acts alone. He then develops a culture and personality explanation of collective liability, and describes the child-rearing practices on which the emotional identification supposedly necessary to collective liability are founded (Cohen 1964:130–3). This is not the place to amplify some of the critical comments I have made on this study previously; its very existence is sufficient to show a way in which evolutionary jurisprudential ideas have found their way into anthropology (Moore 1965:748–51).

There is a distorted self-image of Western law to which the legal systems of pre-industrial societies frequently are contrasted, blurring the analysis of both. This paper is offered as an attempt toward clarification. It will not turn the evolutionary schemes upside down nor inside out, but will try to redefine the problems involved in the analysis of strict liability, self-help, and collective responsibility in such a way as to show the inadequacies of some of the criteria on which these schemes are founded. The phenomena of which they take cognizance exist, but the meanings which they are given are in terms of a traditional conception of our own legal arrangements and their 'opposites' in pre-industrial systems. It is to those meanings that I am addressing myself.

The contention is often made that strict liability for injury and damage characterizes pre-industrial legal systems and that these give little or no attention to the motive behind a damaging act. Elias, and more recently Gluckman, have sought to explain strict liability and modify assumptions about disregard of intention (Elias 1956:135; Gluckman 1965b:ch. 7). Gluckman has reinterpreted strict liability in a social context. One of the purposes of this paper is to review some of Gluckman's ideas on this subject. He has sought to expose the logic of strict liability in terms of the way he interprets the structure of those societies he characterizes as 'tribal,' and has done so very ingeniously, but in my opinion he has generalized too broadly, and I differ with him on some aspects of his explanation.

Gluckman deals with absolute and strict liability in terms of a time-honored issue in jurisprudence: the relationship between intention and responsibility. Carrying this theme further, I shall explore a form of liability in which intention is not germane to responsibility – namely collective responsibility. Like strict liability, collective responsibility has figured prominently in evolutionary thinking about law. The two ideas are in fact connected, since attention to individual moral fault and motive, the antithesis of strict liability, is often associated in evolutionary thinking with the supposed modern importance of the individual.

Maine and Durkheim, for example, though their lines of argument were different and their preoccupations various, had in common the extremely important nineteenth-century theme that the general movement of legal-historical change was from a emphasis on legal community and collectivity to an emphasis on legal individuality. Maine conceived of primitive society as an 'aggregation of families,' modern society as 'a collection of individuals' (1861:126). In primitive society, 'The moral elevation and moral debasement of the individual appear to be confounded with ... the merits and offences of the group to which the individual belongs' (ibid.). Durkheim's formulation saw legal development as reflecting a movement of society from a period of cohesion based on uniformity (mechanical solidarity) to a period of cohesion based on differentiation (organic solidarity). In Durkheim's scheme criminal law was antecedent in development to civil law. Any rule-breaking challenged the very basis of cohesion in mechanically solid societies because such societies were founded on likeness and uniformity. Hence, in Durkheim's scheme, public law developed before private law. Civil, or private, law, the restitutive claims of one *individual* against another, were a later development, characteristic of societies whose cohesion was founded on a highly diversified and specialized division of labor. Law was the visible symbol of different kinds of solidarity, the index of social evolution. The shift from social sameness to social individuality epitomized this development (Durkheim 1893; 1964:64, 130–1).

These ideas have permeated subsequent general discussions of law in anthropology. Whether they are being cited, refuted or amended, they have shaped the direction of many of the generalizations which subsequent generations have made. In *Crime and Custom in Savage Society* (1926) Malinowski tried to turn the Durkheimian evolutionary sequence upside down, and to destroy what he saw as the exaggerated myth of collectivity. The reciprocity of mutual obligations was to serve as a demonstration of the importance of civil obligations in primitive society; the great diversity of individual rights and duties was to show the non-existence of collective ownership. The individuation which Maine and Durkheim saw as the culmination of the legal evolutionary sequence, Malinowski thought he found in the Trobriands.

More recently Hoebel has echoed Malinowski's reversal of the evolutionary sequence. He casts it in terms of 'public' and 'private' law rather than civil and criminal, which latter pair he finds to be merely different degrees of the same thing (1954:28).

Private law precedes public law in Hoebel's formulation. He describes legal development through the ages as a process in which the special private interests of individuals and their kin groups are gradually subordinated to the interests of society as a whole (1954:327). This view of the whole movement of legal development must be understood in terms of Pound's heralding of a fifth stage of legal evolution, the 'socialization of law,' the progressive broadening of the public interest. Pound had said this in 1921, but by the 1930s and 1940s it was not a matter for the future. Emphasis on the public interest was a much invoked legal principle in America in this period and it fitted with the political climate. Hoebel was trained in this general tradition at Columbia Law School, and it appears to have affected strongly his conception of the developmental trend of the law.

For Hoebel law is a matter of culturally determined, enforceable rules, and physical enforcement is the key concept in sorting legal from other norms. Consequently Hoebel sees shifts in the locus of the power to apply force as one of the most significant elements in legal evolution. It moves out of private hands into public hands. Hoebel makes fun of Malinowski for being too tenderhearted to give enough place to force. But in other respects Hoebel follows closely along the lines of Malinowski's reversal of Durkheim. While Durkheim had used 'public law' to mean action on behalf of the collectivity against individual law-breakers, Hoebel uses the term specifically to refer to the development of public officials and formal legal institutions. Part of Hoebel's apparent reversal of Durkheim is due to this difference of definition. Hoebel sees the whole trend of the law as 'one in which the tendency is to shift the privilege rights of prosecution and imposition of legal sanctions from the individual and his kinship group over to clearly defined public officials representing the society as such' (1954:327). The shift from self-help to official action thus occupies the central position in his conception of legal development, and it is this which he characterizes as the shift from private to public law. In the third and fourth sections of this paper I shall deal with self-help and its relation to collective responsibility, and with the concepts 'public' and 'private' law. There are a number of assumptions worth re-examining in Hoebel's sanguine assertion that 'Private law dominates on the primitive scene' (1954:28).

If one is going to talk about public and private law, it is useful to define what constitutes a public. In a sociological view of the law, norms are seen as applicable to particular social relationships. They exist in, and are enforceable in terms of, a framework of defined groups, categories, networks, and the like. Procedure reflects structure. Hoebel looks at law in terms of cultural norms and certain procedures of enforcement. In his legal postulates he touches only indirectly and peripherally on the systems of social relationship which are the context of the norms and procedures.

M. G. Smith has provided what seems to me for certain problems a very serviceable definition of a public. He makes a 'public' equivalent to a 'corporate group.' Smith's model for comparative politics presumes as the basis of social structure a multiplicity of durable, internally organized social units. These 'corporate groups' or 'publics' he defines as 'enduring, presumably perpetual groups with determinate boundaries and membership, having an internal organization and a unitary set of external relations, an exclusive body of common affairs, and autonomy and procedures adequate to regulate them' (Smith 1966:166). In some societies corporations are all discrete units, in others they overlap or some contain others. The corporations within a society may be structural replicas of one another, or they may have varied rules of internal organization and external relations. Smith asserts that 'corporations provide the frameworks of law and authoritative regulation for the societies that they constitute' (1966:119).

Very much in the same vein as this, much of Smith's corporate model is the formulation of Pospisil, who holds that law is to be understood not as a single system but as a whole series of systems, each pertinent to a particular group, the groups varying in inclusiveness. Thus any individual may be a member of a number of groups and subgroups and may be simultaneously subject to the legal systems of each (Pospisil 1958:272–8).

Using Smith's corporate definition of a public, it is not only possible but necessary for public law to exist in all societies in which there are corporate groups, and one is supplied with a formal framework within which some illuminating comparisons become possible. But as we shall see, it is not a framework adapted to all situations. Since Hoebel defines law in terms of cultural norms rather than in terms of groups, his 'society' knows cultural rather than corporate borders. When he speaks of evolutionary development toward systems having 'public officials representing the society as such,' he seems to be thinking of the development of political centralization, and of centralized political entities as equivalent to cultural units. A corporate definition of 'public' permits one to consider the distinction between public and private legal matters in everything from a village in an acephalous society to a sophisticated nation-state. What is public in the context of one group may be a private matter in the context of a larger unit which encompasses it. Public law in this definition may exist in the absence of centralization. The limitations of the Smith–Pospisil model emerge only when one deals with certain non-corporate aspects of law.

In contrast to Smith, Pospisil and Gluckman, Hoebel does not focus on groups or their organization. Hoebel's view of law is very much a mixture of three elements: a cultural-pattern normative point of view, an emphasis on physical enforcement, and lastly a general conception of law as settling 'trouble cases,' disputes between individuals, or between a rather vaguely conceived 'society' (sometimes in the form of public officials) and individuals. Outside the matter of centralization, politics is not part of it.

My general position is that one of the most important differences among legal systems is in the degree to which 'private' disputes between individuals have potential political or structural importance (see Gulliver 1963). Far from agreeing with Hoebel that 'Private law dominates on the primitive scene,' this paper will argue that many apparently 'private' disputes between individuals have a much wider range of potential structural importance in pre-industrial societies than do factually comparable disputes in complex societies. The interlocking of the public and private domains, and the relationship between the personal and political dimensions of disputes, are dramatically demonstrable when one takes a look at self-help and at collective responsibility.[1]

2 State of mind and strict liability

Not only in Pound's evolutionary scheme, but in many other writings there appears and reappears the notion that absolute or even strict liability for injury or damage is some sort of crude, undiscriminating, primitive legal notion, and that it is far more civilized to take motive into account when assessing liability. Elias (1956) quotes with disapproval a passage where Lowie had said, in 1920, 'after all qualifications are made, it remains true that the ethical motive of an act is more frequently regarded as irrelevant in the ruder cultures than in our own courts of justice' (Elias 1956: 135; Lowie 1920:401–2). Elias seeks to redress the balance by showing that in many African law cases *mens rea*, motive and intention play a major part in the outcome (Elias 1956:135f).

A comparative judgment of the sort Lowie made ought to be supported by comparative data if one is to pay attention to it. One need do no more than refer to the existence of a whole range of American cases arising from workmen's compensation to cases involving certain forms of negligence to show that attention to motive is by no means always relevant to liability in Western law. In fact Seavey describes the Western legal tradition in terms of oscillations between, and balancings of, two contradictory principles:

The first concept requires that one who engages in an activity, employs others, or controls things should be liable for harm caused by his activities, agencies or things, even though he is without fault. The second requires that a person whose conduct is not wrongful should not be required to pay for the harm it causes (Seavey 1963:379).

The first principle is said to protect the security of individuals, the second protects their freedom of action. Like many other writers, Seavey too says (p. 378), 'The primitive law stressed security.'

While Gluckman accepts the view that strict liability is characteristic of much of the African law of injury, he argues that the mental elements of an offence are nevertheless always taken into account, even when this is not explicit. Intention and motivation are 'presumed to be what a reasonable man in those social circumstances would have felt' (1965b:213). I interpret his discussion to mean that it is not necessarily the actual thoughts and intentions of the individual that are significant but some legal measure of his motivation. This legal assessment of motive is founded on a reasonable interpretation of the event at issue and the surrounding circumstances. These *may* include actual motive, but Gluckman argues that a far more important element in tribal societies is the relative social position of the protagonists.

Gluckman illustrates his argument about the fundamental relevance of social relationship to legal liability by citing the Nuer rules on homicide as given by Evans-Pritchard and Howell.[2] (See discussion in section 3 of this paper of Peters's revisionist view of the segmentary lineage model.) Gluckman examines the outcome in three different circumstances: where the killer and his victim belonged to two different 'tribes,' where the two belonged to more closely related 'vengeance groups,' and last, where both parties were members of the same 'vengeance group.' In the first instance, a killing between tribes, compensation was not paid, and the outcome was likely to be a retaliatory killing, since a chronic state of feud prevailed between tribes. Here Gluckman says intention is imputed to the slayer from the social situation itself. 'It is assumed,' he says, 'that if a man kills a member of a group with which his own group is at feud ... that he must have done so deliberately ... intention is presumed from action' (1965b:207). In the second Nuer situation, in that range of intergroup relationships in which compensation is paid, liability is absolute. For any homicide, there must be a compensatory payment. But the intention of the killer is relevant to the *extent* of liability. In the third situation, in which a Nuer kills a kinsman, no compensation can be paid, because those who are legally obliged to pay are the same people who would receive the payment (Howell 1954:62). However, the killer must undergo ritual purification. Here it would seem that intention is quite irrelevant to the liability question. It is out of this Nuer material that Gluckman constructs his initial critical argument.

Far from dealing with explicit attention to actual motive as if it represented some kind of intellectual advance, Gluckman simply assumes that there must be a logic to strict liability in the social context in which it occurs, just as there must be a logic to attention to specific motive in the situations and societies in which this is the emphasis. He does not place any higher value on attention to actual motive than on disregard of it. Instead he is looking for the functional relationship between social structure and the rules by which liability is allocated. So far, so good. However, it is with Gluckman's ultimate, more general remarks that I disagree.

Gluckman contrasts the law of tribal societies, 'in which the law emphasized duty to others, with strict liability in transaction and injury,' with the law of more technologically developed societies, which he sees as putting the 'onus on the plaintiff to prove that he had a right to expect a duty from the defendant' (Gluckman 1965b:235). He sees this shift as part of the general change from societies dominated by a model of kinship relationships to a situation dominated by a model of ephemeral social relationships. He sees the complex interdependence of persons in small-scale societies as putting people in certain social relationships under a special burden to be careful in their dealings with one another, even in their thoughts about one another. Gluckman extends to the area of injury and responsibility the emphasis on obligation and good faith in transactions which he finds characteristic of societies dominated by kin relationships (Gluckman 1965b:203). He speaks of the general position of African law as 'applying strict liability arising out of duty to avoid harming others' (ibid.:234).

In my opinion, on the complex society side Gluckman has not sufficiently taken into account the existence of strict liability in our own society, its various *raisons d'être*, and the many strict rules which govern what Pound described as 'relations' (landlord-tenant, debtor-creditor, employer-employee, etc.), rules which apply in Western law irrespective of the will or motive or intentions of the parties to these 'relations.' This passing rapidly over the question of intention in Western law would not matter if it were not for the fact that a great deal of his speculative argument (as opposed to his direct analysis of the African data) is founded on a dramatic contrast between tribal and large-scale societies.

Second, the duty to avoid harming others from which at one point he says strict liability arises (Gluckman 1965b:234) seems to me to be a doctrine inferred by Gluckman rather than coming directly out of the material.

Another rationale might serve better. It seems to me that strict liability, in so far as it results from the general conditions of tribal life, can be more economically explained by interpreting it as a means of assuaging the resentment of those who have been injured or damaged in a social situation in which injurer and injured must go on in a continuing social relationship. A rule that the agency of misfortune pays for it does not necessarily imply special moral or legal duties which have not been fulfilled. But there is good reason why Gluckman finds 'the duty to avoid harming others' a more attractive explanation. It resolves a paradox.

The puzzle that Gluckman set himself grows out of the fact that initially he chose to discuss the problem of legal responsibility in terms of the time-honored differentiation between an intentional wrong and an accidental or negligent wrong. He seeks the logic of a system which emphasizes state of mind to an extreme point in some contexts and apparently disregards it in others. He cites a number of instances of injury in tribal settings in which a man's intention is not investigated, and only his action is taken into account and liability is absolute.

He contrasts these with the treatment of witchcraft beliefs in which, at times, not action but mere thoughts or feelings may be culpable. How, he asks, is this paradox to be understood, that in the same society state of mind weighs so heavily in the one case, yet is quite passed over in the other? In the very same tribal systems in which absolute and strict liability appears as a significant feature, so does the belief in witchcraft, and not infrequently in witchcraft cases people are held legally responsible for state of mind, or mere intention alone. Gluckman resolves the paradox by inferring a legal doctrine that will embrace both kinds of case: the duty not to harm, either by deed or immoral feeling

(1965b:237–8). This duty rationalizes strict liability for harmful acts irrespective of intention, and at the same time rationalizes legal responsibility for mere intention. He has ingeniously reconciled seemingly disparate rules by constructing an inclusive, overriding doctrine.

But can one define in general terms a duty to avoid harming certain others that is special to kin-based societies? One might guess that some such vague general precept is socially universal, and yet that in every society it is also subject to some important exceptions. What evidence is there of a special obligation to avoid harming others in what Gluckman calls 'tribal' societies? How does this special obligation differ from the general condition that all social life requires some control of hostile and aggressive feelings? And if it exists, what is the relationship of this special obligation to strict liability?

In this matter Gluckman's reasoning is similar to that of a common law judge applying principles like those enunciated in Pound's third stage of legal evolution. Every liability is read back as incurred through some moral fault, through the breach of a matching moral duty. This *may* be the way some African societies reason out their rules, but I would contend that this cannot be inferred from the existence of the liability itself. One can rationalize liability for thoughts that harm and liability for unintentional harm by concluding simply that anyone who causes harm must pay for it, by whatever means it was caused. That does not mean that there is an especially extensive duty not to harm. It just means that there is a broad duty to pay.

When Gluckman speaks of strict liability as arising from 'the duty to avoid harming others in thought or deed' (1965b:234), he is by implication connecting strict liability with his idea that there is a general intensification of moral responsibility in tribal society, founded on the nature of multiplex social relationships. I would argue that at best the supposed duty not to harm is only one side of the picture, and that it is useful to consider the possible connections between strict liability and the habit of using force. For example, consider where the 'duty to avoid harming others' fits in with the following statements of Evans-Pritchard:

As Nuer are very prone to fighting, people are frequently killed. Indeed it is rare that one sees a senior man who does not show marks of club or spear.... A Nuer will at once fight if he

considers that he has been insulted, and they are very sensitive
and easily take offence.... From their earliest years children are
encouraged by their elders to settle all disputes by fighting, and
they grow up to regard skill in fighting the most necessary
accomplishment and courage the highest virtue (1940:151).

One gathers from Howell that what the Nuer emphasize is not
care lest they harm one another, but between killing in a fair fight
(*nak*) and killing by stealth or ambush (*biem*) (1954:42). Howell says,

self-help and retaliation are still common enough in Nuerland.
There is still little restraint put on the actions of the young and
hot-blooded by a body of public opinion consciously opposed
to bloodshed as a moral wrong. Nuer will admit that homicide
is wrong (*duer*) [a word which also means 'mistake'] and that
fighting is undesirable, but this is because they realise that these
lead to a most uncomfortable state of insecurity. Nuer are
always acutely conscious of the need for social cohesion. There
is, however, very little expression of an unfavourable reaction
to the taking of life in the abstract, and homicide is not
considered a crime against society. On the other hand, what we
call 'cold-blooded murder', which is extremely rare, offends
Nuer ideas of morality because the victim has had no chance to
defend himself. It is the Nuer code of honour which has been
contravened. People are profoundly shocked in these
circumstances, a feeling which extends well beyond those who
by reason of their relationship to the deceased are expected to
take a vindictive attitude towards the killer and his kinsmen
(1954:244).

Nor are the Nuer alone in such truculent habits. Smith and Dale
say of the Ila, 'Quarrels are of frequent occurrence in a village,
specially when the men are heated by drinking much beer during
a feast. Free fights take place with sticks and spears' (1920, I:417).
They then describe the strict liability of one who kills another.
Elsewhere (at p. 350) they speak of how men enlisted the aid of
their most combative friends when a claim was to be pressed
through self-help. Gulliver tells us of the Arusha, the agricultural
Masai of northern Tanzania,

most homicide occurs as a result of fights arising out of
quarrels, often drunken brawls, for men are prone in this
society to resort to individual violence. *Murran* habitually carry

swords and spears, and all men usually carry a heavy stick; and they are all inclined to use them readily. Although a fight may occur between men who have a long-standing and bitter quarrel, which is the root cause of it, I am not aware of an instance where a man has cold-bloodedly planned to kill his opponent; and in many instances the two men seem to have had little or no previous ill-will.... Whether the act was premeditated, in self-defence, the result of accident or uncontrolled temper, etc, is irrelevant to the settlement processes, although people distinguish these cases from an ethical point of view (1963:128).

Unlike the Nuer, the Arusha did not at the time of observation practice self-help or vengeance in homicide cases. Even of the peaceable Tallensi, Fortes reports 'They are quick to resent a trespass on their rights and readily snatch up a weapon or a missile if they are provoked' (1945:234). He attributes much of the suppression of fighting to the presence of the British colonial administration (1945:236). Hence violent inclinations are not attributable simply to the simultaneous exigencies of self-help, though they may be historically related.

In every respect the Nuer and the Ila, the Arusha and the Tallensi meet Gluckman's definition of a tribal society, of the kind of close, small-scale, technologically simple, kin-based structure he has in mind. How does this material on aggressiveness and fighting fit in with Gluckman's contention that an especially strict duty to avoid harming others in certain social relationships is a necessary consequence of the conditions of life in a tribal society?

One would, it seems, also have to infer from the material on fighting an obligation to be extremely vigilant against any encroachment on one's honor or rights, and an accompanying readiness to protect these by force. The duty to be on the ready and the duty not to harm would seem to have quite conflicting effects – which does not, of course, mean that they could not exist together. Man is not overgiven to consistency, particularly in matters of principle. But can one explain strict liability in terms of a duty not to harm without paying close attention to the concurrent attitude that exists in some societies that one must be ever on the alert and ready forcefully to protect one's interests?

Some instances of strict liability in tribal societies can perhaps be most simply explained by arguing, as I did earlier, that in certain social situations the resentment of the injured or damaged must be assuaged if social relations are to go on, whether or not the injurer was apparently at fault. Perhaps one should also think of strict liability in some cases as more like insurance than like punitive damages. Either of these possible explanations seem to me to be congruent with the conditions of life in tribal societies, and neither requires the postulation of any absolute duty not to harm to support it. They also apply as conveniently to social relations between groups as within them. Both these explanations fit particularly well in societies in which touchiness about insult or injury is part of every man's stance. There is a difference between being obliged to pay for any harm one causes and having an absolute duty not to harm.

The invariable pairing of duty and liability is a kind of common law reasoning which certainly occurs outside the Anglo-American tradition. But it is not universal, nor is it by any means the only basis for the allocation of legal liability, even in our own system. Moral fault is not the basis of all liability. By inferring a stringent duty not to harm, Gluckman is assuming a special moral element to explain a special liability. But absolute and strict liability may simply emphasize causality, not necessarily morality.

If one imagines a restraining duty not to harm at one end of the stick, the right to resort to retaliation and self-help would seem to be the other end, since this involves the condoned use of force by persons who perceive themselves as injured or damaged or insulted. It involves at least the risk, if not the intention, of doing harm.

Though I have indicated my reservations about Gluckman's idea that an especially stringent duty not to harm exists in certain social relationships in all tribal societies, and that it is closely connected with strict liability, I have no doubt that there is some form of restraining doctrine in all societies. Even in self-help systems there are clear limitations on sanctioned violence. One must not harm *except* to right a wrong, or even a score, and then only in prescribed ways and circumstances. There is no way to prove that there is a historical connection between self-help and strict liability, but it seems to me that there is a logical connection. In a system in which there is a good deal of freedom of action to use force in one's own interest, abuse of that freedom may be somewhat curtailed by the knowledge that everyone must pay for the consequences of his actions and that the plea of accident or good intention will not excuse one. Strict liability may be the counterpart of the right to use force (or the habit of using force) in some of the social contexts in which it appears. That strict liability has other forms and other reasons for existence in the same and other contexts is also undoubtedly true. I have no doubt that Gluckman is right about many situations in which strict liability is tied to ongoing social relationships in tribal society. My reservations about his argument refer essentially to the notion that strict liability carries with it a special duty not to harm, and Gluckman has agreed that he would now speak only in terms of a strict duty to pay, not in terms of a strict duty not to harm.[3]

3   Self-help and the principle of expanding dispute

Self-help has at least three important qualities. The first, already indicated, is that it is undertaken in the *name of right*. It is not forceful action admittedly embarked upon solely for naked advantage. It is rationalized with an argument about the protection of rights, the collection of what is due, or the avenging of (or retaliation for) a wrong. A second quality is that self-help is the *intransigent side of conciliation*. Disputes in systems of self-help can be resolved if both parties are willing to do so. Furthermore they can usually find a structural rationale for doing so, not only moral and pragmatic reasons. In other words, societies in which self-help is a widely used form of enforcement normally have well-established conciliation procedures and well-established ideological frameworks which support both conciliation and fighting.

'Self-help' sounds too much as if it always meant enforcement action by a single individual on his own behalf. While the term covers this case, societies characterized as having systems of self-help usually permit the mobilization of a number of persons in an individual's cause, given suitable circumstances. A third, significant quality of systems of self-help thus lies in the consequent *expandability of certain disputes* and the *containment* of others. Some disputes remain disputes between individuals. Other disputes over exactly the same substantive matters expand into confrontations of groups. At that point self-help becomes entangled with collective liability. As we shall see, where the enforcement of rights and the avenging of wrongs has a collective aspect, so do responsibility and liability ordinarily have their collective aspects.

Limitations are frequently placed on the use of self-help in particular relationships. Fortes's scattered material on debt among the Tallensi is a good illustration of: (1) the corporate conceptual framework of a group-backed self-help; (2) the extension for particular purposes of inside-the-corporate-unit status to certain groups and individuals outside the corporate group, i.e., the disregard of corporate borders for certain purposes; and (3) the margin of flexibility and adjustment within the Tallensi theoretical framework (1945, 1949).

Fortes tell us that in pre-colonial times the Tallensi 'tolerated the use of violence as the proper ultimate means of asserting one's rights' and that 'This attitude still survives to some extent' (1945:236). However, group raiding as a mode of self-help against a debtor was not proper within the clan, between linked clans, or between persons in certain kinship relationships (1945:236, 250). Hence clan-linking gave the equivalent of internal standing to external corporate groups in the matter of debt enforcement. Though raiding was not itself an act of war, it often led to war if men were killed. In short, raiding as a form of self-help was an approved method of redress only between groups and members of groups in general hostile opposition, irrespective of the facts of the case of the debt itself.

Inside a Tallensi nuclear lineage or an extended family or between close cognates, borrowing did not give rise to 'debts.' Yet there was an implicit obligation to reciprocate and repay goods or services in some form later on, and if repayment were not forthcoming counter-'borrowing' by the 'creditor' might be used to collect the obligation (Fortes 1949:215). Yet this counter-'borrowing,' a very polite form of self-help, was in no way comparable to the violent kind of armed raiding by a group of kinsmen which might attend the collection of a debt outside the clan (Fortes 1945:236).

It was also a Tallensi rule that mother's brother and sister's son, though they were supposed to be involved in a lifelong exchange of gifts and services, could not contract debts toward each other (Fortes 1949:305–6). Like the instance of linked clans, this is a case in which persons outside the corporate group were accorded internal status in regard to particular kinds of transactions. What was being granted was not membership in a corporation but quasi-status for certain defined purposes.

This kind of legal manipulation of corporate borders is very common in kin-based societies, and in the self-help context it is particularly interesting because it suggests that in self-help 'systems' alternative modes of social control are operative in those relationships in which armed, group-backed self-help is disapproved. Fortes tells us that, among other things, a defaulter in those relationships found it difficult to borrow again (1949:214). In the Tallensi case such group-backed self-help evidently was disapproved in those very relationships in which there were likely to be the greatest number of property transactions. In section 4 on collective responsibility, I shall have more to say about complementary systems of social control, about 'moral' obligations *versus* 'legal' obligations, and about the different modes of enforcing obligations and allocating responsibilities which each implies. For the moment, I shall confine myself to the forced meeting of liabilities by means of self-help.

Despite the existence of theoretical rules about which Tallensi relationships do give rise to debts and which relationships do not, Fortes tell us that in fact 'what happens in practice varies from case to case and from lineage to lineage' (1949:215). Certain very close relationships seem to have unambiguously precluded 'debt,' but beyond that immediate circle of close kinsmen there seems to have been some option about definition. The persons involved could consider either the transaction or the relationship as governing the definition of their dealings as a loan or debt, depending upon the way they chose to interpret the situation. Presumably the relationships between and among clans also shifted over time, and debt relationships could be redefined in terms of changes in alignment or *vice versa*.

It would seem from Fortes's material itself that considerations other than simple theoretical rules about relative social positions governed the actual outcome of particular transactions. The fact that self-help in its more violent forms was suppressed by the colonial power leaves the details unknown for the Tallensi. But the general outlines seem clear enough. A theoretical framework of social alignments existed. Disputes between individuals could expand into fights between groups. Expanded disputes over debts took place between the same sets of allies who chronically made war on one another in other contexts as well. Within each aggregation of allies, disputes over obligations also took place but were not supposed to expand into confrontations of groups lest the alliances be severed. Interpersonal violence between kinsmen or allies was disapproved, though it existed (Fortes 1945:177).

There is very definite information in other ethnographic sources on the containment of in-group disputes. For example, when a fight broke out between two men in a Nuer village, no third person was supposed to take sides (Evans-Pritchard 1940:151). In this way the fight was limited and not allowed to extend beyond the original participants. The alignment of partisans below a certain level could not be allowed vigorous or violent expression unless segmentation were imminent. This is true not only of the violent fights of the Nuer but also of partisanship in more peaceful confrontations in systems in which group-supported self-help is disapproved. Gulliver indicates that among the Arusha (who have a dispute-expanding process but among whom group self-help is forbidden) in a dispute between members of an inner lineage (offspring of one father) the concern of the other members is only in achieving a reconciliation. There is supposed to be no taking of sides. Gulliver explains this on the grounds that 'in practice the number of men in an inner lineage is too small to allow segmentation whilst yet retaining its unity' (1963:76, 135). It would appear from the Nuer example that a group need not be nearly as small as an Arusha inner lineage to take measures to prevent internal segmentation.

The general conclusion which the Tallensi, Nuer and Arusha examples suggest is that the principle of the expandable dispute, so important in legal enforcement between members of different social units, is operative only above a certain minimal organizational level. That level varies from one society to another. This means, in other words, that the principle of expandable dispute need not be consistently applied throughout a social system, but may operate only at specified structural levels. The minimal level of segmentation may vary according to the issue. Subsegmentation which may be allowed to be manifest in peaceful contexts may not be permitted expression in situations of dispute. Such would seem to be the implication of the Tallensi and Nuer data.

Wars, raids, feuds, fights, seizures, and less violent measures all may be forms of self-help in particular cases. In the literature the distinctions among them are variously drawn. Sometimes the terms are distinguished according to the kind of structural unit involved, sometimes according to the style of conducting hostilities, and sometimes – but by no means always – there are differences in the subject-matter of the disputes dealt with in these various ways.

Pospisil states vigorously that wars and feuds are extralegal by their nature, that law is exclusively an intragroup phenomenon because law in his definition exists only where both parties to a dispute are subject to some common authority (1958). He conceives 'authority' very broadly. While Pospisil's definition properly distinguishes certain kinds of structural units from others, and certain modes of resolving disputes from others, it does not follow that dividing the material in this way is the best approach to all problems. Disputes over precisely the same substantive matters may arise between individuals whether they do or do not recognize a common authority. For example, in precolonial times among the Nyakyusa, adultery, bad debts, assault, injury, and homicide were the subject of violent disputes between individuals of the same villages, between individuals of different villages of the same chiefdom, and between individuals of entirely different chiefdoms (Wilson 1951:136f). The common features in these disputes provide a good reason for looking at the social context of all the situations in which they occurred, irrespective of any limiting definition of law.

There is another standard distinction which seems far less absolute when one examines the Nyakyusa material. That is the distinction between 'systems' of self-help and 'systems' in which there is an official adjudicative and enforcing machinery to which an individual can have recourse. Monica Wilson's classic description of the Nyakyusa serves to illustrate the fact that self-help and official action ('recognition of a common authority') can operate within the same social structure. They need not be total alternatives.

In minor cases Nyakyusa disputants would usually settle their differences through conciliation and arbitration. They would ask a respected friend or the village headman to resolve the controversy between them. This method was available not only within a single village but also in quarrels between persons residing in different villages as well. If the headman failed to settle matters, then they went to the senior headman of his side of the chiefdom, thence to the chief of that cluster of villages. Village headmen could not enforce their decisions, but the chief could do so. The cases settled by conciliation were 'mainly disputes over the ownership, destruction or sale of ... minor property.' A small number of minor accusations of assault or insulting behavior also were settled in this manner (Wilson 1951:137, 140–1).

Serious injuries to person or property brought more violent responses. A killing was principally the concern of the agnatic lineage of the victim. These kinsmen either killed the slayer or brought him before the chief, who imposed a fine which went to the relatives (Wilson 1951:149). It is significant in evaluating the chief's judicial role and the nature of such disputes that the option lay with the victim's kin whether to retaliate or settle. Intervillage adultery cases sometimes blew up into intervillage wars, when the wronged husband and his supporters killed a covillager of the adulterer in reprisal. Adultery was sometimes a cover for property disputes, as a man from whom something had been stolen or to whom a debt had not been repaid might go to the thief's or debtor's village and seize the wife of any village-mate of the man who owed him property (Wilson 1951:150).

In pre-European days there appear to have been chronic fights between villages and between chiefdoms (Wilson 1951:25, 150–1, 173). These wars evidently took place in a setting in which there was no total shortage of land in relation to population (Wilson 1951:45–173; Gulliver 1958:3–10). Nevertheless, there were boundary disputes, and there was a continuous and regular process in which villages were moved and lands redistributed among them. This suggests that though there may have been no overall shortage of land, there were temporary shortages of socially valuable land, land in particular locations, which may have been the root of some of these intervillage hostilities, even those which were purportedly over debts, wife abductions, killings, and the like.

The Nyakyusa situation presents a variety of possibilities for resolving disputes. Individuals could reach agreement with the help of neutral friends. They could have recourse to the mediating services of officials, village headmen, senior headmen, or chiefs.[4] Or they could instead, at least outside the village, choose the course of self-help and use force themselves. Wilson does not indicate whether self-help could ever be used inside the village. 'Most Nyakyusa would hold that in the old days quarrelsomeness within the village was bad, that towards members of another village of the same chiefdom it was allowable, and towards members of another chiefdom it was good' (1951:80). Self-help outside the village usually required the mobilization of kinsmen to carry it off. Such action could spill over and involve whole villages in intervillage warfare.

Is it useful to think of the Tallensi and Nyakyusa kinds of expanded dispute as private law, as Hoebel seems to? (Hoebel 1954:28, 322). I think not. Such a view overemphasizes the dispute between individuals which sparks off the larger confrontation, and it ignores the prior or nascent structural oppositions and competitions between groups which are served by enlarging the dispute.

It seems to me that the characterization of primitive law as private law by Hoebel and others has in part to do with certain prevalent ideas about partisanship and impartiality which have their source in an idealization of our own social structure and legal system. Justice and fairness are conceived as depending upon an impartial evaluation of the rights of disputant parties, or the culpability of wrongdoers, by neutral persons. These neutral persons are public officials who represent 'the law' conceived as the norms and interests of society at large. Self-help seems exactly the opposite of this conception of fairness and justice, since it is the purest partisanship. In these models private and partisan are equated. Moreover, public officials are associated with centralized government and the well-being of all, while private causes are associated with the personal advantage of individuals (Hoebel 1954:327).

There is an accompanying conception of Western law in which police and public prosecutors are conceived to move on their own against violations of law, like impersonal angels of justice, punishing wrongdoers on behalf of 'society.' In fact, in industrialized societies, even in criminal prosecutions, officials are frequently set in motion by citizens who have suffered some damage or injury and have complained. Thus Evans-Pritchard (citing Peristiany) goes too far when, in the Malinowski tradition, he says of the Kipsigis, 'almost all cases were civil in the old days, for even when a community punished a man, it was always at the instigation of some person he had offended' (Peristiany 1939:xxv, 185). This is an equation of civil law with action *instigated* by an offended party. It is in keeping with the position Hoebel takes when he says that 'private law dominates on the primitive scene' (1954:28).

It is not solely on the instigation of process or the impartiality of proceedings that analysis should be focused if one is trying to decide whether a matter is one of private or public involvement. The question is what kinds of networks, groups, or administrative structures are set in motion and what kinds of things they do. When a man invokes the help of others, he is likely to avail himself of relationships and structures already existing in terms of other contexts of action. He may mobilize his lineage or his village. He may mobilize local political or religious leaders. His cause then also serves the purposes of others and will reinforce pre-existing groupings, relationships and political positions.

The sociological evaluation of what constitutes a private or a public legal matter depends on the extent of its social effect and its structural importance, not on whether it also serves private interests. Inevitably all public matters – matters connected with the common affairs of corporate units – involve action by individuals, and sometimes that action redounds to their private interest. On the other hand, not all individual action or private controversy has widespread effects. A large area of overlap exists between 'public' and 'private' disputes. Though one can easily identify the polar extremes of public and private matters, many disputes fall somewhere between and one is reduced to identifying their public and private *aspects* rather than allocating the dispute wholly to one realm or the other.

Consequently, I find it completely confusing to use the civil-criminal, private–public dichotomies as a way of characterizing whole systems, or the trend of 'legal evolution' as Durkheim and Hoebel and, by implication, Malinowski have done. There are functional analogues of certain aspects of Western civil and criminal, public and private law in all societies because some of the social problems with which these deal are universal. One cannot characterize whole systems by any of these terms.

In the small corporate groups of pre-industrial societies, and in their relationships with one another, disputes between individuals are far more likely to be disruptive to the social fabric than in impersonal, large-scale societies. In part, this is inherently so because of the small numbers, but it is the more so because of the way in which structurally determined partisan commitments spread the effects of what start as individual disputes. The ways in which that partisanship is determined and the way in which confrontations of partisan collectivities are conducted or prevented constitute a basic aspect of public law in pre-industrial societies.

The question whether a dispute between individuals will be contained between them or will be allowed to expand into a political confrontation depends not so much on the subject of the dispute as on the desirability of the confrontation from the point of view of the social units potentially involved, and on the question whether the rules apply according to which disputes may be expanded, i.e., whether the relative social positions of the parties lend themselves to opposing alignments.

As indicated by the materials cited earlier, the occasions for these confrontations are often personal wrongs against individuals, such as homicide, assault, adultery, and unpaid debts. Since the classic work of Evans-Pritchard on the Nuer, the resolution of disputes arising from such wrongs has been said to depend upon the social distances between the disputing parties – in the Nuer case, on their places in the segmentary lineage system.

E. L. Peters has now proposed very convincingly that this conception of the matter requires revision. In a paper of the camel-herding Bedouin of Cyrenaica Peters gives many examples of homicides in which the outcome does not fit with the segmentary lineage model. Peters shows how the 'irregularitie;' are rationalized away and the conceptual model preserved (1967: 261, 282). Like the Nuer, the Bedouin explain that disputes are resolved in terms of the segmentary lineage system, yet for both peoples the reality of behavior is not always congruent with the segmentary lineage concept. Evans-Pritchard described these disparities as an ideal–real dichotomy (1940:138). Peters has gone much further and argues that the models of society which people use to explain and rationalize their system are not to be understood as a normative framework.

Peters has cast his material as a critique of overliteral uses of segmentary lineage models. I should like to carry a step further the suggestions in his discussion. Building on Gluckman's earlier work on conflicts (1955b) and enlarging on Peters's recent contribution, these expandable legal disputes between individuals may be seen *to be serving complex structural ends, and simultaneously to be rationalized in terms of simplified ideological frameworks.*

Instead of proceeding in the conventional way and asking, 'What are the consequences of homicide in X society?' or even going a step further and asking 'What are the legal consequences of a homicide if it involves persons of such and such social positions?' the whole question can be turned around, and one can proceed from a macrocosm to microcosm. If one looks at corporate groups first and asks instead, 'When and under what circumstances do they mobilize as units against each other? What kinds of events may be used (*or not*) as the occasion for confrontations? How are confrontations rationalized?' one is seeing certain incidents between individuals as opportunities for collective action, and one sees in this collective action an element of choice.

Groups are in competition with one another for power and resources, and individuals likewise compete with one another for valued social positions and goods. These competitions can be long-term or short-term, cool, smoldering, or flaming. But they are always in the background. Peters says of feud:

> Ultimately, feud is a violent form of hostility between corporations which has its source in the competition for proprietary rights in land and water. Thus competition makes it necessary for groups to combine to prevent the encroachments of others in similar combinations and also to expand their resources whenever the opportunity arises (1967:279).

The group decision when it is opportune to expand, or the group decision that there has been an encroachment which must be resisted, is in some (not all) ways analogous to the decisions of individuals to advance themselves at the expense of others, or to react to the self-seeking of others. On both levels there are many choices. On both levels, when action is undertaken it is neatly rationalized, and perceived as justified and proper in the context of some overall conception of how society works.

Many considerations are involved in the question of timing, of when and where and against whom to turn a quiescent competitive position into active hostile competition. The most fundamental of these presumably have to do with the degree of underlying pressure on power and resources, and the degree of encroachment of one's competitors and the opportunities for bettering one's own position. Between counterpoised groups these basic pressures and positions tend to be long-term and the consequence of a cumulative series of events. The issues involved may be so fundamental that they are much more far-reaching than any particular event in the series. Yet active confrontation, if it is to occur, must happen at a particular time, place, and occasion. The legal wrong, because of its specificity in time, place, and circumstances, can provide the occasion for action. The legal wrong, moreover, makes it possible to have a showdown without necessarily acknowledging the deeper long-term motives or objectives which may accompany such action.

It can be put another way. Just as constitutional theories are condensed and simplified ways of thinking about the supposedly fixed relationship of social units, so certain events (in this case legal disputes) can serve as condensed and substitutive media in terms of which it is possible to conceive of, and play out, real social cleavages and structural competitions. Conventional conceptions of social structure serve to make apparently stable, simple order out of very complex, interwoven, and continuously shifting relationships. Disputes between individuals belonging to different groups can serve to bring into active expression some of the conflicts inherent in the social structure itself. Yet these emerge in a disguised form. The open fights appear to be no more than a system of self-help, a part of an orderly method of keeping people to their legal responsibilities. Such a translation of issues provides terms in which not only fights, but also settlements and peaceful intervals, can be arranged. Legal disputes function in this context of groups jockeying for position in somewhat the same way that political issues may in other societies.

From this point of view the apparent inconsistencies Peters has so well analyzed become altogether comprehensible. It also becomes clear that there are two fundamental conceptual frameworks to which conventional indigenous explanations of such confrontations have reference. A segmentary lineage system, for example, is an explanation in terms of relationships, groupings and alignments – what I have called elsewhere the 'constitutional theory' of a society. The other is an explanation in terms of a kind of value order that classifies acts as hostile or friendly. One explanatory frame of reference refers to categories of persons: 'They are allies/enemies.' The other refers to categories of acts: 'Such-and-such an act is friendly/hostile.' One supposedly describes the social placement of people, the other the social evaluation of events. Certain acts are appropriate to certain relationships. The orders of persons and acts are theoretically parallel.

Since the question of alliance or enmity often depends on the context of action between persons, and the amicability or hostility of an act often depends on the context of relationship of the actors, these are two interlocked frameworks of rationalization. I agree with Peters that segmentary lineage systems, like other constitutional theories, are neither sociological models nor norms for behavior but ways of conceiving and explaining the social world. The 'value order' of acts is no more normative than the 'constitutional theory.' It is equally manipulable and sometimes invoked to justify 'righting' entirely fictitious or imputed, provoked, or even anticipated 'wrongs.' Both are ways of conceiving, depicting, and rationalizing action in the social field.

Between groups which have regular encounters or dealings with each other acts which are or can be interpreted as hostile, as insults or wrongs, may be presumed to recur with a certain frequency. They recur irregularly, but presumably in some proportionate relationship to the total number of intergroup transactions.

Provocative occasions may even be conventionalized. The relationships of Bedouins which Peters calls feuds 'are of a kind which requires at least a show of hostility whenever the parties happen to meet.' He then describes unexpected encounters in which potshots and blows were exchanged (1967:268–9). Less improvised and more formal shows of hostility are found in the mock battles of the Ngombe funeral or the Nuer dances, each of which could potentially erupt into real fighting.[5] In short, the raw materials for confrontation, the focusing events themselves, are probably not far to seek if a confrontation is desired.

One of the regularities in hostility and the restatement of opposition is probably in the kind of event over which collective confrontations take place in particular societies. In the impersonal milieu of complex societies, particular wrongs against individuals or legal disputes between individuals are not usually the events which become the rationale for group confrontations. There have been some notable exceptions in the recent riots between blacks and whites in the United States, many of them touched off by just such incidents. Group confrontations within centralized states usually focus around the filling of office. But in societies having the principle of expanding dispute, legal quarrels between individuals may serve groups in their mutual antagonisms.

Deep economic or political reasons for the structural opposition of groups which may lie in the background of such controversies need never be directly acknowledged. The legal dispute between individuals of opposing groups can serve as a simpler, more concrete way of talking about and thinking about alignments based on those more profound problems which are less easily delineated and less easily resolved. Just as the segmentary lineage model serves to rationalize certain social systems, so certain legal disputes can be used to rationalize active structural conflict and bring it to a head at a particular moment. A legal dispute can be used as if it were a condensed replica of a wider and more complicated relationship. Surely one of the most important differences among legal systems must be in the varied ways that legal disputes between individuals can serve these structural purposes in different societies. The basic distinctions delineated here have been between self-help undertaken by individuals and self-help by corporate groups on behalf of individuals. A third possibility, to be taken up among others in the next section, is the case in which a man mobilizes a number of other men to support him in his 'self-help' but the supporters do not constitute a corporate group. In ethnographic fact, all three kinds of self-help may be available ways of proceeding in the same society, or one or another may exist alone, as the only possible or approved form.

4   Collective responsibility and corporateness: collectivities inside and outside

Collective responsibility is a term which usually means no more than that a number of persons are together answerable for certain of the obligations of one or more of them. Sometimes it is even extended to describe the obligations of an individual for a group he leads or represents, as where a man is legally responsible for the obligations incurred by all the members of his household, or a headman for the taxes of his village. In short, like 'totemism' and other nineteenth-century staples, it is a very general term. It covers a wide range of situations in which liability is incurred for the acts of another or others.

Since there are two elements in the term, each requires some amplification. One must ask, what kinds of collectivities may be involved, and to what kinds of responsibilities are they committed? Much of this section will be devoted to expanding on those two questions, using as a base the very loose definition that collective responsibility encompasses any situation in which a number of persons are together answerable for certain obligations incurred by one or more of their number, or their agents. This definition covers such a wide range of ethnographic variety that only a small part of it can be touched on here. Rather than make any attempt to cover the field, this essay will try to identify and analyze some of the variable elements in pre-industrial collective obligation and some of the combinations these elements may form. Distinctions emerge from such an analysis which are usually quite blurred or passed over in the literature. The further development of these distinctions may ultimately supply us with some legal criteria for classifying types of organization, and relationships between organizations.

There are two kinds of collective obligation in situations of self-help involving expanding dispute: the economic liability and the duty to give physical support. When precisely the same group of persons bears both obligations and is a corporate group, that is the simplest and neatest situation. It is neater still if one can say that the obligations are more or less equally and equitably distributed within the group as a whole, and they are mutual and common to all the members of the unit bearing collective responsibility. But such a tidy arrangement is by no means the only form possible.

The allies of a man exercising self-help, i.e., the persons he calls upon for aid in enforcing his rights, need not be a corporate group nor form any part of one. And reciprocally, the persons who are aggregately going to make good any debt or damage his opponent has done may not be a corporate group of any kind either. Gulliver gives us the example of the Jie and Turkana stock associates (1955: 196–200). Stock associates are all those individuals with whom a man maintains reciprocal rights to claim gifts of domestic animals on the more important occasions of social life. A man's stock associates include his close agnates, close maternal kin, close affines and bond friends. Each man has his own assortment, though obviously brothers would overlap in the first two categories. Disputes are settled by payments of stock solicited from the stock associates who in turn expect a share of any payments received. Under the indigenous system of self-help, stock associates were expected to lend verbal, and if necessary physical, support in obtaining compensation.

In M. G. Smith's definition, this kind of non-corporate assemblage would not be a public, nor would the confrontation in a dispute of the opponents and their stock associates be a matter of 'public affairs.' This shows both the limitations and the usefulness of looking on legal processes in corporate terms. The 'stock' associates' Gulliver has described are certainly a major element in the social structure and legal system of the Jie and Turkana. If one thinks of law as having to do with rights supported by the use of force, the stock associates were the major instrument of law in the indigenous system. But they are politically irrelevant. They are neither political units nor subparts of political units. Hence when the supporters of two disputants clash, the fight is exclusively concerned with which individual shall prevail in a particular dispute and which group of followers will share in the proceeds. There are no long-term structural oppositions to be served in the confrontations.

What is useful about Smith's definitional model is that by so emphasizing political units it clearly distinguishes for us a major difference between situations of self-help which involve corporations and corporate affairs, and situations of self-help which do not. One could, in fact, easily define collective responsibility in such a way that it would exclude non-corporate aggregates sharing responsibility, and one would then not have to cope with the stock associates among the Jie and Turkana. However, I think the heuristic value of defined categories is lost if one designs them to exclude related but inconvenient phenomena. I think it important to recognize that from the point of view of the disputants there are some significant similarities between situations of self-help by stock associates and by corporate groups. In both cases there is a dispute between individuals which then expands to include other persons on each side. In both cases force is used (or threatened) in the name of right to settle a dispute. In both cases the brunt of the settlement is borne by a number of people, and, on the winning side, a number of people share in the proceeds.

But the similarities do not necessarily end there. The stock associates' responsibilities fall on them by virtue of their social relationship to one of the disputing parties, not by virtue of their relationship to one another. Something very similar can be true inside a corporate group. The assembling of fighting companions to help to press a claim may take place in terms of a set drawn from an individual's network of kinsmen, rather than necessarily involving the whole of a corporate group.[6]

Smith and Dale say of the Ila, 'When a man induces two or three stalwart friends to accompany him and assist in prosecuting his claim, the other party replies by summoning his clansmen to his aid' (1920, I:350). Such a fight might spread to involve two whole districts, but could be left to be sorted out between the personal supporters of each combatant if the whole of each clan did not see fit to take up the cudgels. 'In any case where a clan takes up a dispute, responsibility is collective and therefore vicarious ... any member of the clan is liable to be punished. The dispute is against a rival clan, not against an individual; the initiative is taken up by common consent, not by an individual, and as the result of due deliberation by the elders' (1920, I:350). One may thus distinguish enforcement procedures that involve an individual's networks and those that involve the whole of a corporate group. The one may, but need not, turn into the other.

On the economic side, the putting together of a collective payment may also take place in terms of a set drawn from an individual's network rather than involve the mobilization of the whole of the group to which he belongs. When a Kipsigis or a Lango had to assemble a blood payment to compensate another group of kin for a homicide he had committed, he had to make a major contribution himself, and then went from relative to relative begging for beasts.[7] These were given him, or refused him, as an individual. His claims for aid against his kinsmen are in this respect (though not in some others) like the claims of a Jie or Turkana against his stock associates.

In contrast to an economic obligation involving ego-centered sets, we find the corporate unity of the Suku. Kopytoff describes continuous sharing and circulation of property within the lineage among the Suku (1964:92–4): 'Obligations contracted by any member bind the lineage as a whole ... self-help may be resorted to indiscriminately against any one of them by a wronged lineage.' The collective responsibility of the Suku extended to

> legal fines and compensations; bride-wealth collected or disbursed; tribute and, more recently, taxes – all these impinge on the lineage as a unit, every member contributing as much as he can convince others he can afford, collecting as much as he can demonstrate he needs. When a person dies, the inheritance reverts to the lineage as a whole.

The corporate (rather than network or set) payment of bloodwealth is also well exemplified by the Arusha Masai. Among the Arusha bloodwealth is always 'paid by contributions from all the sections of the moiety of the killer' (Gulliver 1963:128). The allocation of these contributions is made at a moiety assembly by the lineage counsellors of the moiety.

To what extent can one look upon the property of the members of an aggregate or group as a pool of assets where the members have the right to claim material help from one another in legal settlement and other times of need? The answer is not simply a matter of looking at an ambiguous situation which can be read either way. Many peoples have ideological terms in which assets are spoken of as the common resource of a particular social group – 'cattle of the lineage,' for example. However, the uniformity of such general expressions must not be mistaken for uniformity in the legal rights they subsume. These may be quite varied. There is a distinguishable range of degrees and kinds of property and manpower pooling inside corporate kinship units, and there are also varying types of networks of mutual aid.

Four variant forms of the economic responsibility to aid in meeting legal obligations exist even in the few ethnographic examples mentioned above. The first is that of the Jie and Turkana stock associates, which are not corporate groups and whose assets are in no sense a common pool (Gulliver 1955:196–200). The beasts of stock associates are a resource for an individual. Stock associates are ego-centered aggregates which function as action-sets only on rare occasions at the behest of the ego who constitutes their common point of connection. A second type is that of the Lango and Kipsigis, in which, perceived from the outside, the group of kinsmen is a propertyholding unit liable to bear collective responsibility, but, as seen from the inside, the payment obligations of members are not altogether corporate or collective. Here each individual is the center of a set of concentric circles of kinsmen to whom he may appeal for help. The closer to the center, the closer the relationship, and the more urgent his claims on them. The peripherally related persons in the outer circles are pressed to help only if the inner ones cannot (Peristiany 1939:195; Driberg 1923:208–11). The whole of the group need not be involved. The third type is the Suku, among whom the lineage is a corporate group with assets regarded as allocated to individuals but circulating freely and treated as a common resource for virtually all purposes, everyone chipping in to make payments whenever necessary (Kopytoff 1964:92–4). The fourth is the Arusha, among whom the subsections of a widespread corporate group may occasionally be assessed for special obligations, but whose assets are otherwise quite separate (Gulliver 1963:128).

Throughout these examples there are variations in the social relationships of the persons bearing collective economic responsibility, and the degree to which, and the ways in which, the property involved functions as a common resource and pool for insurance. All the relationships are personal relationships, and most enjoin mutual aid in many contexts. All the property involved is, in fact, in the possession of individuals entwined in these relationships. The pooling aspect resides essentially in the strength, frequency, and nature of the contingent claims to which the property is subject. By way of contrast, there is the collective liability of the business corporation of modern industrial society in which there is a pooling of certain assets by persons who do not necessarily have any other ties or other obligations of mutual aid to one another, and who do not hold specific pieces of corporate property but rather hold shares in the corporation.

By definition, in situations of 'collective responsibility' the property of a number of persons serves as a resource from which to pay legal claims. Yet in all of the situations mentioned, including the modern business corporation, the capital is primarily available for other purposes. I think it can safely be said that the settling of legal disputes is *always* peripheral to the main purpose for which the capital is available, and hence that legal obligations are not comprehensible outside their wider economic and social settings.

It may clarify matters to distinguish three questions and briefly to compare some aspects of the modern business corporation[8] with pre-industrial 'collective liability' on these three points: the question of limitations on liability, the question against whom claims may lie which may be paid out of collective assets, and the question what kinds of claims these may be. We tend to think of limited liability as a modern invention. The shareholder in a business corporation is not liable beyond the extent of his share. The ethnographic data suggest that certain limitations on liability also play a part in pre-industrial collective arrangements.

Let us consider the Jie and Turkana stock associates. Could any man expect or claim unlimited economic help from any particular stock associate? It does not seem so. He expects a *contribution* when he needs it, and presumably that contribution has a relation to at least the following factors: the nature of his past exchanges with that associate – what animals have been given and what received; the means of the associate; the extent of the need; and the prospects of ultimate reciprocation or 'repayment.' Among the Kipsigis and the Lango the blood debtor is in the position of a supplicant asking for help. He may expect contributions from kin, but surely these also are limited by all sorts of norms of standard payment and principles of reasonableness. Moreover, there is a system of priorities according to which contributions are solicited from closest kin first, the implication being that some kind of measure of their means determines how widely requests for beasts may be made. In the Suku case one understands that there is a general distribution of charges, but is there any question of the unlimited liability of any individual or of the group as a whole? I would doubt it. Among the Arusha bloodwealth is fixed at 49 cattle and collected from a wide group. Many equitable principles govern the setting of each contribution. Liability is clearly limited. In all these pre-industrial societies anyone rendered indigent by a legal payment became dependent on the same people who might help him with the payment.

Later I shall argue that the right to expel members is an extremely important element in units bearing collective responsibility in pre-industrial society. It seems to me that this, too, suggests a definite ceiling on liability. Except in the sense of vulnerability to attack in vengeful raiding, kinsmen and associates can limit their liability simply by refusing to support an individual who has imposed too much on their assets.

As for the second and third questions – against whom claims lie which may be paid out of collective assets, and what kind of claims these may be – here there is a most important distinction between aggregates or groups bearing collective liability in pre-industrial societies and certain modern business enterprises. In the pre-industrial situations mentioned here, any claim against any individual who is a member of the relevant corporate group (or has a network of supporting associates) may ultimately be paid out of the assets of other members of that group or network. There is an undifferentiated (but, as indicated earlier, not unlimited) general commitment to aid in times of need. In the industrial business corporation only a claim against the corporation acting through its agents in the conduct of its specialized affairs may be paid out of corporate assets. Corporate business is legally distinguishable from other affairs of shareholders and agents. Corporate assets are similarly distinguishable. And the roles of shareholder, manager, and agent are distinct and may be occupied by different individuals. In sum, I would argue that certain *quantitative* limitations on liability exist both in pre-industrial and certain industrial units bearing collective liability; and that a much more important basis of distinction between the two is that there are many *qualitative* limitations on liability in industrial corporations which do not exist in comparatively undifferentiated societies.

Curiously, even in the pre-industrial world, collective obligations are not always and only to outsiders, though we tend to think of them that way. Even concerning blood payments, a collective obligation can exist internally in a collectivity. Gulliver has described the blood payments made by the whole moiety of the Arusha when homicides occurred within the moiety or maximal lineage (1963:138). Penwill reports something similar among the Kamba of Kenya: 'If a man kills a son or a near relative, the payment must still be made' (1951:82). He then goes on to describe the division of the payments.

Both the social relationships of those collectively responsible and the degree of pooling of property are matters of the *internal* organization of the unit of collective responsibility. But there is another variable of major importance, and that is the character of the *external* relationships of those collectively responsible. How is a corporate group committed to collective liability to outsiders? This may depend on its internal organization; on who is authorized to commit the group – every member or only particular ones; and what procedures commit the group in what instances. On the other hand, the commitment of the corporate group may depend not only upon such internal factors, but also upon the whole character of its external relationships.

Collective vulnerability to violence is one aspect of collective liability in societies in which the expansion of dispute and self-help exist together. In its not uncommon fortuitousness, violence differs in a structurally significant way from negotiated indemnification, which is always systematically and socially allocated within the paying group. When warring or feuding villages raid one another, it can be a matter of chance who is killed, or what property is taken or destroyed, as when a city is bombed in a modern war. Violence is brought to bear by outsiders to whom the internal organization of the collectivity may (but need not) be a matter of indifference. Avenging, attacking outsiders can treat it as a homogeneous indivisible unit; they assault or plunder the most convenient victim rather than seek out the one against whom the immediate grievance lies.

A village treated as a unit from the outside by attackers may show its internal segmentations in later, peaceful settlements. As indicated earlier for the Nyakyusa, intervillage wars were one possible sequel to intervillage homicide in pre-colonial times. But in certain cases, where not war but some compensatory settlement was made between the villages, the offender found himself with heavy obligations. He not only had to pay the kin of the man he had killed in the other village, but he also had to compensate anyone in his own village who had been the victim of a retaliatory attack. He incurred this obligation on the ground that it was his original act which had provoked the retaliatory injury and brought trouble on his village, hence it was his responsibility to pay for it (Wilson 1951:150). Elizabeth Colson reports a similar situation among the Plateau Tonga (1951:121). In both these cases the village was treated as a unit from the standpoint of the attackers, but from within the division between kinsmen and neighbors was decisive.

In making intervillage wars impossible the colonial powers removed one major context of Nyakyusa village collectivity. For the Nyakyusa one might say that there were two levels of collective obligation. The principal collective obligation was that of close agnates, these probably being identifiable as a set drawn out of the network of agnatic kinsmen. However, though villages were not made up of kinsmen, there were occasions when in confrontations, in fights, whole villages supported their members. Two kinds of group were thus involved in Nyakyusa self-help and collective obligation, and members of the two groups had essentially two kinds of obligation. Cattle circulated among kinsmen, and economic aid and physical support in legal dispute were always expected of kinsmen. But neighbors did not have the same stringent duties as kinsmen either in helping their covillagers or in pooling property (Wilson 1951:44–60). Co-residence, or contiguous residence, is often implied by collective vulnerability to violence. Such residential proximity is clearly not necessary to collective economic liability. The hit-or-miss quality of certain types of violence (because of the haste of the attackers, who want to minimize the risks to themselves) is itself a contributor to collectivity. Collective vulnerability to violence in some cases, like the Nyakyusa one, may be one of the most important contexts in which a particular social entity was dealt with as a unit bearing collective liability.

In many societies particular social groups may be freely treated as collectivities by outsiders, who may recover property equally well from any member of the collectivity, and in some cases, may wreak retaliation on any member.[9] However, there are other groups which, though they aid members in case of need, cannot be treated with impunity as collective responsibility units by outsiders (Gulliver 1963:84; Mair 1934:189). And, as seen in the Nyakyusa case, in some societies outsiders may treat a social unit as a collectivity, yet insiders may deal with one another as if there were no collective liability.

Treating a corporate group as a unit bearing collective liability from the outside can be a very effective mode of social control irrespective of whether there is any collective liability from the point of views of insiders. The outsiders can leave it to the insiders to sort out the matter of individual responsibility and to bring culprits to heel. Among the Mbembe of Nigeria, who have a double unilineal system of calculating descent, the matrilineal group was economically collectively responsible to outsiders for any offense committed by a member. Villages tended to be endogamous and were composed of a number of patriclans, cross-cut by shallow, small matrilineages. Movable property was inherited within the matrilineage, land patrilineally. Certain villagewide associations had the responsibility for detecting particular offenses and fining those who broke certain rules. The association 'normally imposed a "fine," seizing any animal ... at random and eating it; and it then became the responsibility for [sic] the offender's matrilineage to compensate the owner' (Harris 1965a:44). Punishing the wrongdoer was then left to

the matrilineage, which normally had the right to punish individuals ... and ... which, in the last resort, might condemn a persistent offender to death. In such case the exasperated matrikinsmen might publicly refuse to pay any more fines on a rogue's behalf and the man would be forced to hang himself before all the people of the village (Harris 1965a:26).

Meek says of analogous examples of Ibo collective responsibility,

> These regulations do not imply that there was any collective ownership of property, or that a person was held morally responsible for the sins of his relatives. They were an obvious method of obtaining redress through those who were in a position to bring pressure. And they were evidence of the strength of kinship and local group solidarity, which, indeed, they served to cement (1937 : 127).

Fortes makes a similar point about the Tallensi:

> Thus in the old days a creditor could raid the livestock of any clansman of his debtor, and not those of a neighbour of his debtor who belonged to a different clan. In the latter case a reprisal raid was the penalty. In the former case the victim of the raid could demand restitution from his clansman, the original debtor; and I know of men who pawned a child or sold him into slavery in order to find the means of repaying a clansman who had been raided, rather than let the affair become a source of conflict in the clan. This is a good illustration, incidentally, of the statement previously made that collective responsibility is not a principle of Tale jural relations. It is not the clan but the debtor himself who is responsible for his debt. Self-help is a technique for putting pressure on a debtor through the mechanism of clan and lineage cohesion (1945 : 245).

Thus even in a society which stresses that ultimate liability is entirely individual it is possible for social collectivities to be vulnerable to seizures of property or other attacks by outsiders because a member has defaulted in his obligations. In many of the pre-industrial societies in which the principle of expanding dispute is allowed expression in self-help, a group bearing corporate liability may be committed to potential liability by any member, acting on his own, without authorization or sanction of the group for his particular acts. It is my hypothesis that *where every member of a corporate group has the power to commit it in this way to a collective liability, a corollary rule always exists whereby the corporation may discipline, expel or yield up to enemies members who abuse this power or whom the corporation does not choose to support in the situation in which he has placed them.*

When a member of one Lango patriclan killed a member of another, in another village, either his kinsmen would join to help him pay the blood money or they might throw him to his enemies. He would be driven away if they felt he had imposed on them too often, or if they felt that they were weak in fighting strength and were in danger of invasion by a strong village and could save themselves only by these means (Driberg 1923:208–9). La Fontaine says that to forestall an avenging attack or save themselves from the payment of bloodwealth the Gisu formerly sometimes killed a member of their own lineage who had killed an outsider. When they thought the killer not worth supporting they did away with him themselves (1960:99). Bohannan tells us that among the Tiv war could be avoided if the murderer's lineage surrendered him to the victim's lineage, or if the murderer's lineage obliged the murderer to kill himself (1957:148). Evans-Pritchard says in his Introduction to Peristiany's book on the Kipsigis, 'public opinion might be expressed actively and collectively by the imposition on an habitual wrongdoer of the collective curse of the village, or by public outlawry of him by his kin which deprived him of their protection and enabled those whom he had offended to put him to death without fear of retaliation.'[10]

These instances support the hypothesis offered above, that a corollary of the power to commit a corporate group is the possibility of being expelled from it. *Expulsion is a qualifier of collective liability*. It also supports the proposition discussed earlier, that there is often an element of choice in the confrontation of groups, and that incidents around which such confrontations are organized may not inevitably cause a confrontation.

Giving expulsion its full importance commits one to consider another proposition: that expulsion may be one of the ultimate legal penalties for breaches of obligations normally thought of as subject to moral or 'social' sanctions only. For example, Gulliver has stated emphatically about the Jie and Turkana stock associates, and the inner lineage of the Arusha, that an individual appealing to these sources for help has no legal right to their aid (1955:203; 1963:85).

In keeping with standard usage, Gulliver by 'legal' means 'supported by the use of force.' He describes non-legal rights as maintained by reciprocity, i.e., by social sanctions rather than legal ones. This is not unlike Fortes's characterization of the obligations of kinship as essentially moral obligations (1949:346).

I would argue that in a number of pre-industrial societies the difference between certain moral obligations and legal obligations is that the application of physical force is the ultimate sanction for the former and a more immediate sanction for the latter. The absence of 'legal' sanctions inside mutual-aid aggregations may be more apparent than real if one gives full consideration to expulsion, selling into slavery, accusations of witchcraft, and other remedies available to such units.

A man who defaults in his obligations to his kinsmen or close neighbors or abuses his rights may not immediately experience anything more than social penalties, but legal sanctions may nevertheless be applied ultimately when his kinsmen are thoroughly fed up with him (Gluckman 1965b:162). When 'social sanctions' imply physical force as a possible ultimate resort, must they not be considered to have a legal element? Penalties attaching to the breach of 'moral' obligations may be deferred, long-term results of the cumulative social record of the individual, not immediate measures undertaken to enforce specific performance of a particular duty, or repair of a particular wrong.

In contrast, 'legal' obligations are those in which such specific performance or repair may be immediately achieved through physical force. 'Moral' obligations are those in which the sanction of social pressure is used to obtain performance. The ultimate penalty for repeated or serious failures in meeting 'moral' obligations may involve force; but such action aims not at performance as its objective, but rather at ridding the social unit of an undesirable member, one who is not sufficiently vulnerable to mere social pressures. The existence of some functional parallels between expulsion and modern criminal penalties is clear. Imprisonment may be a form of internal expulsion. I am not suggesting that what have heretofore been called 'moral' obligations should henceforth be called 'legal' ones. I think the traditional distinction has much to commend it, since it marks differences in the quality of immediate sanctions on breaches of obligation, the difference between social penalties and physical force. What I wish to do is call attention to the existence of legal penalties for stubborn resistance to social penalties. Again and again in the literature, where expulsion is mentioned, or execution by one's own group, it is the gross violator or recidivist who is mentioned. This has a bearing on Durkheim's argument about the presence of criminal penalties in technologically simple societies, and the punishment of the criminal for assailing the basis of group cohesion, part of which is surely conformity without physical force. From the way Durkheim writes, it was not in terms of recidivism that he conceived of primitive criminal penalties, but rather as falling immediately on anyone who broke the rules. That he erred on this score does not matter. What is significant is that he was right about the larger picture, the existence of ultimate penalties for that source of group disruption, the trouble-maker, the individual who will not conform.

Expulsion is surely the ultimate withdrawal of reciprocity, of which there are undoubtedly many more subtle and less drastic forms. In fact, just as reciprocal ties may be established one by one (as between Jie and Turkana bond friends, or those established by trade or agistment in many societies), so presumably can these reciprocities be withdrawn one by one, and not necessarily all together. Sometimes one can distinguish clearly between corporate action in such a case and separate actions by individuals. However, where a corporate group is very small, and the withdrawal of reciprocity involves a number of members, it may be difficult to distinguish one from the other, nor is there any particular reason to do so. Where the aggregate involved is not a corporate group, presumably piecemeal support or withdrawal of support is all the more characteristic.

In citing ethnographies which mention expulsion, on the whole I have not included the very large number of instances of expulsion or other punishment for sorcery and witchcraft, because these are more ambiguous. But it is necessary to mention them, as a great many expulsions come under this heading, and some of them are doubtless also expulsions for faults of character, failure in obligations, or misfeasance, though, of course, other considerations entirely, such as structural competition, or conflict, or catastrophe, may also lead to accusations of witchcraft. Presumably, also, some offenders leave before they are expelled, since it is more graceful to resign than to be fired, less dangerous to retire or withdraw rather than be thrown out.

This raises another point which cannot be expanded on here, but which deserves mention: the question of how much of a penalty expulsion really is. The seriousness of the penalty of expulsion depends upon how easy it is to attach oneself to another community and to what extent one is a second-class citizen in that community. Does one become an 'outlaw,' a refugee or a welcome immigrant? In some societies, such as the Nuer, it appears to be quite a simple matter to settle oneself in one community after another, and many people do so without any stigma attaching to such mobility. In other societies the status of attached aliens seems to be much more precarious than that of proper citizens. Yet on whatsoever basic rule membership in a community is founded, however exclusive it may be, there are ordinarily also other rules under which exceptions are made. Under these subrules persons who do not fit the normal definition for membership can nevertheless adhere to the social unit.

The degree of normal movement among communities varies very much from one society to another, and has also been very much affected by the intercommunity peace established by colonial powers. Communal expulsion in one society is not always equivalent to expulsion in another. Moreover, expulsion may vary in its significance from one moment in political history to another. However, in a society in which it is necessary to belong to a unit bearing collective responsibility or exercising mutual aid, to be expelled from the unit in which one has one's firmest social footing is undoubtedly quite serious, unless one can easily become a member of another.

The penalty of expulsion forces one to consider that a collective obligation, while it may appear altogether collective when viewed from the outside or at a distance, is not so from the inside. Inside the collectivity the actions of members are weighed individually, and often, as indicated earlier, quite specific and varied individual obligations may exist with respect to debts of the collectivity. In the pre-industrial world, when an individual brings about a situation in which a corporate group to which he belongs is involved in heavy obligation, it may honor his claims wholly or in part, or it may turn him out. Certainly, even if he is given help he may be exhausting his potential claims and bringing himself closer to the point of refusal or expulsion. It becomes part of the history of his relationships with his fellows, a history which will bear on all his future dealings. Within the group he is in this way being held individually responsible for what he did, even though his kinsmen (and/or associates) may bail him and themselves out, and he may not 'pay' them for his act at once. The Kipsigis say a man may solicit help in making a blood payment only once; if he does so a second time he is disowned (Peristiany 1939:199). Whether there is usually as clear a measure as one chance for such collective help, or whether in other societies the rules are less precise, there is no doubt that within a group or aggregate bearing collective liability, in the long run individuals are held individually responsible for their actions. Collective responsibility does not exclude or substitute for individual responsibility. Both can and do operate simultaneously at different social levels.

5 Conclusions

The introduction of this paper reviewed some evolutionary or developmental ideas about law, and considered various theses of Pound, Durkheim, Maine, Malinowski, Gluckman, Hoebel, and Smith. The recurrent themes – collectivity and individuality in the law, public and private law, civil and criminal law, and strict liability – crop up repeatedly in contrasts between the law of pre-industrial societies and that of industrial ones.

The body of the paper has examined some aspects of strict liability, self-help and collective responsibility. This examination was undertaken with the idea that by discussing the variety of phenomena to which these very general terms refer, and the variations in social context in which they occur, it could be shown that the evolutionary schemes in which such terms are prominent could do with some revision. I have addressed myself to examining some conceptions of what constitute the basic contrasts between the law of pre-industrial societies and our own. I conclude that some redefinitions and re-explanations are in order.

The evolutionary schemes considered here are all conceived with the notion that there are certain over-riding legal principles according to which (and means by which) responsibility is allocated, and that these principles and means differ according to the degree of development of legal systems. Strict liability, 'private law' (self-help, civil law) and collective responsibility are often mentioned as primitive features. Moral fault as the basis of liability, 'public law' (criminal law, official-enforcement) and individual legal responsibility are contrasted as developments of complex societies. There is some validity to these contrasts and some distortion as well. There is no doubt that in many pre-industrial systems certain kinds of personal injury are treated as cases of strict liability which are not so treated in Western law. There is no doubt that self-help is a prominent feature of many pre-industrial systems, while official enforcement characterizes centralized political systems. Certain obligations which are met collectively in pre-industrial societies are met by individuals in our own.

However, if one puts the problem slightly differently one gets different answers. What becomes apparent is that the questions which lead to these evolutionary answers may not be conceived in sufficiently broad terms. To be sure, the kind of collectivity which is collectively liable has changed very much from pre-industrial society to industrial society, but collective economic liability is an extremely important feature of Western law. For example, if one thinks of personal injury and homicide as exclusively cases for individual liability in Western law, has one not forgotten the importance of insurance companies, business and government corporations, workmen's compensation, and public health and welfare agencies? The standard lay answer which is usually made to such arguments is 'Oh, that's all very well as far as economic liability is concerned, but criminal liability is collective in tribal society, yet is entirely individual in our own.' A significant fallacy is involved in the comparisons usually made. Retaliatory vengeance killing between groups is not at all equivalent to criminal penalty. What is equivalent to criminal penalty is the kind of individual assessment of character inside corporate groups which can lead ultimately to expulsion or execution. This exists as much on an individual basis in pre-industrial society as in any complex one. One can get some very peculiar results if one does not compare comparables.

All this brings us back to M. G. Smith's definition of a corporate group as a 'public' and to Pospisil's conception that law must be seen in terms of the groups to which it is pertinent, and to Gluckman's insistence on the structural context of law. If groups are publics, then social control inside groups must be seen as public law, even if the pre-industrial equivalent involves small groups and modes of social control more suited to small groups than large ones. Though expulsion is often mentioned in ethnographies, too little attention has been given to the theoretical implications of expulsion as a legal measure in pre-industrial society. For example A. R. Radcliffe-Brown mentions expulsion as a sanction but does not develop the point. It is not unless one uses models of society that emphasize the degree of boundedness of groups, and consequently pays close attention to the significance of movement from one group to another, that the variant forms and consequences of expulsion can be given proper weight.

Expulsion may be an ultimate remedy, and in some cases may require provocation over a long period of time to be invoked. But it is there, in the background. Moreover, the issue of expulsion is not always expressed directly in the form which would make it most recognizable to Western eyes as an analogue of criminal penalty. Deaths which give rise to inquests and disasters which provoke witchcraft accusations provide occasions for expressing hostilities, some of which have their root in competition, but others, surely, are related to improper behavior. These are subtle things; issues are mixed; the terms of discussion are mystical substitutes for direct confrontations of difficult questions. Individual dislikes and 'public opinion' are difficult to distinguish. In some cases it may be sensible to consider inquests and witchcraft accusations as quasi-judicial proceedings. They may be quite systematic in appealing for, and testing out, public support. Emrys Peters has made this point about Evans-Pritchard's material on Azande witchcraft. He argues that the consultation of different oracles involves different degrees of publicity (Peters 1963). The social context of the consultation of the oracles may shift to ever-larger audiences, with the consultation of more important ones. 'Public opinion' may thus be tested out, and public endorsement obtained.

It is the mixing of issues and the substitution of issues and the subtlety of personal relationships which make social control in small groups as difficult to study systematically as it is important to study them. But those who, like Hoebel, argue that criminal law and public law scarcely exist in pre-industrial society have never squarely faced the importance of the threat of expulsion or expulsion itself, or, for that matter, the positive importance of membership in good standing in the corporate groups of such societies.

Gluckman has stressed precisely this side of life in pre-industrial society when talking about strict liability. He has very emphatically taken social structure into account. But it is from his conception of the moral underpinning of that structure that he comes to some of his more speculative conclusions. He connects a strict duty not to harm in thought or deed with the fact of strict liability for injury or damage. If one is set on putting the matter into a rights–duties form. I think it simpler to postulate a general duty to make good, or make amends for, any injury or damage one causes in order that social relations may continue. It is not necessary to go so far as to postulate a pervasive strict duty not to harm. My view puts an emphasis on repair, while Gluckman's emphasizes a kind of moral attitude which he considers more stringent in 'tribal' societies than in complex ones. A basic theoretical problem raised by Gluckman's approach – a problem to which there is no easy answer – is the question how one decides what other aspects of social life are functionally related to particular characteristics of law. One methodological route toward such an objective is to try to distinguish separable aspects of the same phenomenon when this is possible.

In section 3 of this paper such a distinction was made between self-help by an individual and what I have called 'the principle of expanding dispute,' in which an individual mobilizes many persons in his cause and confronts a like group or aggregation of persons. In some societies such a confrontation involves the use of force, and may appear as a form of self-help on an enlarged scale. However, the principle of expanding dispute can operate in systems which prohibit violent confrontations between groups, as shown by Gulliver's material on the Arusha.

One of the important qualities of expanding dispute is that the widening of dispute from the original individuals to the groups to which they belong, and to any networks on which they may call, is often a *potentiality* within certain social situations rather than an inevitable rule governed by the relative social positions of the parties, or the subject of their dispute. This bears on two matters. First, it shows, as Peters has so convincingly argued, that such models of organization as segmentary lineage systems must be understood as frameworks of explanation of the social order rather than as sociological norms. Second, I have argued that it shows how an event (in this case a legal dispute) may be used to epitomize or characterize complex, long-term relationships between groups (or categories) as condensed or simplified versions of those relationships. Thus there is a partly symbolic, partly effective connection between certain events and the social relationships they both *represent* and *involve*. This double connection between events and systems of relationship bridges one analytical gap between the conception of social process and that of social system. The dispute between individuals that expands provides both a specific *occasion* for confrontation and a set of concrete, self-justifying *terms* in which the confrontation can be thought of and discussed.

The structured symbolizing habits of societies have received a great deal of attention in their most positive and striking forms. The more arbitrary a symbol, or system of symbols, the more easily it is recognized as such. However, when, as in law, there is what appears to be a rational connection between the reasons given for social action and the action itself, it is sometimes more difficult to analyze the relationship among the rationalizations, the actions, and their setting.[11] Rationalized events can have some of the qualities of symbols. They may be partial or distorted representations of wider issues or structural situations. The relationship is something like that between symbols and referents, but it is more complex because, unlike symbols and referents, the outcome of the 'symbolic' event may in fact affect the social facts of which it is a kind of representation. The substitution of political issues for one another is a familiar form of this phenomenon. A focus of one issue may take out of immediate public discussion a whole series of others, yet in the process of its resolution may imply the bargaining over or settling of issues supposedly not being considered. In law there is the often observed paradox that in theory norms rule the outcome of cases, yet at the same time some cases define norms. So events in social life are conditioned by pre-existent social relationships, yet events may alter social relationships. Legal disputes can be key events of this kind.

When social structures are described it is in terms of the reiteration of certain relationships and processes. 'Structure' is a succinct way of describing a process of repetition. Social relationships are, however, not by any means always repetitive. Legal fights in societies having a principle of expanding dispute figure significantly in the continuous process of definition and redefinition of major structural relationships. Self-help and expanding dispute so conceived can scarcely be thought of as private law. As Gulliver has shown, a major difference between many pre-industrial systems and ours is in the kind of political role that certain legal disputes between individuals have in the former and not in the latter (Gulliver 1963).

The social units to which disputes between individuals expand are sometimes also units of collective responsibility. The material on collective responsibility reviewed in this paper has shown that collective responsibility can operate as a means of assembling capital, and/or manpower, and that it can be a device used by persons outside a collectivity to force the group that has ultimate face-to-face control of individuals to bring pressure on some particular individual. The outsider may be some other group, an individual, or an administrative superior.

Where there is an aggregation of persons who are collectively responsible, they may constitute a corporate group or they may not. In one society they may be answerable only to the member-individual who claims their aid. He in turn may be the only person who is directly answerable to outsiders. In another society the whole collectivity or any of its members may be answerable to outsiders for the obligations of any member. There are a variety of situations intermediate between these two.

Adequate comparisons are possible only if each situation of collective responsibility is examined from at least two points of view: from the standpoint of an outsider dealing with the parties joined in potential liability, and from the inside, from the point of view of the persons so joined. Collective responsibility is as varied as the structural situations in which it occurs. Therefore it is only with reference to a few matters that one can make inferences about the general nature of collectivities so obligated from the mere existence of collective responsibility. In the examples reviewed here, there were only a few striking and general circumstances. One was the universal fact that the collective responsibility for obligations incurred in legal dispute were always secondary and peripheral to the more regular or ordinary functions of the collectivity. The aspect of social aggregates or groups that has to do with legal liability is fully intelligible only if attention is given to the other functions.

Two other general propositions emerged from the material on collective responsibility, but these are more restricted in scope and refer to those instances in pre-industrial society in which the group bearing collective responsibility is corporate. The first is that while liability may be collective from the point of view of persons outside a collectivity, there is nevertheless individual legal responsibility for the same act from the perspective of the person inside the group. The second is that where there is collective liability toward outsiders for the act of a member of the collectivity, the group has the right to expel a member who repeatedly or unwarrantedly puts it in that position, or in a case in which the group does not want to undertake the risks or expenses which it would otherwise incur on his behalf. Both these phenomena are, of course, familiar ones in the ongoing life of many enduring groups in industrial societies in which the issue is generally not legal liability but responsibility and answerability in a more informal sense.

The two circumstances described above – the simultaneity of collective and individual liability, and the corporate option of expulsion – both not only bear on an understanding of collective liability, but as we have seen, also pertain to a number of the issues raised in the introduction of this paper.

In a segmentary society of exclusive, collectively responsible corporate groups, individual responsibility exists essentially inside the corporation. Legal individuality on the whole seems to be a factor of the internal affairs of social corporations. Centralized political organization greatly increases the size of the largest corporate group in society, i.e., it concomitantly increases the size of the unit within which, and in relation to which, there may be individual responsibility. The fact that the milieu within which a person can be held individually responsible greatly increases in size gives an illusory impression of a great increase in emphasis on individual responsibility. In fact, individual responsibility always exists inside corporate groups. The smaller the maximal corporate groups in a society, the smaller the units within which legal individuality is significant.

Political centralization also has the implication that the use of self-help in combination with the principle of expanding dispute is ultimately suppressed for political reasons – to eliminate corporate competition with the superordinate corporation. This changes the character of legal dispute and contributes to the impression of the increasing importance of individuals, since it removes a dramatic function of the corporate group. However, units of *collective economic responsibility* go on being important, and are of as great importance in complex societies as in simple ones. Units of collective force which mobilize to confront other like units come to exist on the level of the maximal political unit only.

It is clear from the ethnographic material available today that what Pound conceived of as four basic stages of legal evolution – payment instead of vengeance, strict law, moral law, and a combination of equity and certainty – can all be found together in pre-industrial systems. These pieces of theoretical pottery, while arranged by Pound in apparently successive stratigraphic layers, can be found glued together to form a single pot. This is not to say that all legal systems are alike, but that the criteria Pound used for differentiating them are not the most useful distinguishing features. His evolutionary criteria are not useful because they are not founded on societal characteristics, and are principles that exist together, not only in that ultimate compound, our own supposedly remarkable society, but also in technologically simple societies. Less severe strictures apply to the legal-collective, legal-individuality discussions of Maine, Durkheim, and Malinowski, because they never abstracted legal principles altogether from the social context in which they occurred. But the analytic fault in their evolutionary statements lies in their being overfocused on particular elements. In the case of Durkheim and Maine their vision of ever-increasing individuality in legal matters was legitimate as far as it concerned the particular problems to which they chose to address themselves. Malinowski looked at quite different materials and redressed the balance somewhat. But surely collectivity and individuality in legal matters are aspects of all systems, not alternative systems. To speak of the temporal precedence in legal development, of civil or criminal law, of public or private law, or of collectivity and individuality, does not make sociological sense. The generalizations couched in these terms use one aspect of a system to characterize the whole, which is a procedure of dubious worth.

Notes

1   The ethnographic examples in this paper are all drawn from African materials for quite arbitrary reasons of convenience. It will be evident from the content of the paper that my main purpose is to indicate what a wide variety of phenomena are subsumed under the terms 'self-help' and 'collective responsibility.' I am sure I have not examined all the variations. I *know* of some I have not discussed. There must be others as well.

2   Evans-Pritchard, *The Nuer* (1940); Howell, *A Manual of Nuer Law* (1954). See discussion in section 3 of this paper of Peters's revisionist view of the segmentary lineage model.

3   Correspondence, 1968.

4   To a similar effect, describing the simultaneous existence of chiefs' courts and self-help formerly in Busoga, see Fallers, 'Homicide and suicide in Busoga' (1960:69).

5 Wolfe, 'The dynamics of the Ngombe segmentary system' (1959), p. 172; Evans-Pritchard (*op. cit.*). See, for example, Lévi-Strauss, *Tristes Tropiques* (1955; 1967 ed.:297), and for Nyakyusa funeral dances Wilson, *Good Company* (1951; 1963 ed.:80); also Fortes on Tallensi wars in *The Dynamics of Clanship among the Tallensi* (1945:242).

6 See A. C. Mayer, for a discussion of set in 'Quasi-groups in the study of complex societies' (1966:98–102).

7 Peristiany, *The Social Institutions of the Kipsigis* (1939:195); Driberg, *The Lango* (1923:208–10); see also Roscoe, *The Baganda* (1911:267), and Mair, *An African People in the Twentieth Century* (1934:188–9).

8 The choice of the Anglo-American business corporation for comparison with pre-industrial collective responsibility units was made largely because it is a form of organization familiar in its outlines to persons not technically informed about legal matters. However, partnerships and other kinds of organizational form should also be considered if the comparisons are to be really comprehensive. Specializations and differentiations of function in complex societies are accompanied by specialization and differentiation of legal obligation. A great variety of industrial institutional forms have to be inspected if one is looking for either functional or organizational equivalence with pre-industrial forms.

9 For example, Harris, *The Political Organization of the Mbembe, Nigeria* (1965a:44); Lawrence, *The Iteso* (1957:257–8); Meek, *Law and Authority in a Nigerian Tribe* (1937:126–7); Kopytoff, 'Family and Lineage among the Suku of the Congo' (1964:91); La Fontaine, 'Homicide and Suicide among the Gisu' (1960:96–9); Fortes (*op. cit.*:236–45); Nadel, *The Nuba* (1947:461); Southwold, 'The Ganda of Uganda' (1965:98); Peristiany, *The Social Institutions of the Kipsigis* (1939:121).

10 Peristiany (*op. cit.*:xxv). For other mentions of expulsion see Gulliver, *Social Control in an African Society* (1963:107); Rattray, *Ashanti Law and Constitution* (1929:289); Mangin, *Les Mossi* (1921; H.R.A.F. tr.:31); Pacques, *Les Bambara* (1954; H.R.A.F. tr.:626); Meek (*op. cit.*:208); Kopytoff (*op. cit.*:91); Cory, *Sukuma Law and Custom* (1953:113–14); Gutmann, *Das Recht der Dschagga* (1926; H.R.A.F. tr.:209); Wilson (*op. cit.*:152); Leakey, *Mau Mau and the Kikuyu* (1952:78).

11 See Gluckman's discussion of the 'extended case' method and of the work of Mitchell and Turner in which disputes are examined as part of ongoing social processes, in *Politics, Law and Ritual in Tribal Society* (1965c:235).

Chapter 4

Comparative studies

Identifying a common link among the three papers that follow,
the conference group gathered them under the rubric,
'Comparative Studies.' Nader's own interest in designing a
research project that would obtain comparable legal data from
several concurrent field studies is evident in her work on the
Berkeley Comparative Village Law Project. It is probably this
interest in the problem of comparability that led the group to
emphasize the comparative aspect of the essays that follow. For
reasons that will be made plain, it is my view that, despite their
form, the papers have more in common as discussions of the place
and nature of concepts in law, than as essays on (or in)
comparison. However, two of the papers do talk directly about
descriptive problems in cross-cultural legal comparison, and the
third compares the varied uses of a single law-related concept
within one society and hence might be characterized as an
intracultural comparison. It will be evident to any reader not only
that comparison has a very different place in each of the papers,
but that deeply imbedded into the two that discuss methods of
comparison, there are differences of opinion about what is being
compared and to what end.

It does not seem sensible to attempt here another brief review of
the past applications of what is called the comparative method in
anthropology, since these have been recently summarized by

Reprinted from Laura Nader (ed.), *Law in Culture and Society*, by permission of the
Aldine Publishing Co.

Eggan (1965:357–72). The comparative studies Eggan cites are very diverse in subject-matter, and in technique, and they vary enormously in scale. They range from the comparison of whole societies, of contrasting social types, of systems, of sequences of development, to small-scale studies of selected variables within limited types, studies of particular institutions, regions, or periods of time. Eggan diplomatically makes no critical evaluation of the validity or worth of the results of the works he mentions. In very general terms he calls for more sophisticated research design and testing. He concludes rather blandly that 'the comparative method is still a useful procedure in cultural anthropology despite the considerable variation in the conceptions held by different anthropologists as to its nature ... the comparative method is not a "method" in the broad sense, but a technique for establishing similarities and differences' (Eggan 1965:366).

Comparison can be said to be simply a technique, but it would be closer to the facts to say that it is very complicatedly a technique. The basic, double-ended dilemma is, *what to compare in order to find out what*. Theoretically, in the social sciences much research proceeds by setting problems in the form of hypotheses. These often concern the causal significance of the association of phenomena or of similarities and differences among phenomena. A class of data is selected to test (or illustrate) the propositions, but in fact what is usually tested (or illustrated) is the association or the degree of similarity. Another comparative procedure is to construct certain ideal types or models, producing them logically on the basis of explicit principles. Then social evidence is examined and analyzed in order to note and explain conformities and divergences from the typology. The objective is to test the adequacy of the principles as explanatory or descriptive devices. What is really tested is the degree to which the model and social realities are congruent.

Where the attempt is to prove, rather than to illustrate, much attention is given to obtaining a suitable number and sampling of instances; when possible, the results are quantified. Comparison may be more or less extensive, more or less rigorous in its attention to precision about comparability, more or less illustrative. A scholar has the methodological option of trying to prove his contentions by checking through all available data and adding up their results, or he may choose instead to illustrate his propositions by selecting what seem to him a few persuasive instances and leave it to others to try to disprove them. Both methods have been used creatively by anthropology, and both have been used in studies that are worthless. Method alone does not guarantee significant results.

Such comparisons as have been made in the published material on anthropology and law have been illustrative. Probably the best-known are Hoebel's comparison of the legal systems of a handful of societies of varied degrees of political centralization and complexity, and Gluckman's comparison of his model of tribal society and its legal concomitants with the data from the Barotse and other pre-industrial peoples (Hoebel 1954; Gluckman 1955a, 1965b). The question is where to move next in comparative work in anthropology and law.

Many of the current apparently technical discussions about legal comparisons are really about what ought to be compared – the what, not just the how. The merits of comparison itself are generally agreed on, and no one could object to a call for more thoroughness, more exactness, greater extensiveness. Where anthropologists differ – and they differ radically – is on the issues: what are *significant* problems, and what is relevant to them.

On the whole, the greatest disagreements and difficulties concerning comparisons do not lie at the comparative stage of study. It is the other stages that have the biggest hazards, the formulation of the problem and the choice of the criteria of relevance on the basis of which data are selected and classified for study. There are no mechanical techniques for deciding what questions to ask and what kind of information is necessary to answer them. The fact that today there are phenomenally improved methods of recording, storing, and retrieving information greatly increases the number, scale, and refinement of possible comparisons. However, it does not in any way answer the fundamental questions of what information to gather and what problems to solve. In this area it is often each man for himself.

The anthropologist with an interest in law must face these basic questions, all the while taking care not to drown in the great oceans of existing information. Most of what is known about law is a huge mess from the standpoint of systematic sociological research. Legal data have been recorded for centuries for myriad purposes, but only relatively recently and to a very limited extent for the purpose of sociological analysis. The question of what can be used of this glut of stuff, and to what ends, raises to emergency proportions the issue of defining problems and determining relevance. The anthropologist is a late-comer into this morass. Because of the nature of anthropology, he may exercise the option of turning his back on the law libraries, but he cannot by doing so avoid the issues involved. They confront him in his fieldwork as urgently as they would in the analysis of the existing sea of legal literature.

In investigating legal phenomena, on what basis is the anthropologist to decide what he is looking for and what to look at? Is he comparing legal concepts or behavior? Are these different from each other, or are they facets of the same entity? Is he comparing whole legal systems? Cases? Rules? Systems of rules dealing with particular substantive matters, land, inheritance, family property transfer, and the like? Procedures? Is he interested in dispute settlement exclusively or in systems of social control in general? There is no end to the possible topics. Each person in the field defines somewhat differently what he is looking at and looking for. There is serious question whether there should be, or even whether there can be, consensus in the discipline about such matters.

Another basic problem in the law field is to what extent the anthropologist should look to the body of established knowledge when he plans a field of study or other investigation, and to what extent he should (and can) maintain a calculated looseness of approach in order to remain open to new observations. Law is a field of social activity that has been under close, self-conscious scrutiny as far back as there are written records. Anthropology has built its own theoretical frameworks and its own literature for looking at social materials. Unless the anthropologist conceives his research in terms of some such body of established knowledge and ultimately in terms of comparative work, there is not only the risk that the information each fieldworker collects will have no comparability to that found by any other, but also the opposite risk that the discipline will never advance but, endlessly naïve, will forever retread the same paths, repetitively discovering the same phenomena. Other dangers attend the formulation of questions too tightly framed in terms of established knowledge. Traditional standardization of the form of inquiry may produce comparability of the data gathered, without such equivalence being a real quality of the phenomena observed. The possibility of having new insights may be inhibited by too narrow a definition of the field of observation, or by too strict an adherence to established ways of looking at the data. The dilemma of legal studies in anthropology is not in these respects different from that of any other research. Comparative studies emphasize all the problems inherent in single studies.

Anthropology advances through an integration of planned, rationally designed research and fortuitous discovery and insight. Since the instrument of this technique is the anthropologist himself, it is important that as much as possible of his reasoning be accessible to those who are interested in evaluating his results. One of the merits of the kind of discussion that took place at the Wenner-Gren Conference, and that is evident in published debate, is that it tends to produce a considerable degree of explicitness about basic assumptions, the general mental models of how things work and why, that underlie a scholar's choice in formulating questions and identifying evidence as relevant. It is for this reason that the discussion of concepts and comparisons that follows is not simply a discussion of techniques. Bohannan's and Gluckman's papers ask, 'What is a valid unit of comparison?' but, in a deeper sense, the answers show differences in point of view about the question, 'What is the subject of study?' Gluckman's paper was presented at the Conference, Bohannan's was written afterward. Since Bohannan's is in a large measure an attack on Gluckman's mode of analysis and comparison, it is only fair to indicate that Gluckman's paper is a response to previous criticisms, not to this particular paper.

A great deal of discussion between Gluckman and Bohannan takes place in the form of an argument about what is a suitable language in which to describe another people's legal system. Bohannan argues that the vocabulary of English jurisprudence is a vocabulary developed for talking about English law and is unsuitable for the description of the folk systems of other peoples. His case is that to describe another people's system one must spell out at length the implications of native terms and categories in order to approximate as closely as possible the indigenous system being examined, and then one must use these native terms rather than substitute English equivalents. Then, and only then, can one begin to think about making comparisons. This part of his argument starts as an argument against an ethnocentric Anglo-American legal vocabulary. Then he faces the difficulties inherent in trying to use indigenous vocabularies when making comparisons. In his paper Bohannan proposes that this problem may be dealt with in the future by means of a 'new logical and independent language,' and he suggests that *Fortran* or some other computer language may be the most suitable medium into which to translate folk concepts for comparative purposes. His argument is fundamentally that English legal terms are so inextricably bound up with the content of English law that they cannot be used effectively to describe another system. The number of redefinitions and qualifiers that must be used to make a term of English law fit an alien legal category is such that, in his view, it is less distorting and less confusing to use certain key indigenous terms and try to describe their referents. This last, since he is writing in English, he does in English words, but with an effort to avoid technical legal terms as far as he can.

Gluckman agrees that the first task of the ethnographer is to describe what Bohannan has called the folk system. He also agrees that vernacular African terms sometimes have no English equivalents, and that in such cases indigenous terms must continue to be used after they have been explained in English. However, where it is practical to use English terms without having to add too many qualifiers – where, in short, there is a satisfactory English equivalent or approximation – he not only sees no objection to using English (or whatever is the language of the investigator), but also thinks it far preferable to do so. He argues that only if the same term is used to cover the notions of diverse legal systems is it possible to discuss where the notions in each system differ, as well as the common elements across the systems. What Gluckman does, further, is to argue that after the notions of an African legal system have been described, they can be compared profitably with those of English law at various stages of its development. Similarly, he also draws on the terms and ideas of Roman law and other legal systems where they seem appropriate.

Presented in this way, there seems a limited area of disagreement between the two. After giving and explaining native terms, Gluckman is prepared to shift to terms of English law more readily than Bohannan, and he has a strong interest in particular comparisons of African with English legal notions that Bohannan does not share. Bohannan explains in English and then continues to use more indigenous terms and makes a studied effort to avoid terms of English law when he can. Both are acutely aware of the difficulties of translation and definition in the task of describing an alien legal system, and both realize that those difficulties are multiplied when the level of analysis and comparison is reached.

Certainly, the English forensic vocabulary does contain many words that may be considered loaded with connotations of English law, though even of these, few have meant the same thing over long periods of time, and many have different legal connotations in different jurisdictions. However, it is useful to recognize that there is also a legal vocabulary of what I can only describe as neutral terms, and there are many combinations of these terms that can be conveniently used by anthropologists in making ethnographic descriptions.

This may not be the place for an extended list, but a few examples may be suggestive. It is a convention of Anglo-American opinion writing for the judge to describe the facts before him initially in such neutral terms. Then he gives the facts their legal significance by recasting into more precise legal language the situation he has just described. An example: two men discuss a possible *transaction*. One of them may afterward claim that they reached an *understanding* about the potential terms of the transaction, and that they *concurred* on those terms. The Anglo-American legal question would be whether in the circumstances this alleged *understanding* and *concurrence* constitute a *contract* or not. In some ethnographic descriptions there would be reason to avoid using 'contract,' but the words *binding agreement* would serve in such cases without much culture-bound loading, while the words 'understanding' and 'concurrence' would serve very neatly to describe reaching an *accord*, or giving *mutual assent* that may not necessarily be legally binding. One of the merits of using such words in ethnographic description is that they force the ethnographer to ask himself what agreements are binding and when and how and between whom they become binding in a particular society.

The word 'transfer' is another very good example of a neutral term, since it tells only that something moves from one person to another or from one place to another. It remains for the ethnographer to describe what is being transferred, how permanently, whether for a fixed period of time or not, whether irrevocably or revocably, whether the transfer gives rights to the transferee, at what point these rights are transferred, whether the transfer creates firm or contingent reciprocal obligations, and so forth. Another useful word is 'interest,' because it is applicable to almost any kind of right. *Transactions*, *agreements*, *obligations*, *transfers*, and *interests* cover a great deal of the legal universe, and they do so with convenient neutrality. There are many other 'neutral' words that are equally useful. Whether their use can capture the full flavor of indigenous categories would be partly a matter of skill in filling in the particular specifications for the system under study, and this aspect is related to the subtleties involved in particular folk notions. The use of well-chosen adjectives and appropriate combinations of nouns can adapt these terms to special ethnographic needs without the awkwardness and confusion caused by using an overabundance of indigenous terms and avoids the perils of Anglo-centrism. Blank-check words have another virtue. Their very emptiness requires the ethnographer to fill in the potential legal connotations of acts that he is in the habit of looking at in other senses. They oblige him to think about the possible legal consequences of mundane behavior.

Hohfeld (1923) proposed another, highly specialized 'neutral' vocabulary for describing *all* legal relationships in terms of the various elements encapsulated in the notions of right and duty. Despite having been brought up, as Hoebel was, in the Hohfeldian religion by Karl Llewellyn, I would reject Hohfeld's terminolgy for ethnographic description for the following reasons. First, it is hopelessly clumsy. Second, it cuts up all legal relations into dyads, which is sometimes a very artificial and distorting procedure. Third, it cuts up legal relations into analytically distinguishable, but not always pragmatically distinct, qualities, until sight is lost of the relationship as a whole. Lawyers, who usually seem to have no need to write gracefully and who are only ocasionally concerned with trying to communicate the flavor of a relationship, nevertheless avoid Hohfeld's system because it is so awkward. In my opinion legal anthropologists should read Hohfeld and then, cheerfully, should do without him.

The dispute between Bohannan and Gluckman about what is a suitable language for legal description is really only the surface of a much more profound difference of emphasis and interest. Bohannan has described the difference in this way: 'The comparatists, from Tylor to Gluckman, want to compare substantive material; I want, rather, to compare viewpoints or theories of substantive material.' Gluckman's statement on the difference in their approach is:

it may well be that we are interested in divergent problems. Bohannan may be aiming to compare folk conceptions in themselves ... I am interested ... in specifying the folk conceptions of a particular people as clearly as I can and then trying to explain why they are as they are, and how they differ from the folk conceptions of others, in terms of economic and social backgrounds.

Implicit in these statements is the basic difference in point of view between Gluckman and Bohannan – a difference only indirectly confronted in the discussion of the language of description and the language of analysis. Gluckman sees the concepts and principles of law as *part* of legal systems, whereas Bohannan is most interested in studying the concepts *themselves*, because he considers them a reflection of the whole organization of the legal system.

To Gluckman, these concepts and principles are manipulable tools within legal systems, part of their equipment, not reflections of their organization. He looks to social and economic backgrounds for broader underlying explanations and describes himself as interested in 'the relation of legal ideas to the general social system of a tribe' (1965b:xiv).

Bohannan is passionately interested in perception, in the way a culture sets up and classifies reality into categories. In his text *Social Anthropology*, while describing Whorf's theory with approval, Bohannan says, 'The proper subject for study – indeed the only possible subject for study – is ... perception' (1963:46). This is his view of culture in general. In another place in the same book he says, 'culture and social action become organized into sensible chunks or schemes that form sensible connected wholes of one sort or another .... It is precisely this system of categories, as it is preserved in the language and recurrent social behavior, that the ethnographer must report' (1963:9–10). He goes on, 'Thus, a language is not merely part of the culture, but is also a reflection of the total culture. It is a reflection, more importantly perhaps of the *organization* of that total culture' (1963:42).

When Bohannan objects to the use of terms other than carefully defined indigenous ones and stresses the theme of the distortions in translations, it is because he sees the categories embodied in indigenous legal language as a key to the organization of indigenous thought. In fact, he emphasizes that 'every culture has 'certain key words in its language' around which the major part of the ethnographer's knowledge of the culture may be communicated (1963:11–12). However vigorously Bohannan argues for a systematic methodology of comparison once these key words are described, he does not provide a way in which the key words themselves can be systematically selected. As far as I can tell, they have to be chosen rather subjectively (1963:12). A careful control of techniques of handling data does not get around the problem of how the data are chosen in the first place. This is a problem of which Bohannan is certainly aware, and he discusses it in his paper. The total pattern of thought condensed into key words is what Bohannan is after as an ideal ethnographic aim. This is what he means when he says, 'I want to compare viewpoints or theories of substantive material.'

Gluckman has an entirely different ultimate aim in mind when he approaches legal materials. The large pattern he is inquiring into is the inter-relationship between the legal system and its social and economic setting. The assumption underlying his work is that these are often related phenomena, and that they are related in complex and various ways. They are not at every point interdependent, but frequently they can nevertheless be shown to be significantly connected. To demonstrate such relationships, comparison is not only illuminating but even essential. Gluckman uses comparative examples to show the ethnographic foundation of his ideas, and he supports his arguments about the relationship of phenomena by offering examples. His technique is one of presenting illustrated hypotheses.

Bohannan is as critical of Gluckman's mode of comparison as he is of Gluckman's mode of description. Some of it he suspects to be too much based on *a priori* categories and concepts. Some of it he finds simply an argument supported by selected favorable illustrative instances. In his paper Bohannan is in effect saying 'You have not proved them,' to Gluckman's hypotheses and ideas in general.

Whatever the ultimate validity of Gluckman's hypotheses may be, it seems evident that the systematic mode of comparison that Bohannan proposes for the future is not a solution to the kind of problem Gluckman has set himself. The controlled comparison of concepts proposed by Bohannan may well prove to be a very fruitful line of investigation. However, it can never be an answer to the problems in which Gluckman is interested. The pursuit of such a study as a key to legal systems is not congruent with Gluckman's conception of the place that ideas, categories, legal principles, and the like have in legal systems.

In Gluckman's analysis law involves, among other things, a hierarchy of principles: some of these low in the hierarchy are very precise and explicit rules, whereas those high in the hierarchy are very vague and general; and in between there are medium-level principles that are more encompassing than a rule for any single set of facts, but less grand and abstract than the highest level principles (Gluckman 1955a:291–326). Anywhere above the lowest level of law (and morality), principles conflict, overlap, have fuzzy edges. Many have a generally definable import; some are multireferential; for others the referents are not altogether precise. The imprecision and multireferential quality increases the higher up the hierarchy of principles one goes. Gluckman's view, which is in accord with the view of many jurists, is that these very vaguenesses of a multiplicity of logically independent principles and the conflicts between some principles are an inherent part of legal systems – part of the living law in terms of which people conduct themselves and in terms of which disputes are settled. The vagueness of and conflicts between principles, the multiplicity of principles, the combination of precise and imprecise principles, give the law the quality of flexibility that enables it to work and makes it applicable to the unbelievable variety of contingencies involved in human affairs. Clearly, if this complex analytical scheme about legal principles is one's point of departure, a legal system is only partly to be understood in terms of its categories. Gluckman wrote in summary of *The Judicial Process among the Barotse of Northern Rhodesia* (1955a; see also 2nd ed., 1967):

> I found a multiplicity of meanings and possibilities of application to the facts of social life inherent in all the key terms of Barotse law .... I was able to accept that this multiplicity of meanings – what the philosophers call 'open texture' – of terms was an inherent attribute of legal concepts .... I tried to work out how the judges manipulated the uncertainty of words. (1965b:22)

Despite the fact that Bohannan casts his argument in terms of methodology, I think the basic disagreement between Bohannan and Gluckman is one over the *significance* of legal categories. They both agree that such categories should be accurately and fully reported. They have some difference about what is the most suitable language to do the job, and Bohannan is critical of Gluckman's style of comparison and of what he perceives as Gluckman's preoccupation with parallels in the history of English law. Gluckman, in fact, was aiming in his books at a 'developmental morphology of law, relating law to techno-economic development' (unpublished lecture). He uses his data on Barotse law to illustrate how they fit into this morphology of development. When he cites other ethnographic data, it is to argue that Barotse law is typical of what he calls 'tribal law.' He did not attempt a systematic march through the totality of the ethnographic literature. It was never his intention to attempt anything of the sort.

But these issues follow from the much deeper difference in approach and interest of the two men concerning what the categories *mean*. Bohannan is apparently convinced that the categories themselves can reveal the 'system,' Gluckman's analysis of how legal principles work would seem to make him necessarily less optimistic about such an outcome.

My own paper is an illustration of the complexities attendant upon any investigation of basic concepts. In looking at descent and legal position among the Lango, I have chosen a vast umbrella concept and have tried to show how many levels of organization and how many kinds of legal rules are framed in terms of it. Driberg's ethnography of the Lango, on which the paper is based, is an old-fashioned, conventional one, not written with any of these problems in mind. Nor do the Lango seem particularly unusual in the fact of their variegated application of descent principles. Though the paper is not to any extent a cross-cultural comparison, the implications of the argument go far beyond the Lango, since the general question raised concerns the manner in which concepts are used in legal affairs. Following one thread, the paper examines the variety of law-related situations in Lango life that invoke descent principles. Following another, it inspects some of the techniques by which legal rules and principles are manipulated. The two are, of course, intertwined.

The legal aspects of Lango descent are approached from the point of view of the practical situations in Lango life, in which descent figures as an element. I do not see how one could reliably delineate a 'Lango concept of descent' without this information. In a fieldwork situation it would perhaps be possible also to elicit statements from informants about what descent is considered to be in the abstract, but this would scarcely be exhaustive. The very specificity that makes case studies more revealing than informants' statements about legal rules makes information about the kind of situation in which descent is invoked more telling than some abstract definition of it. But this is not to say that either terse statements of rules or the abstract definitions of principles are of no importance. They are part of the way people think and talk about social life in general, which is quite distinct from (though related to) the way they deal with it in concrete instances. Law involves both. But it is no small matter to try to work out the relationship between the principles and the supposed 'applications' of them, the concepts involved in law and the uses of them.

It may be, in fact, that the role of certain concepts and principles is less one of defining rights and duties than of defining the general ideological framework in terms of which rights and duties are expressed. Partly it is a question of different levels of specificity. Gluckman has discussed the hierarchy of legal principles to which Barotse judges have reference. Gulliver discusses hierarchies of rules in this volume. Hierarchies of rules are regularly mentioned by judges in British and American courts when several principles apply to a case and some are considered to have a moral or political superiority over others. My paper uses the descent concept to show that certain very general ideas can *reappear at many levels* and in many guises in the hierarchy of legal rules. I suggest that these metamorphoses are separable both for indigenous pragmatic purposes and for the anthropologist's analytic purposes.

Innumerable specific legal rules among the Lango have reference to descent, but, as I have tried to show, descent is not in itself either directly a source of these rules nor in any other way exclusively determinative of them. For example, though the Lango are patrilineal, descent is legally established by the payment of bridewealth cattle, not by filiation. Thus a man's offspring may be members of the descent group of his mother's brother if his mother's brother supplied the marriage cattle with which he obtained his wife. The analysis of the connections among the legal rules, the descent ideology, and the varied courses of action available to people acting in terms of the rules raises questions about the nature of legal rules in general and the legal significance of descent in particular. If the same ideological reference point – descent – is used by the Lango in a whole series of entirely different social contexts and is varied and highly manipulable in those contexts, how is cross-cultural comparison of such an idea to be undertaken? Surely not without detailed attention to the context.

Divergences from what anthropologists sometimes think of as the 'descent ideal' are frequently considered by them to be exceptions to, or inadequate approximations of, the ideal. Some even think they have found a new organizational type where or when they find that divergences are commonplace. My argument is that this is not a matter of ideal–real dichotomies, nor of norms and violations. On the contrary, such 'exceptions' are part of the system. They are legitimate alternatives to other arrangements and there is legal provision for them.

What becomes evident is that among the Lango descent is used as an explicit justifying framework for arrangements that actually are frequently as much based on other exigencies and criteria. When these criteria are lacking, the supposed consequences of relationship do not follow. This means that the idea of descent – that is, the set of inter-related principles of which it is composed – exists concurrently with a more lowly assortment of legal rules, legal legitimators, and qualifying conditions that are the legally and pragmatically effective aspects of the general notion.

The most basic ideas of unilineal descent are very simple and found around the world, yet the jural consequences that are justified in terms of these basic models are very variable. Thus, I conclude that such fundamental ideas in a social system account for only a very limited aspect of its shape. How much lower down the ladder of folk ideas and explanations must one descend before arriving at those that are special to the system (or type of system) being examined? When one gets to these special concepts, what does one know? Are the concepts reflections of the social system, conditioners of perception, or manipulable ideological constructs? Are they perhaps all three? These are some of the questions with which Bohannan, Gluckman, and I are concerned.

Chapter 5

Descent and legal position

Descent systems are part ideas and part social realities. While culturally defined modes of tracing relationship and classifying kin clearly belong to the realm of ideas and ideologies, they serve as rationales of real social arrangements. Legal consequences are often said to flow from descent. Hoebel lists descent among the basic jural postulates of a number of peoples (1954:Ifugao, 104; Trobriand, 191; Ashanti, 253). Fortes puts descent in the jural and political domain (1959:207). Bohannan notes that in almost all societies some legal rights are linked with actual or putative descent (1963:59).

Although the jural importance of descent is frequently acknowledged in this general way, its legal significance can be estimated only by asking first what is meant by descent, and then by seeing exactly what rights and duties are in fact derived from descent in a particular society. That is what this paper proposes to do. The first two sections – this one and the next – define the problem to be dealt with as one of the relationship between concepts and rules, arguing that on one level descent is an ideology, not in itself a set of legal rules; and that certain studies that take as their point of departure the notion that ideological descent by itself has legal consequences are failing to make important distinctions between ways of thinking about social organization and the operative realities. The third, fourth, and

Reprinted from Laura Nader (ed.), *Law in Culture and Society*, by permission of the Aldine Publishing Co.

fifth sections examine the ethnography of the Lango as a detailed illustration of the complex relation between the jural rule level and the conceptual level. The last section summarizes the general significance of the data examined.

I rely on Driberg's description of the Lango as they were fifty-odd years ago, supplemented by some additional data recorded later by Hayley (Driberg 1923; Hayley 1947). I came upon the Lango more or less fortuitously. I had read Driberg's book in the course of collecting comparative material on collective liability in Africa, and it struck me as a concise and uncomplicated illustration of the points I wanted to make in this paper.

What emerges from the analysis of the Lango is the fact that descent, although relevant to many rights and duties, is in the instances examined neither exclusively nor absolutely determinative of them. Descent is seen, not as a principle that has clearly definable, invariable legal consequences, but rather as one of the more significant of a number of considerations pertinent to rights and obligations. Descent sometimes figures more prominently in the conceptualization of rights and obligations than in their operation. These facts – that rights and duties arise from the concatenation of a number of circumstances; that descent is not in and of itself an absolute definer of obligation, but rather a contributory definer of it – bear on the whole question of rules of law and what they are made of.

The present examination of the jural consequences of descent in one cultural milieu is not undertaken to reiterate the already long-established fact that descent systems do not operate as neatly as elementary charts of uterine and agnatic links. That would be a useless and repetitive exercise. This paper will undertake to explore, on the one hand, the concepts, models, and rationales in terms of which Lango rules are framed, and, on the other hand, the operational level of the rules, and the relationship between them.

All jural rules may be analyzed in terms of general principles, categories, and concepts that are not themselves narrow enough to be described as rules. Hoebel, Bohannan, and Gluckman, each in a very different way are seeking this body of material when they respectively pursue the jural postulates, the folk systems, and the hierarchies of principles (Hoebel 1954; Bohannan 1963:13; Gluckman 1965b:295). Legal systems classify types of relationships and types of acts. Any particular case fits within wider concepts and categories. From one view, legal systems are amenable to study purely as systems of classification.

A great deal is known about descent. Descent is an idea woven through many binding relationships and transactions. With descent as a well-marked point of departure, it is possible to have a look at the intricate relationship between the rule level of legal matters and the concept level in terms of which the rules are framed. The rule level has received diminishing attention in some anthropological quarters for both practical and historical reasons.

It was once the fashion to include in ethnographies a section on laws and to give lists of rules worded like the Ten Commandments. These simply stated rules had been extracted from informants, perhaps even suggested to them, and not observed in operation. Only the crudest of hypothetical cases usually were put to informants for their comment. Driberg's book on the Lango is in some respects a museum piece of this method, but happily his ethnographic material is fuller than his law lists. A tremendous reaction against these sterile citings of rules has produced instead an emphasis on case reports. The preoccupation with cases has had a salutary effect. A case is something that really happened, not some abstract precept told the anthropologist, and it presents conflict and crisis situations in condensed form, readymade for analysis.

But as soon as analysis is undertaken, one is returned to the problem of the nature of legal concepts, rules, and settlements. Bohannan (1965:39) has said that in stateless societies trouble cases are settled by compromises rather than by the kind of decisions rendered in unicentric power systems. This, he feels, 'leads to very much less precise statements of norms as law than does the decision-based unicentric solution.' The procedural difference between compromise and decision may well affect the way norms are stated, but there are also many other reasons why many legal norms are imprecise in both types of systems. One of these is the fact that there frequently are many contingencies that affect legal relations, and these make the problem of formulating norms quite complex, as every draftsman of statutes is well aware. I think there is a good reason why norm statements appear least precise in the structurally least differentiated societies – a reason that has nothing to do with particular dispute-resolving procedures. It is this: the more multiplex the social relations, the more contingencies there are that may affect any particular act or transaction. This multiplicity not only makes it difficult to state norms precisely, but sometimes it may even make it impossible, since the assortment of contingencies can vary so much from one case to another. The Lango material illustrates this quite clearly.

The riches of the case method of research should not make one forget that the most important place where legal rules and ideas operate is outside the courts (and other dispute-settlement institutions), not in them. However, in the context of ordinary social life, just as in court cases, legal rules do not usually appear as discrete, simple directives or prohibitions in terms of which people behave. Instead, they appear in clusters, framed in concepts, hedged about with special circumstances, with variations and conditions, with exceptions and accommodations of contradictory principles. Not one rule but a whole complex of rules and legal ideas apply to any social relationship, and some of the rules are alternatives.

Unsatisfactory studies of the rule aspect of law have generally been the result of the naïveté with which rules are sometimes conceived and treated, simply and one at a time. Instead of assuming that legal rules are simple and definite and certain, and can legitimately be considered one by one, it is more profitable to start with very different assumptions. One must postulate a *complex of rules* for any situation and also assume that there is in many legal relations a measure of indefiniteness and uncertainty, and that these qualities are essential to the operation of legal systems.

In introducing Cory's book, which attempted to codify Sukuma law, Mr J. P. Moffett, Local Courts Advisor to the Government of Tanganyika, said, 'one of the principles of the Rule of Law, fundamental to the British way of life and an indispensable part of any system of British administration, is that the law should be certain' (Cory 1953:xi). This kind of statement may be found in many judicial opinions on both sides of the Atlantic. Certainty is one of the themes of the Anglo-American legal creed. But a major task of the legal scholar is to apply himself to the study of those very aspects of the law that do not comfortably fit such a conception.

Gluckman has illuminated important facets of this problem in his study of Barotse judicial process. He has shown the indefiniteness of the high legal principles and the way these are used as a tool by Barotse judges (1965b:295f). On the lowest level, in application to the facts of a particular case, he shows how legal rules appear very precise. The apparent precision comes from the facts of the case and the necessity of decision. In a particular dispute, by definition, there is a specification of all the conditions that surround the dispute. Any attempt to generalize about rules at a level lower than the 'highest principles' and higher than the facts of a single case show that indefiniteness at this intermediate level derives not only from the vagueness of legal principles, but also from their very multiplicity. Indefiniteness at this level also flows from the endless variation of factual possibilities.

Any attempt to state normative rules at an intermediate level (that is, without narrowing the statement down solely to the facts of a particular case) requires that one try to specify a whole range of possibly relevant conditions, contingencies, and alternatives, which are always part of the complex of rules, concepts, principles, and facts that bear on legal relationships. Ordinary people acting in ordinary social situations usually take the whole complex into account. They act in terms of it. One of the purposes of this paper in tracing the theme of descent through Lango law is to show in what varied ways descent figures in such rule complexes. Three aspects are of particular concern here: the justifying, legitimizing, and symbolic frameworks in terms of which rules are conceived and expressed; the rigidity, flexibility, or manipulability of rules; and the contingencies that affect obligations.

A minimal definition of descent

In a paper published in 1964, L. L. Langness makes an analysis of a New Guinea society in which he touches on the connection between descent and law. He deals with descent in terms that I think confuse some of the very issues he sought to clarify. He contrasts the ideological definition of local units as patrilineal descent groups with their actual genealogical composition, describing this as a contrast between *jural rules and statistical norms* (1964:163). Underlying his analysis is the not-unusual conception of law as a set of rules that are obeyed or disobeyed with statistically measurable frequency. He conceives of patrilineal descent as such a 'jural rule.'

Langness's 'detailed quantitative description' of a New Guinea people is offered in order that 'whatever discrepancy exists between the sociological facts and the cultural ideology can be made apparent' (1964:164). He sees the problem of analysis as twofold. First he mentions Barnes's discussion (1962:5–9) of whether it is profitable to use models developed for African segmentary systems in examining New Guinea societies, and second he asks 'whether one is discussing, in the New Guinea case, jural rules or statistical norms.' And he adds, 'It seems in fact, that the comparisons made are often between jural rules (ideologies) of the lineal segmentary societies of Africa, and presumed (but not actual) statistical norms of New Guinea' (1964:163). The key to his conception of the problem lies in his speaking of jural rules as identical with ideologies.

Langness describes one of four subgroups of a tribe. The Nupasafa group is localized, corporate, exogamous, and a 'patrilineal descent group ... *by ideology* (dogma)' (1964:165). The Nupasafa group considers itself to have been founded by an ancestor named Gooyi. It consists of a total population of 232 persons. Langness carefully distinguishes the local Nupasafa group with which he is concerned from a much larger non-localized category, the Nupasafa 'clan,' which would include all those persons who on the basis of descent might call themselves Nupasafans. Confining himself to the local group, he indicates that nearly all male residents claim to be members of the subgroups founded by Gooyi's five sons, though they cannot all show a genealogical connection. Thus they are all ideologically members of Nupasafa, which is conceived as a descent group. When Langness gets down to genealogies, he explains that there are 35 adult male agnates, 15 non-agnates living in Nupasafa. Sifting these down by eliminating adolescent, aged, or ineffectual individuals, he judges that the active core consists of 30 males. These constitute the fully participating nucleus of the Nupasafa group, and of these 10 are non-agnates. The grounds on which these non-agnates were resident varied. Some were the children of people who had settled there as refugees from war defeats, some were subject to sorcery in their own communities, two had Nupasafa wives and still claimed land in their own communities, and one had a father who had once been temporarily resident in the community, which was considered sufficient reason to allow him to attach himself to the community.

All non-agnates considered themselves full members of the local Nupasafa group. All were addressed by kinship terms. The two married to Nupa women did not, of course, claim common descent, but the others evidently did. When pressed, they would admit that they were not actually descended from the Nupasafa ancestor, but it was clear from the shallow memory of genealogies exhibited that this point would soon be forgotten and that they would be totally assimilated in a generation or two. Immigrants assimilating in this manner observed all the Nupasafa rules of exogamy and would have found it unthinkable to marry a Nupa girl. Langness argues from these data that 'the sheer fact of residence in a Bena Bena group can and does determine kinship' (1964:172).

Langness argues that

> To say that Nupasafa group is patrilineal in terms of its 'core' may be descriptively adequate, but the implication that Nupasafa group is truly a 'patrilineal descent group' with the connotations that are usually associated with the term, and which might easily result from such a description, is a very serious over-simplification. (1964:167)

He returns repeatedly to what he considers to be the African model:

> It may well be that the number of agnates living elsewhere than in their natal group may be significantly larger for a New Guinea group than an African one, or that genealogical depth is greater or remembered more precisely in an African group, but this does not necessarily mean an absence or weakness of the dogma of patrilineal descent. What it does mean is that the dogma of patrilineal descent operates weakly as only one principle among several, rather than as the sole principle implied in the African materials. (1964:171)

Apart from passing introductory allusions to African segmentary models, Langness never makes absolutely clear what he conceives the African situation to be. In fact, many of the points Langness has made about the Nupasafa can be illustrated easily from the African materials. A serious difficulty would seem to arise, not from differences between African and New Guinea ethnographic data – and there certainly are important differences as well as parallels – but from the conception of descent that Langness has chosen to use. He takes the position that there is a jural-ideological model in which true genealogical descent, and descent alone, gives a person legal rights in a patrilineal descent group. I think this is the way he conceives the African systems.

Since the Nupasafa do not fit this model, Langness ends by classifying them as *quasi-unilineal*. He says, 'the fundamental problem is the discrepancy between ideology and statistical norms.'

I would argue that descent ideology and jural rules are distinct concepts and cannot be used interchangeably, as Langness has done. In my view descent ideology in its most basic form is an *ideology of identities*, a model of relationships in the sense of *homologies*, not of behavior. As such, it is an idea that can be used in many different ways, and it is enormously adaptable and manipulable. It may be used literally to define the membership of social categories or units. It may be used symbolically to represent identities of interest or category that, in fact, are not genealogical descent relationships at all. It would appear that it is used for both purposes by the Nupasafa. But Langness considers only the literal use as fitting the 'descent ideology.' He treats the metaphorical use of descent (to assimilate non-agnates into the group) as a statistical deviation from the 'jural rule,' from the 'ideology,' as he uses those words.

I. M. Lewis's recent paper approached descent in an entirely different manner. His was a much more flexible conception of descent, though it, too, was very much tied to the idea of descent as a principle of social organization. He inquired into the question of 'how unilineal descent varies in different unilineal descent systems, and how such variations can be assessed, or measured,' adding parenthetically, '(if indeed this is possible)' (1965:87). He begins by asking the question, 'are some societies more or less "strongly" patrilineal or matrilineal than others; and, if so, in what respects: and, further, by what criteria can such differences be objectively established?' (1965:87)

Lewis touches briefly on a wide range of applications of patrilineal descent principles in segmentary lineage systems. He starts off with 'national' genealogies that embrace the whole society or culture, then he moves down a level to maximum corporate groupings. He struggles with the problem of the 'functional significance of descent' in politico-jural and religious contexts and tries to make tests of consistency and exclusiveness of application. He presents a whole smorgasbord of variations in uses of patrilineal descent, essentially to demonstrate the hopelessness of trying to make a total quantitative evaluation of the overall significance of descent in any particular society, let alone in comparisons between societies. He touches on matrilineal societies to the same effect.

Throughout his paper Lewis speaks of descent as an 'organizing principle'; this is the aspect that interests him. For example, he argues that 'The fundamental test of the functional importance of unilineal descent in a particular society must surely be the extent to which it is empirically the organizational basis for social activities in the widest sense' (1965:94). Lewis is well aware of the idiomatic use of descent to represent relationships founded on other bases, but his preoccupation is with organization, rather than with ideology. The problem he set himself was an impossible one, and he carried the test of 'strength' of unilineality bravely through a maze of facts and asides, to a very sensible conclusion: that is, that it cannot be measured.

If descent ideology is approached as an ideology of identities that can be adapted for use as an organizing principle, rather than as an organizing principle in the first place, it is not difficult to cope with the varieties and irregularities observed by Lewis and Langness. The basic element of the ideology of descent is a way of thinking about the procession of the generations. It postulates certain identities between ancestors and descendants and consequently also categorizes contemporaries. In no way does this minimal model itself dictate what specific social consequences this series of identifications shall have. Descent is essentially an infinitely expandable system of identities. As it has to do with sequences of generations, it often gets involved with facts and myths about sex and procreation, with rules of incest and exogamy, and with the distribution and handing on of property and status. Social units may describe their boundaries in terms of it.

The regulation of these matters involves jural rules. However the rules are not inherent in the system of identities itself. The jural rules may or may not be built partly or wholly in terms of the descent ideology or rationalized by it. Even if descent is invoked, the model itself is non-specific in these matters, and *quite a variety of jural possibilities can be built on the same minimal descent base.*

One way to sift out the connections between descent and law in a particular society is to examine the rights and obligations of individuals, two legal questions being asked throughout. First, is descent by itself the effective source of the rights involved, or is descent operative only when combined with other factors?

Second, is descent (with or without other elements) the only source of the rights involved, or may the same rights be acquired by alternative means not involving descent at all?

These questions are not answerable unless one distinguishes among the ideological, the jural, and the statistical or behavioral levels of analysis. Thus far I have spoken of the ideology of descent in its minimal and fundamental form, isolating identities as the lowest common denominator of descent ideologies. Built on this basic set of identities are elaborations special to particular cultures. For example, a conception of society at large and of its component parts may mix basic descent principles with others to arrive at a constitutional theory of society. This is a *way of thinking* about social organization that may be more or less metaphorical. It is only on the jural level that one finds those practical binding rules that actually regulate the 'on the ground' operations of a particular society. These rules may be stated in terms of the descent ideology, but they vary greatly from society to society, whereas the minimal forms of descent ideology (the identities between ancestors and descendants) by definition are very much the same in many cultures. On the statistical level one investigates the incidence of action under the various alternative jural rules, not simply violations nor the extent to which a population fits or does not fit preconceived notions of what constitutes a 'descent group.' The basic descent ideology, the constitutional theory, the jural rules, and the statistical frequencies should be kept conceptually distinct whenever this is possible.

The Lango: descent and constitutional theories

In so far as a society has a conception of what constitutes a formally legitimate political subunit and what is the proper relationship among such subunits, it has a constitutional theory. A constitutional theory 'explains' the vagaries of the political reality by describing in very general terms the model system within which political events supposedly take place. Some cultures seem prone to conceptualize their political relations in terms of a single dimension – segmentary lineage systems, for example. Others, like the Lango, do not rationalize the whole in such unitary terms, but simply operate with a varied set of interlocking constitutional categories and principles.

The fact that a constitutional theory is couched in terms of one repetitive idea does not mean that the whole polity is really operationally organized on the basis of only one principle. It suggests rather that there are political reasons for emphasizing unity and minimizing diversity by means of the *model*. For example, for some purposes the Inca conceived of their empire as everywhere subdivided into units of 100 taxpayers, these being included in larger units of 1000 taxpayers, which in turn were grouped into units of 5000 taxpayers, and so on. Each larger unit was contained in a still larger one, until the whole empire was encompassed. This categorization produced an apparent organizational homogeneity from top to bottom, from emperor to merest villager. In fact, the decimal conception concealed real diversity. It provided a simple set of terms in which an empire of many disparate and relatively autonomous local units could be conceived as a single integrated whole.

Apparent formal unity is achieved in some other constitutional theories by representing the relationships among the large-scale constituent parts as if they were homologues of relationships within entities of the smallest scale. Hilda Kuper (1961:40) indicates that the Swazi kingdom is for some purposes represented in sayings and customs, as if the whole Swazi nation were a magnified model of a single homestead with the king at its head. (This is not to say that other constitutional conceptions were not available to the Swazi and invoked when convenient.) Segmentary lineage systems are another instance of this use of the internal organization of a small unit to depict the relationship among larger ones, since relationships *between* lineages are represented as relationships between ancestral individuals *inside* lineages.

This use of the internal organization of small units as a descriptive model for the depiction of the entities of large scale produces a repetitive pattern in which each level of formal organization seems built out of the same elements as every other one. By this means differences of kind seem reduced to mere differences of scale.

Why did the Lango not develop some such unitary overall conception? Was there anything about the decentralized Lango system that would have precluded the development of a fixed model of the relationship among villages? They had patrilineal clans which segmented. Why did they not develop a segmentary lineage system? One can only guess at the answers.

M. G. Smith (n.d.) has argued that a segmentary system of the

Nuer type cannot develop where lineage groups are structurally differentiated from one another by such matters as differential marriage rules. The Lango system has another differentiating characteristic that would seem to be inconsistent with a segmentary lineage rationale: unstable military alliances among villages. No descent rationale of alliance is possible where alliance is unstable.

The Lango were organized into named exogamous patriclans. Genealogical connections were recognized among some, but not others, and there was no overall 'national' genealogy or other total descent framework into which they were fitted. Some clans were subdivisions of others, having segmented and broken off. These named subdivisions could intermarry (Driberg 1923:191).

The economic basis of Lango life was a system of shifting agriculture combined with cattle-keeping. The Lango lived in villages that were chronically at war. Each village tended to have a numerically dominant clan. Driberg (1923:71) gives figures on one such village in which 67 men belong to one clan, and the remaining 26 belong to 7 different clans. Villages were led by the head of the dominant clan and had local fighting alliances with other villages under the leadership of one of the village heads. Numbers of these village groups would join forces from time to time under a common temporary leader. Such alliances were constantly changing (Driberg 1923:206–8; Hayley 1947:56–8).

Village composition was not altogether stable. The Lango rule of residence appears to have been one of considerable flexibility. Usually the eldest son continued to reside in the village of his father, but other sons did not always remain (Driberg 1923:71). There were many reasons why a man might take his family and move from one village to another, or why several families might start a new village. An individual or group might leave because of internal disputes, or because when the village moved to a new site the place selected did not meet with everyone's approval, or because there was illness in the family, or on the advice of a diviner (ibid.:71). There seems to have been no binding obligation of any kind on the Lango to remain with a particular village if he thought he would be better off elsewhere.

Villages moved every three or four years. Consequently, land was frequently redistributed, and adjustments could be made easily as the composition of the village altered. Each man had his own plot (Driberg 1923:71). There was no land shortage, and individual 'ownership' was temporary and more or less equivalent to the period of cultivation. Evidently a village that moved retained rights in the land it had abandoned for a year or two after moving, but thereafter lost all rights to its earlier site and fields. Agricultural land, then, though it was the basic means of production, was not really an inheritable asset of a descent group or a village; it could be temporarily inherited (ibid.:175). But clearly such rights were no more durable than the occupancy of the site by the village itself. Clearly, also, land distribution would have been no impediment to additions of persons to the village. The social composition of the village could change without affecting existing land rights in any way.

Four named geographical territories were distinguished by the Lango. These were the largest categories that ever acted as a unit. Driberg (1923:191 footnote) tried to discover a genealogical rationale for these divisions but was unable to find any. Nearly all the clans were represented in all the regions. Three of the territories regularly functioned as ceremonial units, the local clans coming together at one place for the age-set initiations. These took place in a four-year cycle, and there were 4 age sets, linked alternately. A nine-year gap was observed between cycles. The period of the initiation ceremonies was a time of intratribal truce, culminating in a raid against another tribe. Groups of normally hostile Lango villages co-operated peacefully in the age-set ceremonies and the raid.

The age sets had a major ritual function in the annual rain-making ceremonies. These also took place at one traditional site in each of three of the geographical sections mentioned earlier. The fourth region appears to have been less cohesive and organized. There the ceremony was performed clan by clan (Driberg 1923:248–63; Hayley 1947:63–80).

Clans were bound together locally into what were called *etogo* – sets of clans whose initiated males met periodically to partake of a ritually killed animal. Women and children also attended these ceremonies, but sat apart. The *etogo* group controlled the spirits of the dead, and in this capacity it performed essential services for the living. Clan dead were dangerous only to their descendants. Hence, when the occupants of the spirit world became troublesome and brought a man illness or misfortune, he turned to the members of his *etogo* group for help. Since other clans were immune from the acts of his clan spirits, they could take measures to scare away the ghost without fear of reprisal. The *etogo* also performed ceremonies at ordinary funerals and played the major role in the great burial rites for the tribal dead held every two or three years (Hayley 1947:17–21, 63–71).

A man belonged to the *etogo* group of his father. However, if he moved away from his own *etogo*, he could attend the ceremonies of the local *etogo* in the place to which he moved, although not as an initiated member. His son, however, could later be initiated as a full member. At initiation into the *etogo*, each boy was sponsored by a ceremonial father of the linked age set. The sponsor belonged to a clan other than that of the boy, yet the boy was not allowed to marry his adopted father's daughter. The same adopted father sponsored him at the age-set initiation ceremonies (Hayley 1947:63–71).

In sum, the localized segment of a clan, one basic unit of social cleavage, was connected with other clans through the regional organization, the age-set structure, the *etogo* groups, and the kinship networks established by exogamous marriage. The ceremonial system tied the whole bundle together in periodic ritual observances. Certain of the constituent elements of Lango society are evident from this summary. However, it omits two very significant facts of life for the Lango: the village and the military alliance of villages. There is no evidence on the question whether the smallest groups of allied villages were also the members of the *etogo* groups, but Hayley (1947:57) feels that such a presumption fits with the logic of the system.

The constitutional theory of Lango society could be described as founded on patriclans and age sets (which existed both in localized subunits and in dispersed form), these in turn functioning in the context of villages, village military alliances, *etogo* groups (united for minor ritual), and regions (united for major ritual). Every male belonged to every one of these units. His place in the polity depended upon how he fitted into or manipulated his membership in these constitutional categories. I consider the constitutional categories themselves as much a part of the Lango legal system as the narrower rules under which individuals acted within them.

Although the *types* of categories and connections were fixed in the Lango system, both the composition of social units and their particular relations with each other could shift within the system. Village alliances were variable. Patriclans could split or fuse. Not only the relationships among groups, but also, as will be shown, the relationships of individuals to groups was not absolutely fixed, despite the importance of the descent element threaded through the system.

It remains to be seen whether the place of descent in constitutional theories is a useful criterion for distinguishing organizational forms. It also remains to be seen whether particular sorts of constitutional forms can be consistently correlated with economic, social, and historical circumstances as Sahlins (1961:322–45; 1965:104–7) has sought to show. It may turn out, instead, that some constitutional theories are a formal dress that may clothe quite varied types of social arrangements. These questions lie beyond the scope of this paper. For present purposes it suffices to suggest the usefulness of employing the concept of constitutional theory in order to place notions of legitimate overall organizational form in the comparative law framework where they belong.

Clans, cattle, and contingency: variations in the descent formula

The legitimation of membership in the descent group

Technically defined, each Lango patriclan was composed of persons whose mothers were married with cattle belonging to the clan, plus other individuals – such as war captives – who were adopted into the clan. Where there was no cattle payment, children belonged to the mother's clan. However, the initially 'illegitimate' children of women who later married into the clan became full clan members through the marriage payment. Payment also made it possible for kinsmen who were not clan members to father children who were. A mother's brother could provide his sister's son with marriage cattle, whereupon the children of the sister's son would belong to the patriclan of the mother's brother.

There is nothing unusual about these facts. But from a legal point of view, this classic case is instructive. What it shows is that it is not patrilineal descent principles by themselves that have legal consequences in Lango society. The addition of new members to the patriline, while *conceived* in terms of genealogical descent, is only *legally effective* through cattle payments. A woman's lineage had full primary rights to her reproductive powers and to her offspring unless these were transferred to another lineage through the marriage payment. The formal device by which the transfer of rights in offspring is made from one patrilineage to another serves in the ordinary case to legitimize patrilineal descent. But the same device by which descent is legitimated serves also as a means of deviating from genealogical descent when it is convenient to do so. Thus the very legal formalities that make descent principles binding are the means by which the descent rule is made manipulable.[1]

Because the ordinary Lango case is one in which cattle payment and descent go together, these elements are noticeably separated only in the exceptional cases. But from the legal point of view, it is useful to treat them as analytically separable elements in all cases. The purpose that is served in distinguishing descent from its formal legitimations is obvious as soon as comparative studies are made. A look at the New Guinea societies in which not marriage payment, but long residence and the allocation of land are the legal legitimators of descent makes it clear, not only that descent systems frequently have built into them legal legitimators quite separate from genealogy, but also that these legitimating procedures may be quite different in different societies. (See Meggitt 1965 for a beautifully clear description of the operation of a New Guinea system.) It makes one wonder, in fact, whether all unilineal societies do not have some such formal means of adjusting genealogy to convenience. The extent to which this is done in any particular society is a statistical question, which may be some index of social change or type. However, the very existence of the legal device shows something of the complexity of operational descent 'rules.' They are founded on a multiplicity of circumstances of which genealogy is only one.

Legal adjustments in the definition of the descent group to accommodate demographic change

A Lango clan could split by dividing its cattle. If the seceding group also adopted a new name and new food taboos, it could thereafter intermarry with the remainder of the clan with which it had once been united. In such cases separation and social autonomy (and its validating symbols) were more important that common descent interpreted in strict accordance with genealogy.

New clans also could be formed through the coalescence of branches of two old ones, and the fused clan could then intermarry with either of the original clans (Driberg 1923:191). Hayley confirms this report by Driberg, giving a number of additional details. He evidently witnessed a case of incipient segmentation in which a clan had grown to proportions such that half of it did not feel itself closely related to the rest. They were awaiting a case of incest to formally declare the two divisions distinct clans (Hayley 1947:41).

In the previous section we saw that descent ties that did not follow the lines of genealogical patrilineality could be created through cattle transfers at marriage. Here we see that genealogical descent ties already acknowledged and existing in a clan could be *unmade* by splitting cattle holdings and by formal declarations. Physical separation could be effected without formalities. However, social separation sufficient to permit marriage could be managed only on the occasion of a precipitating case and through public statements and formal symbolic acts. Here again, as in the matter of individual membership, descent grouping is seen as an arrangement that could be modified by procedures involving manipulation of the symbols of legitimation.

Contingencies relating to the assembling of bridewealth and the distribution of an inheritance

Family composition, prosperity, and degree of internal harmony, are all factors that bear on what are often thought of as descent-determined rights and obligations. The priorities for the provision of a Lango boy's marriage payment were as follows. The obligation (moral?, legal?) lay primarily on his father. If he had no father or if his father were poor, he could appeal to other agnatic relatives. If they could not help him or were dead, he might then turn to his mother's brother for help (Driberg 1923:155). Usually, in point of fact, the animals received for a man's sister were the actual source of his marriage cattle, but as male and female children cannot be counted on to arrive in pairs, the other means existed.

Lango exogamy had a characteristic that seems logically consistent with the marriage-payment arrangements. The rule was that a man could not marry anyone in his father's *or* his mother's clans. This would seem to fit with the position of the

Lango as a potential quasi-member of his mother's patrilineage, should it honor his contingent claims to marriage cattle from maternal kin.

The rules of inheritance were also consistent with this close tie to maternal relations. A man's eldest son was normally his heir. But if the eldest son were a ne'er-do-well, another son could be chosen. In the absence of sons, or suitably responsible sons, the inheritance might pass to the deceased's brother's son or, if he were ineligible, to the deceased's sister's son (Driberg 1923:174). The wives of the deceased could choose among the various possible heirs the one with whom each decided to live. The general order of eligibility for inheritance was the same as the order of claims or appeals for aid.

The heir was selected at a ceremony held from four to sixteen months after a death (Driberg 1923:168). Livestock were the principal inheritable property and were distributed by the clan after the selection of the heir. Customarily goats were inherited as they had been distributed in the decedent's lifetime among the houses of his wives, and cattle were inherited in accordance with the distribution of milk among the various wives. The heir got what livestock were left, and he held them subject to certain rights of his siblings. He was under obligation to help provide his unmarried brothers and sister's sons with marriage cattle. His uterine brothers (whether or not they were physiologically sons of the same father) and the sons of a uterine sister had claims on him prior to those of any sons of other wives of his father (Driberg 1923:174).

On an ideological plane, the cattle of agnates among the Lango may be regarded as symbolic of the real, genealogically traced patrilineal descent group. But then, with only the slightest legerdemain, the symbol itself could be used jurally to create or break membership. This is the kind of legal fiction Sir Henry Maine was talking about. It is possible to argue that all this does is to extend the mantle of descent over a few instances that would not otherwise be included or to allow for other unusual circumstances. One can stress the contrast between the ordinary routes to membership and the less usual ones and make much of the usual rule fitting the patrilineal paradigm, treating the others as deviations from rules postulated as 'ideal.' However, I think such a procedure is distorting; it overstresses the ideology and undervalues jural rules. The same reservations apply to the acquisition of cattle; what may be statistically exceptional among individuals – the young man without sisters or helpful agnates, the war captive, the orphan, the irreconcilable dispute between brothers, the shrunken or overgrown clan – may be part of the ordinary experience of every village. Certainly the rule of exogamy that barred members of mother's patriline as well as father's was part of the ordinary experience of every individual, and the contingent claims for assistance and inheritance that lay against the mother's patriline was a part of general knowledge, as were cattle dealings outside the agnatic circle. These must all be taken into account as aspects of Lango descent.

It seems to me to be a serious mistake ever to consider a complex of jural rules, such as the rules that govern membership and rights in Lango patriclans, without considering as *built in* to the basic rule those devices and extensions by which it is adapted to the vagaries of reality. The ideological model is one thing; the jural rules are another. When one gets down to the legally binding rules, patrilineality among the Lango had its own local twists, its own accretions to the bare-bones model, its own local forms of manipulability.

Descent group cores and clusters of contingent claims

Neither the Lango definition of bridewealth obligations nor the determination of inheritance distributions is governed solely by a fixed gradation of closeness of agnatic relationship. Individual character, emotional preferences, accidents of family composition, wealth, and competing claims, all affect who pays what and who gets what. The priorities are as much determined by the contingencies as by a descent formula.

Clearly not all rights in cattle were strictly agnatic rights, either for brideprice financing or for inheritance. Nor can one look upon the clan cattle from a jural point of view as 'owned' in common by the descent group – though Hayley (1947:46) speaks of them in this way. Ideologically the cattle wealth of agnates may have been identified with the descent group. But in jural fact there were simply many separate networks of claims, each nucleated around the holdings of individuals. This situation is in some respects the obverse of Gulliver's concept of 'stock associates,' which he developed in connection with his analysis of the Jie and the Turkana. Gulliver (1955:196) defines 'stock associates' as the circle including all people with whom a man maintains 'well-recognized reciprocal rights to claim gifts of domestic animals in certain socially defined circumstances.' What is being described here for the Lango are circles of *stock claimants*.

Each individual's stock holdings were at the center of a set of concentric circles of *contingent claimants*. The more peripheral the claimant, the weaker was the claim. Certain agnates, at least theoretically, were supposed to be closer to the center. One could perhaps postulate theoretical reciprocity over the long term among agnatically related descent lines, but this is quite different from the expectation of actual reciprocity between particular individuals in their lifetime.

If the whole of a localized Lango descent group were depicted as concentric circles of contingent claimants, one would probably find that certain people had only a few peripheral claims and that others were close to the center of many claim circles. That is, there would be persons who had high-priority claims on a number of cattle-holders, and persons who had only weak peripheral claims where they had any. There would, of course, be mixtures also – individuals who had some high-priority claims and some peripheral ones as well. The fortuitous composition of families would have much to do with these variations.

Such inequalities of position were not mapped out individually in the Lango fieldwork, but they follow from the descriptions of the system. This finding has significant theoretical implications, since it adds an inside perspective to the conventional picture of agnatic descent groups in which everyone is seen from the outside as jurally equivalent to everyone else. Perceived instead from the inside, in terms of concentric contingent claims, a picture emerges of internal differentiation in the descent group, not only of property, but also of rights. One sees the descent group as having a *core* – a core of persons who have many overlapping claims of high priority against one another. On the edges of these dense clusters of overlapping claims are persons more peripherally attached. Very likely aliens (non-members of the locally dominant descent group) also fitted into the periphery of some claim circles, as did non-resident affinal kin. This cattle-claim model could be elaborated for other types of rights, and one would, I think, find similarly variable concentrations of other overlapping and multiplex ties. (See Pospisil (1963) on variations of individual wealth among the Kapauku.)

Presumably, with the vagaries of birth and mortality and the ups and downs of stock breeding, to say nothing of disputes among brothers and variations of individual character, the lineage core thus identified would not be stable over long periods of time. Shifts in the relevant contingencies would alter the alignments of priorities, and so on. Surely this Lango continent cattle-claim complex is a common enough aspect of corporate unilineal groups to merit analysis as a legal type. In it, descent operates as a guideline for priorities of contingent claims rather than as a clear determinant of ascribed, invariant, and enforceable rights.

Law as a rule-complex pertaining to a field of action

The whole matter of stock rights among the Lango is further complicated because it was possible to acquire cattle in various ways that did not depend on inheritance or claims on the generosity of kin. It was a common practice to place cows with friends .for long periods of time, and this custom also served as a means of obtaining cattle, for if the cow calved more than once during the period of care, one of the calves was given to the friend in payment (Driberg 1923:92–3). Cattle borrowing was also very common. A man might borrow cattle, giving as security the promise of betrothal of his daughter or even of an unborn daughter (Driberg 1923:155).

Cattle also could be bought with grain (Driberg 1923:92–3). This not only has implications of opportunities for the buyer, but also reflects on the whole notion of communal ownership by the clan of the seller. Hayley (1947:46) notes: 'he would always inform at least his brother should he intend to kill or sell an animal.' Inform? Under what circumstances, one wonders, could the brother object, and could he implement his objection beyond making his wishes known? One senses in the whole description a distinct conflict between agnatic claims and individual autonomy, with shadowy areas where it was not clear which was paramount. When observed, then, the Lango had within their legal system at least two competing sets of rules – those relating to contingent kinship liens and those pertaining to the discretionary rights of the individual in property in his possession. Any picture of the descent-connected kinship rights in cattle is incomplete unless the countervailing individual discretionary rights are also considered.

The Lango possessor of beasts held them under a great variety of conditions. The extent of his discretionary power over their disposition, however, depended not only on the manner in which he acquired possession – whether by agistment, as a brideprice payment, by inheritance, and so on – but also upon his family situation, the urgency of the claims upon his animals, whether by wives or marriageable sons or by other persons.

When the possessor of cattle does something with them that alters existing legal relations he is acting in a legal field of choice. Multiple ends and means confront him, and he picks his way, usually in a manner that can be rationalized by some legal principle. At the risk of exciting the ire of colleagues who see red whenever universality is mentioned, I would venture to say, not only that all legal systems have such areas of discretionary action, but also that it is over the very stuff of these fields of action that a great many disputes arise. Writers on economic anthropology are aware of the importance of the weighing of alternatives. Legal anthropology could profitably give more attention to these problems. Lawyers are all very acutely aware of choice as an aspect of law because much of their professional life is spent, not simply in settling disputes – which seem to have become the focus of legal anthropology – but in giving advice, advice about legally legitimate choices open to a client who wishes to achieve certain ends. The legal choices available to the Lango possessor of cattle did not involve his consulting Dibble, Dibble, and Dabble; he had to make his decisions himself. But the fundamental element of choice is similar.

One way of looking at legal systems is to identify and analyze the legal rule complexes that surround particular fields of action. Seen this way, the law is not a simple normative standard one does or does not conform to. It is much more complicated than that.

Village membership: descent group membership

Expulsion: the loss of legal claims on the descent group without the loss of nominal membership

Perhaps an even more telling aspect of the jural implications of Lango descent emerges when one examines the occasions and causes for which a Lango could be abandoned or expelled from the community by his patriclan, from which he normally would expect to receive help and protection. The most extreme example of obligation is perhaps that of collective liability for homicide, yet on close scrutiny one discovers that such liability is not precisely collective, that it is not absolute, and that a man's agnatic relatives may decide not to back him in certain cases.

Driberg first describes the rules in terms of conventional collective liability terms. He tells us that when a man of one patriclan killed a member of another, the interclan dealings that followed were all directed toward the repair of the damaged patrilineage as a corporate unit, the replacement of the lost individual. The Lango equation was the familiar one: men are produced by women who are obtained by cattle. As indicated earlier, membership in the patriclan itself was calculated in these terms rather than in terms of descent itself.

The rules governing compensation followed logically. When a member of one patriclan killed a member of another, and the killer was known, cattle had to be paid in compensation by the kin group of the murderer to the kin of the decedent if blood vengeance were to be averted. The killer tactfully went into hiding until a settlement was concluded between the clans, when he could again emerge safely (Driberg 1923:210).

The injured kin group had lost a member. It was compensated in the currency that could replace the dead individual through the birth of new ones – that is, in cattle, which could be used to obtain a bride for a man in the decedent's kin group and hence to increase its numbers. The Nuer were more direct in this matter than the Lango, using the payment to buy a wife to marry to the name of the deceased. But the essential basis of the Lango practice was clearly the same, for if the Lango murderer had a marriageable sister or daughter, the deceased's brother could accept her instead of the cattle as full requital (Driberg 1923:211). The seven head of cattle that were the standard number paid were more or less equivalent to the brideprice, which Driberg cites as ranging anywhere from 4 to 10 head (1923:157).

Liability for payment was not inevitably collective. It rested initially on the murderer himself. His relatives took all the cattle from his herd if he had the necessary 7 animals, or they took his sister instead. But, if he had neither, Driberg notes that the obligation to pay was shifted to his agnatic relatives (1923:211). Primary responsibility thus rested on the actor, contingent but ultimate responsibility on his kin group. Viewed from the outside, the fundamental obligation was from one patriclan to another, and the debt was paid in cattle, the core of the clan patrimony.

But from the inside of the patriclan, the obligation rested on the individual who had committed the homicide. Where possible, all the animals came from his herd. Only if he did not have them and had no available sister did his close kinsmen help him out. Even then there was a question; his kinsmen had a choice. They could help, or they could deliver him to his enemies. In this respect the position of the kinsmen is quite different from that of the killer. He has a binding and inescapable obligation to his enemies. Among his principal assets are his claims for aid from kinsmen. But these are contingent claims, which the kinsmen may or may not honor. They are under no absolute and unambiguous obligation to him. He can exhaust his claims on them.

Driberg tells us that

> whether the offender pay the full compensation for his offence himself, or whether he is assisted by his relatives, both the family and clan are poorer by the loss of so many livestock, and consequently, the crime of an individual weakens the whole clan. The offender is accordingly in temporary disgrace for weakening the clan, and if the offence is serious, is publicly reprimanded by the clan headman, not (be it noted) for his offense, but for its communal consequences: and a hardened offender who squanders his patrimony or constantly requires assistance from the clan is driven away or eventually given up to the vengeance of an injured claimant. (1923:208–9)

In so far as it exists, the collective liability then is not an automatic consequence of membership in a descent category, but rather it follows on being a member *in good standing* of a patriclan in a particular localized group. The descent model (with the jural elaborations indicated earlier) defined the membership, but not the conditions for remaining a member with full privileges in a localized segment of the clan group. Hayley (1947:58) tells us that 'Unsociable individuals were driven away,' driven out of the village. Expulsion seems to have been a recourse available for a wide range of reasons, from shirking one's share of the communal agricultural work to mere quarrelsomeness. It could also be resorted to for unwarranted exposure of the village to the vengeance of another village (Driberg 1923:208; Hayley 1947:59).

Membership in the community or expulsion from it were not

the only possibilities. One could be a community member and yet be tenuously attached. As indicated earlier, rights of members were characterized by shifting concentrations, overlappings, and priorities. Certain persons had many strong claims, others had few weak ones. The material on expulsion suggests that individual behavior as well as agnatic position was important in these matters. A 'slightly attached' community member might seek his fortune elsewhere, given any provocation to do so. Whether he moved voluntarily or was expelled, his clan membership would remain fixed for purposes of exogamy but would not carry with it the rights in a particular community previously associated with it.

Villages and village alliances: the structural basis of legal enforcement

One of the interesting features of Driberg's account is that in part of his book he presents the blood feud and compensation obligations purely in terms of clan liabilities, yet when he gets down to procedure, he makes it clear that not only the clan, but also the village as a whole was a liability unit.

The elders of each village, together with the local clan head and sometimes with the leader of the group of allied villages, settled all disputes between local people. Within their villages their decisions are described as binding and respected. A complainant from one village could even recover against an inhabitant of another village by bringing his case before the elders of the defendant's village; this course was effective, provided the two villages were friendly and within the same alliance district. However, notes Driberg,

> should he sue at a hostile village, or at one under another *rwot* (leader of a group of allied villages), his prospects would not be so bright, as, though the elders might find in his favor, they would be unable to enforce their decision if the defendant were unwilling to come to terms, and the defendant would certainly be supported by the younger warriors anxious for a fight. Hence, though custom has evolved an elastic scale of fines and compensations for various offenses, recourse had often to be made to violence to obtain satisfaction, and in case of murder or even adultery it was easier to make war on the village rather than to await the result of a lawsuit which would probably be unfavorable or inoperative....

This has resulted in the principle of the communal responsibility on the one hand of the family ... and of the village on the other. A weak village in which lives a defendant sued by a member of a strong fighting village would insist on the defendant's punishment to save themselves from invasion, and to save the defendant, his relations and clansmen, if he is poor and has not committed an offense which is incompoundable, will help him to find the necessary amount of the fine or compensation. (1923:208–9)

Villages evidently fought as units and were raided as units; presumably attached elements were as involved as dominant clan members. Here edges of any purely clan definition of the blood feud become blurred. The fighting was carried on between villages, not simply between patriclans. Clearly much depended upon the strength mustered by each side of any intervillage dispute, leading to what Gulliver has called essentially political processes of dispute settlement (Gulliver 1963:297f).

Conclusion

Descent ideas appear in Lango rule complexes in many varied forms. The Lango evidence shows, on the one hand, that there were simple techniques by means of which the definition of descent and patriclan could be adjusted to fit variable social circumstances (cattle transfers, patriclan fission and fusion). It shows, on the other hand, that there were conditions under which not the definition of descent, but its social concomitants were adjusted or changed (contingencies, withdrawals or expulsions from a village). The law can have it both ways. In some instances the covering concept for a rule has an adjustable definition. Yet in others the concept is not tampered with, but the rules under its cover are adjusted or countervened.

In reviewing the Lango material, it is extremely difficult to isolate any significant rights or obligations, with the possible exception of some ritual ones, that may be said to flow absolutely from descent and from descent alone. Even the rule of exogamy, excluding as it does the mother's patriline as well as the father's, goes beyond descent for the definition of its scope. Lango jural rights and obligations connected with descent commonly involve other elements to make them operative, or they may be derived from alternative sources. These are the circumstances that give perspective on the difference between ideology and the jural rules. Ideology sometimes has descent and its elaborations as the be-all and end-all. The jural realities are always far more complex.

A way to approach the problem without overweighting descent is to say that many Lango jural rights depend on *social identity*, and that descent is an element in that identity. This formulation puts descent in its place as a contributory definer of the legal position of individuals and stresses that it is generally far from the sole determinant.

Gluckman (1965b:14) has spoken of rights and obligations associated with social positions. I use 'social identity' to mean all those descriptive aspects of an individual's social positions that attach to his person, as well as some other elements that refer to his character. Social identity is a composite. As a concept it lends itself to the discussion of component parts. Some aspects of identity are permanent – one's sex, for example. Some may be changed, such as residence. An individual's reputation is part of his identity, and it may have a crucial bearing on his rights in the social community in which he lives. Yet reputation is not comfortably encompassed in the concept of social position.

Another way of stating the matter is to say that in a society where significant jural rights are tangled in multiplex ties, there are likely to be multiple sources of jural right. Descent, for example, may be an effective source of rights only in combination with coresidence, frequent social contact, a history of mutual support, and so on. A great many elements in an individual's social identity may have to fit to make operative rights that seem ideologically to stem from descent alone. In a single-interest-tie situation jural rights emanate more often from single sources. In Western law a man may sue another as the holder of a negotiable instrument; it is not relevant to his rights as holder where he lives, whom he sees often, what he does for a living, or whether he is faithful to his wife.

A problem of jural analysis is imbedded in this multiplicity. A training in Western legal systems pushes one in the direction of trying to specify the sources of right. But it may not always be possible to do so in the precise terms one is accustomed to expect. The Lango rights derived from coresidence in the same village serve as a good example of the problem. Coresidence in a village carries with it rights to land, agricultural assistance, co-operation in herding and care of cattle, and support in intervillage dispute. Since most covillagers belong to the same clan, clan membership and village membership usually run concurrently. But of course, villagers who were non-agnates could enjoy the same benefits of communal life.

There are two ways, at least, to read this state of affairs. One can argue that the rights went with coresidence and had nothing to do with descent, since non-agnates enjoyed them. Instead, one can argue that attached non-agnates were treated for village purposes as quasi-members of the dominant clan. Which was the indigenous rationale? If I read him correctly, Driberg implies that it was the first − that village residence was treated as the key principle. The situation could have been rationalized in terms of descent ideology, and it evidently was not. Thus another related and jurally significant piece of Lango social identity was membership in a village. What does one do with Nupasafa, where membership in a village *was* rationalized in terms of the descent ideology? Is the jural situation substantially different as a result?

What about rights to cattle? A Lango man's best bet was his father's obligation to provide him with a wife. Beyond that, about all one can say is that descent gave a man a position as a legitimate *claimant* to the assets and assistance of his close agnates for particular purposes, the most ordinary and urgent of which was the financing of his first marriage. But there is a difference between contingent claims and absolute rights. There could easily be claimants with higher priorities. A father's brother might have a son of his own of marriageable age. A young man was in real trouble if he had to go so far as to depend on the generosity of his mother's brother or his sister's husband (Driberg 1923:67–8). These might simply refuse to help.

The right to claim assistance from agnates in the assembling of the brideprice is clearly related to descent. But a weighing of competing claims is involved that is not settled by descent principles at all. Once a man's father failed him, his rights were not clear-cut. The distribution of the brideprice is clear enough, but the assembling of it is very muddy. Even for the much better reported Nuer, Howell writes (1954:97): 'There are no set rules governing the actual assembling of bridewealth cattle, and in any case the circumstances are too varied to warrant generalization on the subject.'

The raw fact of descent identity itself gave him the right to claim help but by itself would not assure him of receiving help. Many things must have weighed in the balance, including the ties other than descent ties that he or his father had to agnatic kin and the history of their relationships. The fact that agnates could refuse to supply bloodwealth, or other indemnity, to redeem someone they thought contemptible is indication enough that more weighed in the balance than descent alone. Rights to the assistance of agnates seems to have been conditional and contingent.

In some respects the situation may be analogous to the obtaining of credit in Western society. Credit is not obtained as a matter of absolute right; it depends upon the likelihood of ultimate repayment. It also depends on the lender's having available capital that he does not intend to expend in some other manner. The whole business career of the borrower may be reviewed and may have relevance to his success or failure in obtaining the loan. Particular aspects of an individual's social identity may make it more or less likely that he will receive credit. As I see the position of the Lango seeking the help of his agnates, common descent gives him the position of a legitimate claimant, who may be more or less favored, depending on the surrounding circumstances.

One could generalize about the Lango that membership in a localized patrilineal clan provided the ordinary way in which an individual acquired rights in a village and the usual means by which he could gather cattle when they were needed. Nevertheless, the jural rules amply provided for other entirely legitimate possibilities. One out of every 4 males living in the village Driberg gave figures for had availed himself of some of these alternatives.

Descent identity, normally acquired by birth, was permanent. Yet while descent identity could not itself be lost, the rights and claims ordinarily associated with a particular group of agnatic kin could be lost. These rights could be rendered worthless or nugatory through the misfortune or decease of the agnates or the existence of prior claims. They could be lost if one did not get along with one's agnatic kin. Substitute arrangements could usually be made and legitimized by regular procedures. The permanence of descent identity was thus not matched by any invariable permanence or certainty of what appear to be descent-engendered rights. One could move to another village if one's chances seemed better there.

How, then, are the statistical facts to be interpreted? If an ethnographic description of a village indicates that the community is prevalently composed of agnatic kin, though there are present a substantial number of resident non-agnates, what is to be made of the classification? What Langness has done in his New Guinea case is to say that the ideological-jural rules require patrilineality and patrilocality, hence non-resident agnates must be explained away as deviations from the rule. He opposes the 'ideal' (jural) and the 'real' (statistical). Lévi-Strauss's dichotomizing into mechanical and statistical models is adequate for some purposes, but not for this one. As Scheffler (1965:301) has noted, 'although people may discuss their economic, political and other relations by means of kinship norms or rules we should be careful not to imply that in so doing they are attempting to attain or maintain an ideal state of affairs, not even that seemingly implied by the norms or rules themselves.'

A rule may be stated in very rigid and mandatory terms yet have built into it numerous means of adjustment. The techniques by which this may be done include at least the following; there may well be others.

(1) Fictional or formal extension of the rule. Fictions and formal devices can exist by which the rule can be nominally adhered to while being actually circumvented. The Lango adoptions of war captives or the rule that children of a marriage are assimilated to the lineage that provided the marriage-cattle are extensions of this type.

(2) A loose application or discretionary interpretation of the rule. The existence of exceptions can be ignored and tacitly denied by behaving as if they do not exist – as if the rule, in fact, encompasses them. The rule can be applied metaphorically. This would appear to be the Nupasafa situation in which non-agnates behave as agnates do and are assimilated as quickly as their origins can be forgotten. This intentional ignoring of the facts may be done in general or only in specific contexts. However, the decision when the rule shall be applied may be in the discretion of a person or persons who may make adjustments according to their own lights. An example is the Lango agnates' option to support or surrender an accused kinsman.

(3) Other rules may exist that may be resorted to instead. This characterizes the Lango residence and cattle resource arrangements.

Any of these three ways of rationalizing can be used to justify the same set of facts. They may all be used simultaneously, in fact. I think they must be regarded as different techniques for accommodating reality and as an essential part of the basic system of jural rules, not simply as deviations or exceptions from an ideal. I do not know what significance, if any, the use of one rather than another of these techniques might have, but it is a question that might be worth further inquiry. Formal extension or loose interpretation does more lip-service to the exclusiveness of a patrilineal-patrilocal descent group ideology than would the open acknowledgment of legitimate alternative arrangements. But if the alternative rules are regarded as second best and there is a strong preference for maintaining membership in a patrilineal-patrilocal descent group, is there any less value given to the patrilineal ideology in the last instance than in the first two? The question, in a sense, concerns the meaning of the situation in which there are preferential rules in one case and prescriptive rules in another, yet the same statistical distributions occur in each. I am suggesting that the distinction that Needham has made between prescriptive and preferential marriage rules might usefully be investigated with reference to other rules. There seems a great variation from society to society in the *apparent* mandatoriness of particular rules. There may even be variations within a single society of the perception of the degree of mandatoriness or of the relevant contingencies.

Social identity, the multiple source of right, and surrounding political circumstances, are all contingent factors in the Lango system that affect the enforcement or application of rules. However, the fact that rules are multiple and highly conditional in operation makes them not less but more significant as subjects of study. Legal reasoning of the sort that is common in Western courts, and that has been described by Gluckman for the Barotse, has its analogues in the justifying rationales of social systems quite outside of juridical institutions such as courts. Social arrangements, like court decisions, are usually conceived in terms of justifying principles, not simply as expedient or practical matters. Descent is often used as such a principle. Systems of legal principles, concepts, or 'beliefs' (rather like systems of religious belief) provide descriptions and explanations of the nature of the social universe, and at the same time provide means for manipulating that very social universe, so that those who want to can try to make it bend to their advantage.

Descent ideologies and their elaborations are in part symbolic or metaphorical representations of social connections, in part categorical definers that affect social relations. There seems to be a two-way interaction between social structure and ideas about social structure. Any analytic framework that deals with the matter as a one-way flow at this stage of knowledge has serious limitations. The dichotomizing of descent analysis into the ideal/jural and the real/statistical implies that social arrangements are simply imperfect approximations of ideal models which follow from supposed jural rules. But in fact, jural rules, though they may be stated in terms of ideology, invariably provide one way or another for the complexities, irregularities, and manipulations of real social life. By distinguishing the jural aspects of descent from the ideological and statistical, one places oneself in a better position to inquire into the relationship between justifying ideologies and social arrangements.

Note

1 This point adds a dimension to the Leach–Fortes debate on the relative importance of kinship, descent, and affinity as 'crucial' links between corporate unilineal descent groups. The manipulability of descent-group composition, as well as local constitutional theories, may bear on the relative emphasis given to one element or another in particular structures (Fortes 1959:193–309; Leach 1961:114–23).

Chapter 6

Politics, procedures, and norms in changing Chagga law

In his book on the Arusha, the agricultural Masai of Mount Meru, Professor Gulliver concludes with a general theoretical statement in which he suggests a way of classifying processes of dispute settlement. Gulliver says that there are 'two polar types of process – judicial and political – between which there is a graduated scale where, ideally, particular systems could be placed according as to whether they were more judicial or more political in their nature' (Gulliver 1963:297).

By a judicial process Gulliver means,

> one that involves a judge who is vested with both authority and responsibility to make a judgment, in accordance with established norms, which is enforceable as the settlement of a dispute [p. 297].

> The purely political process, on the other hand, involves no intervention by a third party, a judge. Here a decision is reached and a settlement made as a result of the relative strengths of the two parties to the dispute as they are shown and tested in social action. The stronger gains the power to impose its own

Reprinted from *Africa*, 40 (4) (October 1970:321–44) by permission.

Author's note
This paper was prepared on the basis of work done during 1967–8 under a scholarship from the African Studies Center at the University of California, Los Angeles, and on my first three months of fieldwork in Tanzania in 1968 under a grant from the Social Science Research Council. I am grateful to Professor P. H. Gulliver for his kindness in having loaned me the Figgis and Griffiths reports.

decision, but it is limited by the degree to which its opponent, though weaker, can influence it. In this case the accepted norms of behaviour relevant to the matter in dispute are but one element involved, and possibly an unimportant one [ibid., p. 298]

Gulliver's polar types are founded on three criteria: the importance or unimportance of the relative social *strength* of the parties; the presence or absence of a *judge*; and the importance or lack of importance of *norms* as the bases of dispute settlement. At the 'political' pole of his continuum there is no judge, the strength of the parties' political support is the principal determinant of the outcome, and norms are of little or no importance. This situation is closely approximated by the Arusha. At the judicial pole the situation is reversed. There is a judge. He determines the outcome, but his decision is made on the basis of norms, and the relative political strengths of the parties is of little or no importance. Gulliver considers the Lozi of Zambia, as described by Gluckman, to be very close to the judicial ideal type (Gluckman 1955a). He makes it clear that he conceives of the polar extremes as theoretical models only, that probably all settlements are in some measure affected both by norms and by 'political' considerations. He says, 'the processes of dispute settlement in any society combine in some degree both judicial and political elements' (Gulliver 1963:299). There is nothing rigid about his formulation, and it would be misrepresenting him to suggest that there is. Since this article was first written, Professor Gulliver has published a further short discussion of processes of dispute settlement which appears to be a modification of the statement in *Social Control in an African Society*. (The new discussion appears in L. Nader (ed.), *Law in Culture and Society* (1969:11–13).) No longer using the 'political' and 'judicial' types, he now contrasts 'negotiation' with 'adjudication.' Moreover, he describes this distinction as heuristic and exploratory and no longer identifies the types with ethnographic examples such as the Arusha and the Lozi.

While these modifications remedy some of the limitations of the earlier statement of polarities, they do not affect the main concern of this paper, namely the appropriate frame of reference for the analysis of relationships between judicial decisions, the political setting, and the statements of behavioral norms. For this problem Professor Gulliver's earlier formulation or, more precisely, the criteria on which it was founded, provide the basis for further discussion. His framework of ideal types has indeed accomplished its heuristic purpose as it stimulates one to consider further the nature of the fundamental variables embodied in the comparison.

Gulliver's initial way of putting the whole matter emerges directly out of the Arusha ethnographic material with which he was centrally concerned. In its indigenous form the Arusha Masai society had neither chiefs nor judges. Legal disputes were argued out (and most still were in 1963) at public meetings at which each party appeared with a flock of supporters. Not only the disputants, but also supporters and spokesmen, participated actively in argument and settlement of cases. Partisanship on one side or the other depended on social ties, hence significant political groupings and relationships were brought into play. The outcome of dispute depended to a great extent on the quality and quantity of support a man could muster. Although norms were invariably mentioned in argument, Gulliver concluded that they had negligible effect on the ultimate outcome (ibid.:241). From these practices Gulliver abstracts the type that stands at the political pole of his continuum.

As I understand it, at the very least, three matters were being considered when an Arusha dispute was being thrashed out. The first was the dispute between the parties. The second was the relative pre-eminence of the spokesmen, counsellors, or notables on each side and the groups they represented. And the third was the leaders' maintenance of their positions of leadership in their own groups. In contrast, is the only matter involved in a judicial proceeding the dispute between the parties? To make an analysis of the political implications of judicial proceedings that is comparable to that of the Arusha, must one not say that in a judicial proceeding in addition to the sifting of the dispute between the parties, there is simultaneously a demonstration of the authority of the judge or court? The question of the nature of the authority depends on its political source, and the whole political setting in which it is operating. There is thus a political dimension to all judicial proceedings. The Lozi court, the *kuta*, was, after all, made up of royal councillors. When the *kuta* made decisions it was exercising one power of the Lozi crown. Surely *both* Arusha and Lozi procedures of dispute resolution are intimately tied to the political systems in which they are imbedded.

This is not to suggest that Gulliver is in the least unaware that judicial proceedings can have political implications. In fact, he explicitly mentions this possibility, but he treats such instances as a deviation from the ideal. His ideal judicial type is removed from any political context. To my mind, it thus loses one of the central analytical characteristics of any system of authoritative decision-making. I am emphasizing that the procedural characteristics of both modes of dispute settlement, the Arusha type and the Lozi type, are closely tied to their political contexts. This being so, in making comparisons it is necessary to give equal analytic attention to the general political background of enduring procedures of dispute settlement, whatever the society one is looking at. Every Arusha case is an occasion for political confrontation and challenge. Every Lozi case is an occasion for the redeclaration of political authority.

Gulliver associates the extent of the 'political' element in judicial decisions with the degree of the judge's departure from an ideally impartial norm-applying position. Such an ideal type implies that the proper application of norms by judges can be clear cut, purely an exercise of prescribed authority. At one point Gulliver makes the analogy between a court applying norms and a government agency fixing the price of a commodity according to an economic index (1963:235). I would argue, following Gluckman and many others, that the judicial use of norms is ordinarily a complex discretionary matter. If the magistrates' courts in Arusha are as mechanical in all instances as Gulliver describes them as being in brideprice cases, they are very unusual.

In many courts and in many cases there are wide choices to be made by judges among applicable norms, and suitable ones could be found to rationalize a variety of decisions. Norms are often general and subject to a considerable range of interpretation. Even where the applicable norm is clear, alternative decisions are often possible on the ground of the adequacy or inadequacy of the evidence. There is also in the background the possibility of judicial innovation. All these complicate the process of decision, and make norms something less than automatic guides to decision. But whatever the *real reasons* for a judicial decision, norms are frequently explicitly cited or referred to by implication to support decisions. Often this is taken at face value. It is assumed that the norms cited by judges determine their choices. But the place of norms in judicial decisions is much more complex than that.

The ideal polarity between political and judicial types makes a dramatic contrast. But as soon as one comes to analyze real societies it is much more useful to consider separately the very criteria that the ideal types combine. In order to make an analysis it is essential to distinguish among *procedures* (judges or other), the *reasons for outcome* (norms or other), and the *political implications* (strength of parties, relation to political setting). Whether these vary together or not is in itself an important problem for investigation, rather than something that can be assumed. The question, what varies with what, can be examined only if the elements of procedure, reasons for decision, and political implications are kept analytically distinct. The postulation of a continuum with two poles is a convenient model by means of which to suggest that two variables covary in a complementary fashion. But if, as in this case, there are more than two variables, because each type is made up of several variables, the image of the continuum may not be as illuminating or as appropriate, though it gives the appearance of providing for all possible combinations.

Like the ideal types, the notion that one can place 'systems' along a continuum has implications of homogeneity and unity within such 'systems.' Yet there may be many modes of dispute settlement in one society. I would argue, for example, that courts are a highly specialized institution which probably never constitute the entire mode of dispute settlement of any society. When Gulliver writes about the Arusha, he is looking at the whole range of dispute settlements in Arusha society, but when he takes Gluckman's presentation of the Lozi *kuta* as an illustration of its opposite, he is using a discussion of a Lozi court only. Hence the two ends of his dichotomy in this sense are not comparable.

If one accepts that in many societies there is not a homogeneous 'system' of dispute settlement – for example, that there may be different ways of settling in and out of court – it follows that different parts of the 'system' may vary in their degree of resemblance to the 'political' or 'judicial' type. Moreover, the political implications of dispute settlement may vary not only from one procedure of settlement to another, but from case to case. Heterogeneity in procedures of dispute settlement, and in content of cases, makes it very difficult to place societies having such varieties of dispute settlements in any simple comparative series.

In this paper I shall compare some Chagga legal processes in different historical periods. Fortunate accidents of the historical record make it possible to follow the changing career of Chagga chiefs as settlers of disputes from pre-colonial times to the point in 1952 when most of them lost their judicial powers. It is by definition a useful case for examining the political context of judicial activity. Throughout the period examined, a period which stretches from about 1890 onward, there was considerable heterogeneity in the Chagga processes of settling disputes. The emphasis here will be on the relationship between the changing political position of Chagga chiefs and the concomitant changes in the procedure of dispute settlement in which they were key figures. I shall also indicate some of the political uses of judicial office in particular cases. In the course of presenting this material, some comments will be made about the use of norms by judges. The typological opposition of norms and political considerations as the alternative determinants of decisions (and settlements) deflects attention from the fact that norms can and often do function in judicial decisions as justifications for decisions made on other grounds. Such a use of norms is usual, not exceptional. The Chagga material, like much other evidence, suggests that judges often use norms to legitimate their decisions very much as disputants use norms to fortify their arguments.

Thanks to Bruno Gutmann, an energetic missionary who lived in Chaggaland from 1902 to 1920, we know a good deal about Chagga law both before and during the period of German administration. There are also accounts of various pre-colonial travelers, of which perhaps the most useful is Johnston's (1886). It must be emphasized, though, that there were many autonomous chiefdoms in Chaggaland (in 1924 there were still 28. Dundas 1924:50) and that there was variation among them, so that what follows about the early period refers largely to the area around the Moshi Chiefdom that Gutmann knew best, and that Johnston visited in 1885.

Mount Kilimanjaro, the huge, glacier-topped mountain on which the Chagga live, is very benign to her dependants. The glacier provides an unending supply of water in the form of rushing streams that cut deep gorges into the sides of the slopes. These gorges came to be the natural boundaries that marked the divisions between many of the Chagga chiefdoms. A good many of the administrative boundaries of the present date back to these beginnings. Where water did not flow on its own, the Chagga channeled it to their banana groves in an elaborate system of water furrows.

In pre-colonial days the Chagga were cattle-keepers and banana-growers. Land was abundant. Cattle were numerous, and the warrior age-groups of each locality kept themselves in good fighting shape in innumerable interchiefdom raids and wars. In 1885 Johnston made some patronizing comments about this state of affairs. 'Why,' he wrote, 'in the midst of such superb scenery, with smiling plenty exhibited on every hand could these silly savages think of nothing but mutual extermination' (1886:177). The answer was partly that cattle-raiding had obvious and immediate rewards, as did the capture of slaves to sell to traders from the coast, and the capture of women, who did a great deal of the gardening and domestic work. An indirect benefit from being successful at this kind of war was that a strong chiefdom frightened off counter-raids, and also attracted alliances and immigrant lineages. A show of strength produced more strength. Allied chiefdoms sometimes formed fighting coalitions (see Stahl (1964) for details of shifting alliances in various periods). There was thus a level of political activity above that of the autonomous chiefdom even in pre-colonial times.

Chagga chiefs took a cut of all the good things. They controlled the slave and ivory trade. They collected some of the spoils of war, the cattle, and the slaves, and the women. They were entitled to a share of any beer brewed in the land, and of any animal slaughtered. The perquisites of office also included the right to requisition labor to cultivate the chiefly fields, herd the chiefly cattle, and build the chief's huts and enclosures, and whatever fortifications he saw fit to construct. Yet, for all that, there were political weaknesses in the chiefship. Many a chief spent part of his reign in exile (Dundas 1924:285). There were endless plots about succession, and wars between chiefdoms over local dominance. Plots against incumbents involved not only competition among lineages within a chiefdom, but treasonable alliances with outsiders as well. This very insecurity and weakness can be shown to have had very significant implications for the process of law-enforcement and dispute settlement in Chaggaland.

Take, for example, the case of a man named Kisiho in the 1860s, who violated the rule that a share of beer was due to the chief. Presumably this was a symbolic act of rebellion, as he was promptly and summarily executed. But in return his lineage[1] killed the very henchman of the chief who had executed him. Moreover, the lineage picked up its belongings, herded its animals together, and started to migrate to another chieftaincy. The chief then had to make conciliatory gestures to win them back, and on their return concluded a blood alliance between the chiefly lineage and the fleeing lineage (Gutmann 1926:247–8; H.R.A.F.tr.:222).

The inescapable conclusion that one must draw from this sad tale of banana-beer and disaster is that in the mid-nineteenth century local lineages were in a chronic state of potential secession or treason. If they chose to, they could take their cattle and go. They would find themselves welcome in another chiefdom. The chief, then, was always in some degree having to pay political attention to the delicate question of asserting power in such a way as not to alienate the lineages on which he depended.

The continuous tension between chiefs and subjects and the autonomy of the lineages in dealing with their own members is shown by another case cited by Gutmann. A young man was expelled from his lineage because, wanting revenge on some of his lineage-mates, he had revealed to the chief the number of their cattle and various other facts about their property which the chief had used as a pretext to seize some of their wealth (Gutmann 1926:236–7; H.R.A.F.tr.:210). The informer used his right of asylum and took refuge with the chief. After a time he fell slightly ill. The chief, who found his uninvited guest a political embarrassment, sent for his clan fellows to tell them to take him back to lineage territory. It was a Chagga belief that no man should die in the land of another lineage. The man was not very sick, but his illness provided the chief with an occasion to get rid of him. His lineage came for him, but they made it plain to the chief that 'if we kill a dog that bites us, you will not have a chance to make a legal case out of this.' On his own lineage territory the man did not last another day, and the chief and everybody else thought this was only natural (Gutmann 1926:237; H.R.A.F.tr.:210).

Clearly in the pre-colonial period the lineages had a great deal of freedom of action. They had powers of coercion over their own members and considerable leverage against the chief himself. While blood revenge was not the order of the day, it did happen, and there were circumstances in which it was even condoned by the chiefs (Gutmann 1926:243; H.R.A.F.tr.:216). Blood revenge was unpardonable only if undertaken after the culprit had been given asylum (Dundas 1924:290). Normally chiefs gave asylum for the payment of a cow and a goat. Then the chief negotiated the payment of bloodwealth in cattle, sheep, or goats. He also took part of the bloodwealth payment for having loaned his good offices to the negotiations.

According to Gutmann, the *amount* of the bloodwealth payment was not subject to negotiation. The task of the chief was to persuade the victim's kin to agree to accept the payment in lieu of revenge, and to persuade the slayer's kin to produce the payment. In the settlement of blood disputes, the chief was lending his authority to make negotiations possible and to make the outcome binding. Yet he was also a go-between in a bargaining procedure in which the alternatives appear to have been payment or revenge.

In less lethal matters the chief had a somewhat more judicial role. Cases were heard on the Chief's Lawn, an area before the chief's house where representatives of the 30- to 45-year-old age-group and warriors from the subsections of the chiefdoms assembled to debate cases (Gutmann 1926:310, 590f; H.R.A.F.tr.:278, 529f). Each subsection usually contained members of several lineages, and had a warrior age-group under the leadership of *mchili*, or headman. There were no true villages in the early days and there are none today. Johnston said in 1886,

> there is no such thing as a congeries of habitations forming a town or village in our sense of the word. Each family lives apart with its own two or three houses for men, women and beasts, surrounded by its plantations and gardens, with plenty of room for expansion all round ... each separate state of Caga may be looked upon as a huge straggling city, one vast capital of huts and gardens, equally inhabited and cultivated throughout its extent (pp. 250–1).

The 'room for expansion' is now gone, but otherwise the description still fits.

Cases that came to the Chief's Lawn for decision had already been thrashed out before, sometimes several times over. A person who had a claim was first supposed to try to settle matters directly and amicably with his opponent (Gutmann 1926:599; H.R.A.F.tr.:537). If that failed the two might agree to meet with an arbitrator who would hear out their disagreement privately and settle it if possible. Another route open to them, assuming they belonged to different lineages, was to have the two lineages negotiate the matter. A third possibility was to bring the matter to the section lawn. There an assembly of section-mates was presided over by the local *mchili*, or headman (Gutmann 1926:590; H.R.A.F.tr.:529). As far as one can tell, assemblies on the section lawn seem to have been very similar to those Gulliver described for the Arusha. The body of men hearing the case was well acquainted with its details beforehand. The disputants presented their arguments to friends and neighbors ahead of time over beer (Gutmann 1926:591; H.R.A.F.tr.:530). Presents to the *mchili*, the headman, were also in order. If the decision of the section lawn did not close the matter, it might then be brought to the Chief's Lawn.

There the procedure was a curious one. Ordinarily the chief remained in his hut during the presentation of a case, but was kept closely informed of what was going on. When the assembly had reached a decision, the chief was told about it. He then played whatever part he chose in the whole affair. He either emerged and made further inquiries and reopened discussion, or he remained in his hut and negotiated with the two warriors assigned to represent the parties, and the speaker of the day. He then decided the amount of the payment that was owed by the losing party, or whatever other details of settlement there might be. The speaker announced the decision. The chiefs apparently liked to emphasize that they were only following the decision of the Lawn Assembly (Gutmann 1926:593; H.R.A.F.tr.:532). But there were occasions when the Lawn Assembly was deadlocked, or there were accusations of undue influence or threats, or other occasions when there was difficulty in reaching a decision in the Assembly, when the chief, or his brother, at the request of the Assembly came out, heard the case, and made the decision himself (Gutmann 1926:596, 713; H.R.A.F.tr.:536, 636). On other occasions the chief was persuaded to intervene in the decision by pressing secret requests by one of the parties (Gutmann 1926:596; H.R.A.F.tr.:536).

When the chief was coyly veiling his own part in the proceedings by concealing himself or by insisting that his decision on the penalty was no more than a carrying out of the will of the judiciary assembly, the procedure shows that the chief had ready means of avoiding apparent responsibility for the decision made.

He decided cases and took responsibility when there was an impasse, when he was asked to, and occasionally when he chose to, but on the whole he leaned heavily on the junior elders and warriors on whom his power depended.

The principal business of the chief and the age-groups in the Lawn Assembly was simply to establish officially the claim of one of the parties before them. The question of enforcement was a separate issue (Dundas 1924:290). Sometimes the losing party accepted the decision of the Lawn of Justice and voluntarily met his obligation. But sometimes the accused party refused to appear altogether. Of those who appeared, some refused to accept the judgment of the assembly. Then there was a question of whether the winning party would be left to his own devices or whether the chief and his men would intervene on his behalf (*loc. cit.*).

If the chief chose to lend his authority to the process of enforcement, he could order the two warrior spokesmen of the parties to go, together with the guards from the chieftain's lawn, to the homestead of the loser and confiscate the required number of cattle (Gutmann 1926:596; H.R.A.F.tr.:536). But if the loser were a rich man with a strong lineage that threatened to emigrate as a body if there were any property confiscated, the chief preferred tactics of persuasion (*loc. cit.*). Obviously there were persons against whom the chief could use force and others against whom he could not easily risk it. Such was the weakness of the Chief's position, that decisions made on the Lawn of Justice were not equally enforceable. He had not only the political positions of the parties to consider, but also his own.

That the chief sometimes used force vigorously and decisively on his own behalf was seen in the case mentioned earlier in which a chief had a man executed for not paying his beer tribute. But chiefs were evidently more cautious about using force where their own interests were not directly involved. Self-help *after* judgment was what followed in many cases, and this remained so for many decades, far into colonial times (Dundas 1924:290).

A winning party did not, however, necessarily resort to the risky business of taking by force whatever compensation he was owed. He had another means of coercion. He could swing the cursing pot in the marketplace and subject the recalcitrant loser to dreadful conditional curses. This form of cursing was a legitimate, public use of vengeance magic. The men who owned the cursing pots could lend them only if the chief gave his consent. Once this official consent was obtained, the borrower embarked on a long repetitious course of publicity and ritual. He went to the market of the chiefdom where all the women bought and sold their wares, and there he announced to all and sundry his intention of using the pot on the next market-day. If the threat did not produce results, four days later the curser took his place at the market and let the curses fly: 'May the milk you drink from the cow you owe me destroy you and make you urinate blood. I am sending you the destroyer so that you may beget a child without arms, legs and eyes. May whatever you touch cause you to bleed,' and so on. Curses and explanations were repeated for seven days in a row in the most public circumstances available. A postscript was always inserted in the curse to exempt the curser from the dread forces released from the pot, since these were known to rebound against the user from time to time (Gutmann 1926:624; H.R.A.F.tr.:560f).

At the first sign of not feeling quite well a nervous debtor might pay up. But a man with staying power had time on his side since ordinarily, in this kind of case, the pot was deactivated and pacified after two months whether the reluctant party had paid up or not. This pacifying of the pot took place partly to keep its dangers under control, partly in order to make the pot available for the next creditor.

The cursing pot had other uses as well, the most important of which, for the present discussion, was that it served not only as a method of enforcing judgments, but as a method of *settling disputes*. An accusation on the chief's Lawn of Justice was not necessarily concluded by a decision of the chief and his assembly. Instead an accused person might challenge his accuser to swing the cursing pot against whichever one of them was lying. This legal wager was decided when either a person or an animal died in the household of either party within a prescribed time, usually by the next cultivating season. The loser then had to pay two sheep in addition to whatever he owed in relation to the original dispute, to compensate the innocent person for the worry the curse had caused him. The winning party had his victory proclaimed in the presence of the chief on the Lawn of Justice.

Another way in which disputes were sorted out was by means of the *kimanganu* ordeal. The chief had a supply of dried leaves of a local plant which, when properly cooked with water, and drunk, caused intoxication and partial poisoning. It was a Chagga truth-drug whose effect was supposed to be to remove the subject's ability to conceal the facts. Once under the intoxicating influence of the drink, the subject was questioned, and from the interpretation of his answers (garbled or not) his guilt or innocence was established. Some people recovered quickly from the *kimanganu* ordeal, but others were sick for weeks. In some cases the *kimanganu* was said to cause an extraordinary swelling of the testicles and sterility ensued. This possibility had the understandable result that many an accused person confessed before being subjected to the ordeal and paid off whatever beasts were demanded rather than risk illness (Gutmann 1926:670; H.R.A.F.tr.:602).

The wager of the cursing pot and the *kimanganu* ordeal and other similar wagers and ordeals employed by the Chagga were procedures that settled disputes without involving an open decision on the part of the chief and his assembly. Of course, the chief decided who was to interpret the signs of the results of these magical techniques, and he could also arrange, in the case of the ordeal, that an innocuous herb was substituted for the poisonous one. But he did not have to make an open choice between the parties.

Looking at all these Chagga settlements of dispute that were proclaimed on the Chief's Lawn, whether it is the age-group assembly, the swinging of the cursing pot, or the ordeal of the truth-decoction, all can be interpreted as ways of removing from the chief the onus of decision. To be sure, he did decide some cases in person. To be sure, he did bring the force of the spear down on some people. But the system was one in which he could often makes his moves covertly. He did not often have to take a stand openly and assume responsibility for it. The political weakness of the chiefship turned all these procedures into occasions which while acknowledging the honoured position of the chief did not force him to make a show of authority. Publicly acknowledged authoritative decisions were made by *groups* of persons.

The concealment behind an assembly is in some ways analogous to a decision that alludes to norms, the one being a consensual basis composed of social elements, the other a normative basis consisting of ideological components. Both involve supporting decisions on a wider base than the power or judgment of one man. In the case of the chief's emphasis on the decision of the assembly, the wider basis is *socially consensual*. In the case of an allusion to norms, the wider basis is *symbolically consensual*.

The chiefs seem to have been too insecure in pre-colonial times to rely solely on symbolic consensus.

What happened when the Germans moved in? At first there was armed resistance from some quarters. The Chagga were tough opponents. They had had guns from their slave-trading friends for some time. In fact, in 1885 they had already had British government Snider rifles that had been traded for ivory (Johnston 1886:252). Some Chagga chiefdoms joined the Germans in fighting rival chiefdoms, thus serving their own as well as German purposes. Once military defeat was complete, and the Germans had terrified everyone by publicly hanging a number of chiefs they thought 'disloyal,' some of the remaining chiefs settled down to a period of unprecedented security. Their quiet was here and there marred by some lethal mutual intrigues in the traditional style, poison, or throwing a chief's heir down a gorge on the rocks, being favorite techniques.[2] But on the whole, chiefship was stronger than before, if not steadier. The Germans backed the chiefs with force. There were no more serious wars between chiefdoms to worry about (see Stahl 1964; Dundas 1924; and Gutmann 1926, to this general effect).

One major political consequence of the German presence had to do with the political level above the chiefdom. The Germans rewarded one Chief Marealle of Marangu, a man who had shown himself to be loyal and helpful to the Germans when their campaign against Chagga resisters was not going too well, by making him a kind of paramount chief over Vunjo and Rombo – all of Eastern Kilimanjaro (Dundas 1924:103; Stahl 1964:322–35). He thus became superchief over an enormous territory and over many other chiefs who had previously been his equals. Marealle's ascendancy was not without its uneasy moments and he spent some time in exile, but his power and importance are well remembered on the mountain even by people whose knowledge of Chagga history is quite hazy. This may be in part because the First Paramount Chief of all the Chagga who came into office in 1952 was a descendant of 'the great Marealle' and emphasized his connection with his illustrious ancestor.

Inside all the chiefdoms the German peace brought with it a considerable expansion of chiefly power, and a recasting of the chiefly role. The Chagga chiefs were expected to produce corvée labor in quantity and to collect taxes from their people for the German administration. With this came a firm power to punish tax-evaders. The lineages could no longer retaliate or move as easily as they had done in pre-colonial times. Tax collection had its profitable side. Corvée labor could be used for chiefly projects as well as colonial ones. Moreover, it was German policy to allow the chiefs a proportion of the taxes to make them more assiduous in collecting them. They were supposed to have 5 per cent (Raum 1965:177). Gutmann says that, in fact, the chiefs collected seven times as much for themselves as for the Germans (Gutmann 1926:390; H.R.A.F.tr.:351). Tax collection also had another aspect that contributed to structural change: the fact that following the German model, taxes were collected household by household, rather than as a lineage obligation (Gutmann 1926:382–5; H.R.A.F.tr.:343–5; Raum 1965:198).

In the light of these changes, what happened to the chief's court, to the Lawn of Justice and its doings? Gone was the custom of having the chief keep to his hut during the deliberations. Instead the chief presided over his own court and gave the decisions himself. He consulted with those present when he chose, but these were a very different array from the age-group assembly of earlier times. There were ordinarily present at the chiefly hearings, village officials and their assistants, confidants of the chief, and those guests who just happened to be around (Gutmann 1926:310; H.R.A.F.tr.:278). It was clearly an assemblage of persons who were in one way or another beholden to the chief or dependent upon him, his administrative subordinates and his intimate associates. Moreover, the pressing of a claim, which in pre-colonial times had invariably involved a man's lineage and its secular leaders as well as the claimant himself, could now be carried on by an individual, without involving the lineage.

Although the German presence effectively enlarged chiefly authority by backing chiefs with force, and by giving them means of bypassing lineage organization in tax and legal matters, thus weakening the lineages, at least in theory the Germans removed from the jurisdiction of the chiefs' courts the handling of capital, witchcraft, and political cases. These fell under the official jurisdiction of the German District Court (Raum 1965:184). But as there were estimated to be about 28,000 Chagga households, many of them physically distant from the centers of German administration, one may wonder how inhibiting the official restriction was in fact (Gutmann 1926:586; H.R.A.F.tr.:527).

Below the chiefly level, the traditional informal hearing

continued as before. The local headman, the neighborhood elders, and the local lineages all heard cases and decided them as informally as previously. The colonial presence undoubtedly affected this level indirectly, but detailed information is lacking.

Just as the chiefs availed themselves of their enlarged tax-enforcing power to line their own pockets, so did they exercise their stiffened authority as upholders of law with an eye to personal profit. An extreme instance that gives some of the flavor of the period was the action of the Chief of Machame who, in 1907, announced that evildoers were abroad in his chiefdom and the whole population would have to take the poison ordeal to ascertain who was guilty and who innocent. Anyone willing to confess straight away could, of course, pay a fixed fine in cattle instead. An excellent, if temporary, source of chiefly income was thus provided (Gutmann in the *Evangelisch-lutherisches Missionsblatt* (1907) as cited by Raum 1965:182). Another chief made a new rule that he be paid a head of cattle for every betrothal in the chiefdom, thereby acquiring part of all bridewealth payments (Gutmann 1926:216; H.R.A.F.tr.:109).

There were other more modest cases of chiefly greed. In one case that Gutmann heard, a poor man had repaid a cattle debt by giving his creditor his young daughter. After a time the creditor had the girl properly circumcised and married her to his son, though she was very young and, to Gutmann's appraising eye, not very well developed. This was an economical arrangement that saved the father from having to pay bridewealth for his son. But to the considerable inconvenience of all concerned, the girl was miserable and ran home to mother. The father-in-law, now once again a creditor, brought a case against the girl's father. It was heard before the Chief of Moshi. The complaining ex-father-in-law asked not only for the cow he had lost in the transaction, but for all the offspring the cow had produced in the time elapsed. 'No,' said the chief, allowing him only one cow on the ground that he had married off the girl at too early an age. The chief asserted that because he had sinned against the laws of growth, he had forfeited the right to profit from growth. However, as the girl's father had no cattle, the chief stepped into the breach, and paid the debt. But in return he appointed himself the girl's bridewealth guardian in her father's place. Eventually when she married, the chief would probably get his cow back and a good deal more (Gutmann 1926:128–30; H.R.A.F.tr.:111–13).

This case is not only interesting because of the insight it gives into the active role a chief could take in a settlement during the German period, it is also a clear example of one use of norms in decisions. The chief cites the principle that one should not sin against the laws of growth and this gives the whole decision an appearance of justice. However, while this principle may justify the decision, it does not explain it. Sinning against the laws of growth rationalized but did not require reducing to one cow what the creditor was allowed to recover. Moreover, this principle does not even begin to explain the rest of the solution, the payment of the debt by the chief and his self-appointment as bridewealth guardian of the girl. The suspicion lingers that the debt may have been reduced to one cow because the chief decided to pay it. But the reason the chief stepped in at all is probably that the complaining creditor was from another chiefdom, a fact which elevated the case of the runaway bride to the level of international diplomacy, and made it more important that the debt be paid.[3]

In German times, as before, it was necessary for chiefs to have allies, now no longer for military reasons, but still for political ones. Major questions about succession, about which chiefdoms should be consolidated with which others, about which chiefs were to be more powerful than others, continued to ferment. What in the pre-German period had been settled by a combination of wars and diplomacy, was now settled by intrigue, diplomacy, manipulation of colonial officials, and sometimes by threats and murders. There were many replacements of chiefs and changes in the air. The missions contributed to the complication of the political picture. Lutherans and Catholics were each assigned exclusive areas in which to proselytize. The areas were defined by chiefdom, so each missionary's interest in expanding as much as possible the area assigned to his church, was identical with the interest of the local chief in expanding his domain (Stahl 1964:134, 140, 199, 268, 324). On the whole, for those chiefs who succeeded in playing the game, by obtaining German approval without losing local support, and who held off or frightened off their rivals, it was a time of unprecedented wealth and power.

The changed political position of chiefs in the German colonial period had certain clear general effects on judicial action. First, the procedural change indicates that along with greater political security came far greater personal authority in the judicial role. Second, while some legal decisions undoubtedly favored those lineages or persons whose support the chief sought, and others lined the chief's pocket, what seems most evident is that as far as the political game went the highest stakes were played for outside the judicial role, and outside the chiefdom. This does not suggest that there were no politics played in the court. What it does suggest is that if one is looking at 'the processes of dispute settlement' as a *whole*, one must go beyond the settlement of ordinary law cases in courts to get a complete picture. The channeling of different kinds of disputes into different kinds of institutional frameworks for resolution involves sociological problems of considerable importance. It is only in terms of that kind of broad overview that the highly specialized role of courts can be understood.

Many more changes came to Chaggaland under the British. The forty-five years of British colonial rule, from 1916 to 1961, encompassed a period during which fundamental changes took place that affected the political position of Chagga chiefs, changes as fundamental as the coming of colonialism in the first place. The period stretches from a beginning in which local chiefs were relatively strong, at least within their own chiefdoms, to a time when an attempt was made to cut their power to the ground. This happened well before independence. It was the consequence of changes inside the tribe that tended toward the concentration and centralization of power on a political level above that of the area chiefdom. I have already commented on the existence of interchiefdom politics in pre-colonial and German times. Well before the arrival of the British, the ascendancy of Chief Marealle over all Eastern Kilimanjaro had faded. When the British took over, though there were stronger and weaker chiefdoms, there was no comparable officially recognized right of any chiefdom to tax or govern others. The British originally recognized 28 autonomous chieftaincies. Yet the level of interchiefdom politics was nevertheless to loom progressively larger and larger in Chagga political life. It was accompanied by a structural change in Chagga judicial office. From a time when the chiefs were the highest judges in each chiefdom, local chiefship survived into a period when it lost all its judicial power.

The political changes took place in the context of a phenomenal rise in population and a basic alteration of the economy brought about by widespread coffee planting. A German population estimate of 1912 put the number of Chagga homesteads on the mountain at 28,000 (Gutmann 1926:586; H.R.A.F.tr.:527) while a British District Officer's population estimate in 1953 was 230,000 (Johnston 1953:134). If one were to guess that each Chagga household had 4 or 5 members in 1912, then that would be about a doubling of the population in that period. Such figures are, of course, highly conjectural. However, anyone who has taken genealogies would be inclined to suspect that the increase may have been even greater. Prosperity, peace, increased medical facilities, and education probably all combined to produce this explosion. This population increase combined with the consolidation of chiefdoms (28 independent chiefdoms in 1924 were reduced to 19 by 1930 (Annual Report, Northern Province 1929:2)) meant that many chiefs in 1930 were ruling over larger political units than their chiefly forefathers had done.

The chief was also operating in an entirely different economic situation. In pre-colonial days, throughout the German period, and for a decade or so beyond it, cattle were a major form of wealth. Everyone had ample land on which to grow bananas and vegetables and grain. Land was plentiful. There was no reason to accumulate more than one could use. Unoccupied land could be had for the asking, or sometimes even without asking, just by cultivating. With the stepped-up planting of coffee in the 1920s, and an increasing population, land became the most precious form of wealth, and sizable amounts of cash reached everyone on the mountain.

A few Africans had tried to grow coffee in the German period, but were discouraged by taxation and marketing problems. Charles Dundas, the British administrative official who took over in 1917, wanted to help them, and with his encouragement the Chagga resumed coffee cultivation. In 1924 under the leadership of Dundas's former interpreter, Joseph Merinyo, an African coffee-marketing association was organized, the Kilimanjaro Native Planters' Association. Despite the fact that European planters were alarmed and protested, the colonial government supported the Africans and the Association grew and prospered. In fact it boomed. With the income from coffee Chagga subjects, not just Chagga chiefs, had access to substantial amounts of cash. Moreover, coffee brought with it a centralized interchiefdom organization, the K.N.C.U., that marketed coffee and regulated related matters. Probably more than a quarter of the population was producing coffee. Land replaced cattle as the most precious form of wealth. By 1932 the Kilimanjaro Native Co-operative Union, as it then became, had a membership of 11,500 Chagga. (In 1930 Griffiths (p. 129) estimated that there were 14,000 Chagga families involved in coffee-growing.)

This centralization of some economic affairs had its political and judicial parallels. At the end of the 1920s a Council of Chagga Chiefs came into existence. Initially it was not a higher executive authority over the individual chiefs constituting the council. Each chief was still the superior authority in his own chiefdom. But in 1929 the Native Treasuries of all the chiefs were amalgamated into one 'Treasury of the Chagga Council,' and the same year the Court of the Chagga Chiefs came into being. This was an appeal court for cases heard in the local chiefly courts. It was also empowered to hear some cases beyond their jurisdiction, and cases to which chiefs were parties (Annual Report, Northern Province 1929:2).

It seems more than a matter of coincidence that in 1934 the Council of Chagga Chiefs should have petitioned the British government to appoint Chief Petro Itosi of Marangu, a descendant of Marealle's, paramount chief over the whole tribe (Johnston 1953:135). The British refused as they were pushing another candidate, whom the Chagga rejected. The Chagga remained without a paramount chief until 1952, but the pressure towards centralization continued.

The Council of Chagga Chiefs came into ever-greater prominence in running affairs on the mountain. The politics in the council ultimately became of greater moment than the politics in the chiefdoms. The colonial government's Native Authority Ordinance 18 of 1926 had provided for tribal councils (Hailey 1938:441) and the Chagga chiefs subsequently availed themselves of their right under this ordinance to legislate rules. Some of these rules were clearly made to enhance chiefly power. For example, a rule was passed that transfers of land could be made with the authority of the chief (Hailey 1938:848). Though it sounds like a liberalization of the policy of land tenure, as if it permitted sales of entailed land or something of the sort, what it amounted to in practice was an increase in the chiefly power over the distribution of land. The following case from Kilema shows how this kind of rule was applied to extend administrative control over the allocation of land, a matter which had once been largely a matter of lineage discretion.

The complainant in the case, a man named Ndepachio, was suing the headman of the village because the headman had given someone else a piece of land Ndepachio said was his. The original owner of the land had given it to Ndepachio for one cow, but had done so without telling the chief or the headman of the village about the transfer. The chief of Kilema ruled that as the 'secret' transfer of land was an offense, it was hence invalid, and that the headman could consequently give the land to someone else. The chief conceded that the complainant ought to be able to recover the cow he had paid, but ruled that he had no right whatever to the land (case no. 117, Kilema, 1936).

By means of such making of rules and interpretation of rules, the chiefs gained expanded control over the distribution of land. 'Norms' have many uses. The indigenous prerogatives that chiefs had always had over the territory they ruled were more and more interpreted as rights to all unclaimed, unoccupied, or unused land. In Gluckman's terminology a chiefly estate of administration was being expanded to include an estate of production as well, in as many cases as could be interpreted this way. Chiefs' requiring to be kept informed was not only a means of enlarging chiefly control over land distribution. It also enhanced the chiefly income, for a man receiving land from the chief paid a gift of a cow to the chief and of beer to the headman. The gift was treated as confirmation of the transfer (Figgis (1957:93) says Dundas officially eliminated tribute and *upata*, the gift of thanks, but they still existed in 1957 when Figgis was writing).

Since the British were not as broadminded as the Germans had been about chiefly tax collection, and put all taxes into a Native Treasury, out of which the chiefs were paid salaries, the chiefs sought other ways of augmenting their income. The device of requiring that the chief's permission be obtained for any number of things was convenient towards this end. In a 1930 case (Mwika, Kitabu cha shauri 1927, case no. 7 of 1930) a chief fined a man for having taken a cow that had been declared by the court to be his in a previous case. The objection was not to the self-help. That was all right. What was not all right was to undertake self-help without *informing* the chief. The chief wanted not only to remain in touch with his subjects, but also to use his information for his own gain.

The rise in population substantially affected the administrative position of the chief and his access to information. In ruling over more and more people, since there was no substantial change in modes of transport and communication, chiefly control inevitably became more and more diffuse, and came to be delegated to an even greater extent to the headmen of the sections. Some of the struggle to hold on to chiefly power was focused on keeping the headmen in line, and the chief's court was used as an instrument to this end.

A number of law cases in the 1930s and 1940s concern the abuse of official position by headmen. In one, for example, a headman was prosecuted because of a goat and seven shillings that he had collected from the complainant and another person, having told them he had been sent by the chief to obtain these contributions from them (Kilema, 1947, case no. 92). He had evidently been involved in extortion of this sort several times before and had been warned by the chief that it could not continue. His technique on other occasions had been to tell people that if they paid him a suitable sum he would see that they would be exempted from personal tax on the ground of poverty. The headman in this case was fined and dismissed from office. Informants suggest that this was because he had gone much too far, not because the practice of obtaining 'contributions' and gratuities of this sort was unusual.

In another case, a headman, who was also a shopkeeper, fought with one of his customers (*Mwika Shauri Book 1927*, case dated 1931). He chased him out of his shop and beat him with a weight from the shop scale. The victim brought a case against the headman. The chief fined the headman, and also reprimanded him both for his violent behavior, and for being a bad example to others when he ought to have been a good one.

Balancing out the cases in which chiefs curbed the violence and venality of their headmen are many more in which headmen's acts are upheld and their authority reinforced by chiefly judgments. In their roles as organizers of corvée labor, the headmen often had recourse to the chief's court to ask the chief to penalize people who failed to attend to assigned public works tasks such as the digging of water furrows and the building of roads or schools (Kilema, 1947, cases 114, 117, 174; Kilema, 1937, cases 18, 56; Keni-Mriti-Mengwe, 1947, case 125, are only a few of the many examples).

Procedurally, the chiefs' courts in the early period of British colonial rule differed in general terms only slightly from those of the German period (Dundas 1924:287). The chief, or sometimes a deputy of his, presided. He was assisted by one or two or sometimes a handful of elders, often lineage heads or other important men. The British, on their guard against chiefly autocracy, insisted on the presence of some elders. This was clearly also in keeping with earlier custom. Sometimes headmen were also present if the case was a particularly important one. The parties presented their cases informally and answered questions by the elders. Opinions were then rendered by the elders after which the chief gave judgment.

Two important procedural shifts took place after this early British colonial period. One had to do with the role of the elders and the other with the keeping of records. In the early period the elders had much more autonomy and a more active role in the whole proceeding and the making of decisions (Dundas 1924:287). As time went on the chiefs, though they often acted through deputies, tightened their control over the courts including their control over the appointment of elders. One of the constitutional reforms of 1946 was the introduction of the principle that elders in the area chiefs' courts should be elected by the people, not appointed by the chiefs. Johnston, the District Officer, comments that thereafter 'in practice "election" was often nominal only' (1953:135).

Written records of all cases in the chiefs' courts were kept from the late 1920s on, and a great many of these records are still in existence and accessible. These often mention various sorts of informal hearings before kinsmen, local elders, and neighbors which preceded bringing the case to the chief's court. Field observation confirmed the continued importance of these informal procedures today.

The cases which have been presented here are a very few, selected out of hundreds of others, because of their direct reflection of certain political aspects of Chagga judicial office. On the surface, at least, many of the others do not seem to involve special political issues. They are bridewealth cases, agistment cases, loans, disputes over the boundaries of land and such. These may have had local political significance but one cannot tell from the decisions themselves. The clearly political cases such as those described here speak for themselves about the ways in which chiefs could and did use their position as judges to define and enforce their power.

How did they come to lose that power and the judicial role that helped make it effective? In a very condensed form what happened was this: In 1946 under pressure from the few very powerful chiefs, from the new educational élite, and from the Colonial Government, the Chagga Council agreed to a constitutional reform in which it abolished itself. The mountain was divided into 3 sections administered by 3 separate Divisional Councils. Each of these was to be headed by a Divisional Chief, elected by the Chagga Council before it disbanded. But the catch was that above the Divisional Councils the 3 Divisional Chiefs were to rule over all of Kilimanjaro, aided by a small special council which they virtually controlled, and from which the local area chiefs were excluded. The Divisional Chiefs also had judicial functions. In short the local chiefs became subchiefs (Johnston 1953).

By permitting a higher level of government to come into existence the local area chiefs took a step towards their own undoing. The real focus of power was now elevated to a higher organizational level, and the local area chiefs' strength faded accordingly. The reform was presented as one necessary for administrative efficiency. It also served very effectively the ends of those chiefs who were elevated to the Divisional Chiefships. They had been very powerful members of the Chagga Council, hence their election was the culmination of long years of political maneuvering. (Two of these were men who had been candidates for the paramountcy in 1934.) This was the beginning of the end. The pyramiding of power continued, for very soon afterwards a popular political movement called the Kilimanjaro Citizens' Union began a campaign for the election of a paramount chief. Despite its seemingly traditional objective, it was essentially anti-chiefly in sentiment, or at least it served as an organizational focus for the very widespread feelings against chiefs found on the mountain. The movement was organized by two commoners; one was the same Joseph Merinyo who had started the coffee-marketing organization. They had as a candidate a man who fulfilled the requirements of chiefly legitimacy, being a grandson of the Marangu chief whom the Germans had made a paramount in their time, but who had never been an area chief, who had lived away from Kilimanjaro during much of his adult life, and who had been educated at a British university. He thus combined the qualities of modernity and tradition and yet was untainted by any association with the actual exercise of chiefly power, something for everyone. The bid for traditional support was absolutely fundamentalist. The Union promised the lineages a restoration of their old prominence (Keni-Mriti-Mengwe Political File Letter no. 72; Figgis Report 1957–8:27, 34, 41 speaks of the fact that the 'clans' were the subject of a modern political revivalist movement). The Union could thus be against the abuses of traditional chiefly power, yet be reassuringly traditional. On the other hand, there was a bid for the support of the educated élite with promises of modernity and efficiency. The Citizens' Union Candidate ran for the Paramountcy against the 3 Divisional Chiefs and won the election. In 1952 he was duly installed as the first (and last, as it turned out) Paramount Chief of all the Chagga.

As early as 1950 one of the planks in the Citizens' Union platform had been the separation of the executive from the judiciary. The government had proposed it earlier in the year and had met with 'a mixed popular reception' (Johnston 1953:136). However, the Citizens' Union took up the cause and eventually put it through. One of the first acts of the Chagga Council under the administration of the Paramount was to separate the judiciary from the executive in as many chiefdoms as could be persuaded to do so. The chiefs were to be replaced by magistrates. Appointments to the Magistracy were to be made directly by the Chagga Council, and appeals from the magistrates' court were eventually to come before a committee of the Council. The change was very soon put into effect in 7 of the 16 chiefdoms, and others followed later. It was the end of the career of Chagga chiefs as judges.[4]

Conclusions

What conclusions does a review of this Chagga historical material suggest? What does it imply about legal typology? Certainly any simple opposition of ideal types is difficult to use. How is one to place a complex of varied dispute settlement techniques in a bipolar continuum? How is one, moreover, to classify simply a complicated historical sequence?

Reviewing this part of Chagga history makes it amply clear that judicial activities must be considered in terms of political context. The political setting in which courts operate is generally the source of judicial authority and indeed in a large measure determines their character. What is most striking about the Chagga historical sequence is that basic changes of legal procedure invariably accompanied other basic changes in political organization. Crudely divided, these may be said to fall into three phases: *the pre-colonial* in which the chief's pronouncement was often, in form at least, an enunciation of the collective judgment of the age-group assembly, and disputes were often settled in other ways that avoided the open exercise of chiefly authority; *the colonial period until 1952*, in which the chief, or his deputy, made his own decisions, in consultation with a few advisers, to whose opinions he accorded greater or lesser importance as he chose; and *the end, from 1952*, when judicial decisions were no longer to be made by chiefs, but by magistrates appointed by the Chagga Council. To this one may append the more recent formal shift to a national judicial system since independence.

These judicial changes were all ancillary to shifts in the direction of political consolidation of smaller units into larger ones and of increasing centralization of control. In pre-colonial times the largest corporate unit was the chiefdom, consisting of localized lineage settlements unified by a cross-cutting age-grade system and common loyalty to a chief. Unitary action under chiefly leadership was taken regularly when the fighting age-grade was mobilized for cattle-raiding and slave-raiding wars. Chiefly political maneuvering lay in alternately cajoling and commanding subordinate lineage and local groups, in maintaining a monopoly on the slave and ivory trade, and in control over other external relations.

During the first part of the colonial period, before the widespread cultivation of coffee, control in the hands of the local chiefs not only continued, but was intensified. The military age-grade lost its former significance. Obviously, both the sources and expressions of chiefly power shifted because of the presence and policies of European administrations. Chiefs, backed and directed from the outside, used their taxing, their labor-mobilizing, and their judicial authority to consolidate their positions within their chiefdoms.

Later, in the second colonial phase, the introduction of coffee cultivation and the marketing of coffee from all chiefdoms through a central co-operative brought connected political developments. It brought changes in the direction of a progressive consolidation of all the chiefdoms into a single administrative unit. Ultimately, from 1946 on, all Chagga chiefdoms were joined and capped by a completely centralized Chagga administration.

Local chiefs were concomitantly downgraded. Today all Tanzanian chiefly offices have been abolished and political centralization is being pressed on a national scale.

Basic alterations in the processes of dispute settlement were precisely parallel to these basic political changes. Both colonial governments and the Chagga chiefs themselves treated the courts as an important arm of their political power. Should anthropologists do any less? Presumably not. (See Barnes (1969) to the same effect on the political use of courts.)

Some may reply that Gulliver was using 'political' in a different and special sense. So he was, some of the time. In the typology Gulliver applied 'political' to the kind of dispute settlement used by the Arusha, in which political groups confronted each other, but also to any biased decision by a judge. I suggest that these two uses are very different and should be emphatically distinguished. The biased decision of a judge and the pressured settlement worked out between two political entities are combined in Gulliver's scheme not because of any positive similarity between them, but because, according to his criteria, they are both examples of disputes decided on some basis other than norms. The 'judicial' type presumes that norms can be 'applied' very simply and of themselves can determine the outcome of cases in ordinary judicial proceedings. One can take too literally the occasions when judges use norms to explain their decisions. Judicial explanations are not always adequate sociological explanations of judges' choices.

Considering the Chagga and Arusha examples there seems no reason to try to characterize one process or period as more 'political' than another. It may be useful instead to separate some purely procedural distinctions from other criteria. On this basis two kinds of settlement are distinguishable immediately: the settlement arrived at through bargaining between opposed social units, and the one arrived at through authoritative decision. The political implications of each are a separate issue.

In analyzing the Chagga chiefly role as it moved from presiding *in absentia* over somewhat Arusha-like bargaining procedures in the age-group assembly, to a period of more authoritative judicial decision, it would be impossible to say which process of dispute settlement had the greater political implications. Their bargaining procedures and authoritative decisions were equally imbedded in the political background.

There is obviously no necessary connection between bargaining as such and politics. In our society many disputes are settled by private bargaining that never expands to involve political units, officials, or public issues. But bargaining procedures can be political, and it is a very important point that Gulliver makes when he emphasizes that the most mundane law cases can be an occasion for political confrontation in acephalous societies. Arusha disputes certainly did involve politics. Bargaining, then, as a means of settling disputes can be but is not always political.

Authoritative decisions of disputes are another matter. Except for arbitration situations, where the parties themselves endow the arbitrator with decisive power, the authority to settle disputes and enforce the settlement is generally allocated in some political context. Chagga chiefs acting in their capacity as judges were asserting political prerogatives. The Chagga magistrates who replaced them in 1952 were exercising authority allocated to them by the Colonial Government, the Paramount Chief, and the Chagga Council. Every settlement of dispute by such an authority is political at least to the extent that it reiterates the right to exercise authority and asserts the legitimacy of the political entity that allocated the authority.

That political entity may be more or less well established. Its power may be expanding or contracting. It may be fighting to maintain itself or it may be virtually unchallenged. These considerations affect the decision of dispute, both in shaping the regular procedures and in coloring the decisions of particular issues.

To recognize this political element is to recognize that there are always several things going on simultaneously in the public resolution of dispute. One of these is the reiteration of persisting relationships that obtain in the society quite outside situations of dispute. To the extent that it is regular and public, procedure is bound to embody some aspects of political organization. This is true whether the proceeding is entirely a confrontation between opposed parties and their supporters, or whether it takes place before a judge or other authority.

A second thing that is going on in any law case is the struggle between the parties over particular issues. If the position of the parties, the authority, or the nature of the issues (explicit or implicit) are a matter of concern in public affairs then the struggle between them may be a political matter in itself. Thus the political qualities of a dispute may reside in three distinct elements: *the procedures*, *the persons*, and *the issues*. In particular societies or particular cases, these may not all be obviously separated because of replications among them. But for comparative analysis these distinctions are necessary. One can easily see their applicability to the various historical phases of the Chagga data, and the variety of Chagga cases.

In bargaining procedures at the 'political' end of Gulliver's continuum, the pressured settlement is the result of the ordinary procedure. It follows from the procedure in the ideal type, from the nature of confrontation itself. At the 'judicial' end of the continuum the pressured or biased decision, the 'political' element, is a deviation from the ordinary procedure, an improper departure from the ideal type which 'ought' to make its decisions on the basis of norms. Thus Gulliver has addressed himself to the question of the 'normal' relation between politics and procedures at one end of the continuum only, the 'political' end. It is quite natural, since Gulliver's ethnographic focus is on the Arusha, that the 'political' type should be more closely worked out than the 'judicial' type in his discussion. But clearly the ordinary relation between politics and procedures is as deserving of attention at the 'judicial' end of the continuum.

As was implied earlier, an inspection of the Chagga material suggests that it may not be as useful analytically to postulate a system of decisions entirely based on norms as one might at first suppose. Judicial decisions often are not 'simple' applications of norms. Yet the complex structure of normative decision only emerges if one approaches the whole question by separating the *reference* to norms in legal disputes from the issue whether norms actually *determine* the outcome. The determining place of norms in judicial decision cannot be assumed. It must be examined.

Obviously, the reference to norms is commonplace in judicial reasoning. Many of the Chagga cases alluded to in this paper referred to norms. But given what we know of the political setting in which they were made, it would seem that the norms were sometimes more justifications than reasons. The most venal of Chagga chiefs making the most self-interested of decisions usually did so while invoking accepted, or at any rate, politically legitimated principles of conduct. In other cases the same chiefs may well have been invoking norms more disinterestedly, but that is not to say that the norms mentioned invariably determined the decision. In either kind of case, the form of the decision and the reasons for decision not only can be, but ought to be separated for analytic purposes.

The analogy to the use of norms in bargaining procedures is clear. Gulliver tells us norms are always cited in argument in Arusha disputes, but cannot be said to determine the content of settlements (1963:241). It is surely as important to distinguish the reference to norms from the determinants of decision in judges' opinions as it is in bargaining settlements.

But it is certainly true that judicial decisions ordinarily *refer* to norms, and refer to them as if they were the ground of decision. Why is this done? Where judges have the power to *force* compliance with their orders, why does tradition so often require that they give explanations and rationales of such orders? These explanations would seem to be, at least in part, a way of soliciting approval for the exercise of authority, a way of legitimating it.

Norms are many things at once. They are, of course, in part, commonly stated rules and principles for conduct. But as such they are also a part of that body of ideas that represents society and social life as if it were an orderly system. Commonly stated norms are one part of the 'collective representations' of society. Whether particular norms are or are not specifically the reasons for a particular court decision, the *reference* to norms places the court and its decisions in a wide framework of legitimacy. Using Smith's Weberian nomenclature (1956) it can camouflage any exercise of power as a simple exercise of authority. The reference to norms removes the onus from the judge. *It seeks to tie a particular decision by a particular judge to the concept of the social order itself.* So interpreted, the reference to norms is as much a justification for the existence of the court, for the very power to exercise authority, as it is a justification for the particular decision.

In pre-colonial times when Chagga chiefs announced a decision, they emphasized that they were merely expressing the collective will of the assembled age-grades. In later times, when there were no such assemblies, their allusion to ideal norms of conduct would seem to have somewhat the same function. The analogy to our society is clear. By alluding to norms, the judge is saying that it is not the judge but the 'law' that decides cases. The allusion to norms is in many respects an enunciation of *symbolic consensus*. One may learn a lot about norms from cases. But it is not always possible to learn much about the reasons from the norms a case cites.

Certainly, at least from German times to the present, there is evidence that norms have been regularly invoked for Chagga decisions. But the inspection of even a few Chagga cases involving the scope of chiefly power and headmen's authority demonstrates the fallacy of taking normative statements literally as the simple bases of judicial decision. I infer that these particular political cases demonstrate crudely what is often more subtly present in other judicial cases, a difference between rationales of decision and reasons for decision. Only by treating judicial explanation as analytically distinct from the reasons for judicial action will it be possible for anthropologists to study legal institutions and legal 'events' as they have other facets of social life.

This is not to say that the norms cited by judges are invariably detectable as rationalizations, but they often are. Nor is it to say that when judges make decisions they invariably do so out of the crudest 'self-interest.' Their decisions may be affected by the way they perceive their role in complex social and political circumstances, and these perceptions may weight their choices in subtle ways. Some of these matters are accessible to sociological investigation, and involve categories of judges, and categories of cases, not simply variations of individual motive. As Gluckman has shown in *The Judicial Process* judges must choose among norms, some of them conflicting, many of them vague and ambiguous, and must decide which to apply to the case before them. Judges, in short, have very wide opportunities to make choices in deciding cases. Yet they almost invariably explain their decisions as if there were no choice, as if the decision followed inevitably from the very existence of the norms cited.

The relationship between norms and judicial decisions is extremely complex, much more complex than judicial opinions make it seem, and much more complex than Gulliver's 'judicial' type makes it seem. One cannot simply make two categories, biased decisions and norm-applying decisions. Even the most biased decisions usually are affected by some norms, and some biases ordinarily affect norm-applying decisions. Decision-making is not in any circumstances a simple process, and judicial decisions are no exception. When anthropologists are looking for sociological explanations of witchcraft or religious phenomena, they do not hesitate to probe beyond explicit indigenous assertions. The legal pronouncements of judges, however rational and logical in style, should be accorded investigation of the same depth.

Unpublished sources

Case Files Kilimanjaro Primary Courts. A large collection of these files is in the Faculty Library of the Law School of the University College, Dar es Salaam. In theory, this collection includes all files earlier than the mid-1950s. In fact, some early files may still be found at the courts on Kilimanjaro themselves. Records date from the late 1920s onward. Post mid-1950s files are all still in the courthouses on Kilimanjaro. The cases are all recorded in Swahili. About 19 courts are involved. There are thousands of cases in all.

File of Political Correspondence, Baraza of Keni-Mriti-Mengwe
    Letter no. 71 is dated 13 January 1958 and is from an elder in the entourage of the Paramount. It declares that all lineages should have their original common land, and that the matter of the restoration of these lands to the lineages Kimaresi and Mtaresi should be reserved for discussion until the Chairman of the Kilimanjaro Citizens' Union, N. P. Njau, could come to Rombo and hear the matter.
    Letter no. 72 dated 25 January 1958 is from N. P. Njau, and concerns a meeting at which it was decided who was to be considered head of the Makidoho lineage, of which there were 3 sublineages having from 31 to 51 members each. It is partly a record of the meeting, partly a letter of advice.

Figgis. T. F., *Chagga Land Tenure Report 1957–58.* Mimeographed report. Survey done at the behest of the government. Copy in the possession of P. H. Gulliver, School of Oriental and African Studies, University of London.

Griffiths, A. W. M., *Land Tenure, Moshi District.* Typed report of District Officer, 1930. Copy in the possession of P. H. Gulliver, School of Oriental and African Studies, University of London.

Minutes of the Chagga Council. Available at the offices of the Kilimanjaro District Council, Moshi, Tanzania.

Annual Report, Northern Province for 1929 dated 16 January 1930.

Typescript in National Archives, Dar es Salaam, file no. 18693, vol. 1919. Some of the details in the typed reports were edited out of later printed versions, hence where available these typescript originals were consulted.

Notes

1   There are problems concerning the designation of the agglomerations of Chagga kin. The literature in English refers to them as 'clans' as do the Chagga when they speak English. For the most part, they are named exogamous patrilineal units able to trace relationships within them. Hence 'lineage' is probably the most appropriate name for them. But not infrequently there are several branches residing in different parts of the mountain. The relationship between such branches is not always traceable although kinship is acknowledged. Whether they are alluding to all the branches or to one localized branch only, the Chagga use a single term whether they are speaking Kichagga, Swahili, or English. But the significant unit in social life today is the localized branch, the lineage. A census conducted in 1968 showed that of 172 households, over half were living in localized agnatic clusters of kin of 14 households or more. Of the 172, 150 households were in clusters of 5 or more. There were only 8 solitary households without agnatic kin immediately around them. Of the smaller clusters, many have hived off from larger lineage groups living quite nearby.

Presumably the localization of lineages was at least as great, if not greater, in earlier times.

2   One man in Mwika today describes how the heir of the chiefdom of Nganyeni was killed by aides of the chief of neighboring Kinyamvuo. The Chief of Kinyamvuo, Mangi Lengaki, then became chief of both. This took place in German times. The heir was thrown into a gorge when he was on his way to Marangu to visit Marealle.

3   Admittedly this is a secondhand account, and hence may be incomplete, but I wanted to include a case of this period, and it is doing double duty. I have read and heard enough Chagga cases (and American ones) to know how often a general principle is invoked to explain quite specific decisions, decisions that the principle itself could not *determine*, but does justify or rationalize.

4   Liebenow (1958) reports that by 1958 all but three had replaced the chiefs with magistrates (p. 76). But I found that the minutes of the Chagga Council of 3 May 1961 indicates that there were still six chiefdoms in 1961 in which the chiefs appointed their deputies as judges and that the Council agreed at that date that there should be magistrates all over the mountain.

Chapter 7

Law and anthropology

The classification of legal systems

Since this is the first article on law to appear in the *Biennial Review*, it seems fitting to consider at some length the major themes that have preoccupied anthropologists working in the law field before presenting a summary of the literature of the last two years. The limitations of space make it impossible to write a comprehensive history. Rather than presenting a catalog of names, I have undertaken a more expanded discussion of the work of a few people whose books encompass the major themes of the field. Even in reviewing the current literature, I have chosen to omit most of the purely descriptive works in favor of those that raise analytic problems. I assume that others find it as difficult as I do to make sociological sense of lists of disembodied legal rules floating on their own, cut off from the social body of which they were once a part. Hence, though I shall mention some work of this kind, I shall pass over most of it. Comprehensiveness has been sacrificed in the interest of comprehensibility. The selected Bibliography at the end of this paper includes some of the significant works that could not be discussed in the body of the article.

Examining different approaches to the classification of legal systems may give us some idea of the magnitude of law as a subject, and of the ways in which anthropologists have perceived

Reprinted from *Biennial Review of Anthropology, 1969*, edited by Bernard J. Siegel with the permission of the publishers, Stanford University Press. Copyright © 1970 by the Board of Trustees of the Leland Stanford Junior University.

the field as a whole. No society is without law; *ergo*, there is no society outside the purview of the 'legal anthropologist.' It is not merely difficult but virtually impossible to control the full range of the available ethnographic information. Every good ethnographic description contains a great deal of legal material, whether or not it is explicitly called 'law.' (Nader, Koch, and Cox 1966 have tried to sort the specialized works from the others in an annotated bibliography.) Not only does every society have law, but virtually all significant social institutions also have a legal aspect. This means that to master the whole legal system of one society, procedural and substantive, one must master the whole institutional system of that society – from citizenship and political place to property and economic relations, from birth to death, and from dispute to peaceful transaction.

One's approach to classifying legal systems may thus depend on whether one sees the problem in terms of the kinds of society in which law operates, or in terms of the distribution of specific procedures or concepts or rules. The first, the attention to social context, is very much the anthropologist's approach, the second very much more the approach of the scholar-lawyer who specializes in comparative law. There is some overlap, of course; but whatever is special about the anthropologist's point of view lies in his tendency to see the legal system as part of a wider social milieu. And since anthropologists have differing ideas of what makes up the mainspring of the social clockwork, they also differ in their approaches to classifying legal systems.

Because law pervades so much of social life, the major writers in the field have used a variety of approaches to the material, classifying it differently for different analytic purposes. There have been essentially three kinds of classification: (1) a dichotomy founded on the basic differences in social organization between technologically simple and technologically complex societies; (2) an evolutionary series focusing on legal concomitants of the development from decentralized to centralized political systems, e.g., enforcement procedures, courts, and codes; (3) a procedural dichotomy, which contrasts dispute settlements hammered out or bargained out between the disputants themselves (often with supporters and allies on each side) and dispute settlements made by a third party having authority over both disputants.

The first kind of classification mentioned above might be called the Maine–Durkheim–Gluckman tradition. These men cut the cake in half. They divide societies into two great types, and see the development of law as closely related to the differences between these types. For Maine (1861), the division is between kin-based and territorially based organization. Durkheim (1893) distinguishes societies on the basis of their having either mechanical or organic social cohesion – a cohesion founded on a multiplicity of identical units as against one based on the integration of differentiated units. Gluckman (1955a, 1965b, 1965c) sees a division between 'tribal' societies and differentiated societies: tribal societies have a simple technology and a social system dominated by multiplex relations; differentiated societies have a complex technology and a social system in which single-interest relations are of predominant importance. Gluckman (1965b) has argued that differences in social context between the legal systems of tribal societies and those of differentiated societies not only have procedural consequences, but also are marked by certain differences in basic legal concepts.

Another tradition of classification is exemplified by Diamond and Hoebel, two writers very different from each other but having in common the fact that they both classify legal systems into a whole social series (Diamond 1935, 1951, 1965; Hoebel 1954). To Diamond, who is an orthodox Lewis Henry Morgan evolutionist, the series is either historical or quasi-historical. He attempts to identify what he considers to be the legal concomitants of each stage, from savagery through barbarism to civilization. Courts, for example, are said to appear at the first agricultural stage. As constricted as one may find the Diamond framework because of its adherence to the rigidities of an early evolutionism, and irritating as is its use of isolated traits taken from all over the library (the world), there is no doubt that many of the kinds of questions Diamond has raised have not yet been thoroughly investigated by other anthropologists. It is not yet possible to specify in detail in what kinds of social settings 'courts' are found, or the conditions that produce hearing processes of various kinds. The careful comparisons that have been made for kinship institutions have never been made for legal institutions.

For Hoebel (1954), the social series is both morphological and historical, and consists of a sequence from simple to complex, from decentralized to centralized, from what he calls 'private law' to 'public law.' As he sees it, the great historical change is from systems of self-help operating in the absence of government to systems of law enforcement by public officials in centralized polities. He emphasizes the development of the organs of government and their role in enforcement. Hoebel's series is orderly and consistent in so far as this criterion is used; but it is far less clear when he also tries to take into account the system of cultural values in each society he describes. On occasion Gluckman (1965c) has also looked on the field as a series, largely in terms of techniques for maintaining order in societies ranging from the stateless through chiefdoms and kingdoms. (For an attempt to sort out societies and legal systems on the basis of complexity, see Schwartz and Miller 1964.)

The third kind of classification again divides the field of inquiry into two types, but narrows the subject to 'dispute settlement systems,' rather than looking at the whole field of law. Gulliver (1963) calls his two polar types 'political' and 'judicial.' In the political type of dispute settlement system, there is no judge; disputes are settled by a mutual testing of the two parties' social strength, and the outcome is not determined by norms to any significant degree. In the judicial type, there is a judge, who has the authority and obligation to hand down a decision settling the case on the basis of given norms. Gulliver postulates a series of gradations between the two polar types. Bohannan (1957, 1965, 1967) has made an analogous but somewhat wider division, which applies as much to disputes between groups as it does to those between individuals. He divides power systems into unicentric and multicentric types. In unicentric power systems, there is a central locus of legal authority, which settles disputes through the exercise of that authority. Bicentric or multicentric power systems, which include the law of stateless societies and international law, are characterized by the absence of any superordinate authority. All these typologies narrow the focus to certain differences in the settlement process, rather than treating the wider field considered by the classifications mentioned earlier. On this dispute settlement side of procedure (as opposed to the enforcement side), Gluckman (1965c) has followed Llewellyn and Hoebel (1941) in placing the champion-at-law, the intermediary, the negotiator, the mediator, the conciliator, and the arbitrator on a scale of increasing authoritativeness – a series culminating in the judicial process itself.

Obviously, all of these various classifications are coping with a series, either by setting up a graduated progression from one pole to another or by characterizing the two poles themselves. It will also readily be seen that the core of most of these systems of classification is legal procedure, perhaps because the relationship between political structure and procedure comes through clearly. The general classification of substantive rules and concepts is a much more complex task, and is much less frequently tackled by anthropologists, though Gluckman (1965b) attempted something of the sort when he sought to identify some of the legal concepts peculiar to tribal society from his Barotse material.

The underlying premise of all of this classification is that there is an intimate relation between law and society, that law is part of social life in general and must be treated analytically as such. Though the cruder contrasts between the legal arrangements in 'simple' and 'complex' societies have been known for at least a century, much remains to be worked out about the range of variations and combinations. But that is by no means the only task ahead.

Definitions of the law

Besides examining the classification of types of legal system, we can get some idea of academic preoccupations in the field of law and anthropology by looking at the various ways in which the field has been defined at various times, considering not only formal definitions of law, but the kind of work people have actually done. This exercise is not intended to arrive at some better definition, nor to produce a critique of past ones, but rather to look through these definitions at the historical development of the subject, in order to see how it arrived at its present state.

Though some detailed descriptive works existed on the law of exotic peoples (e.g., Barton 1919 on the Ifugao, and Gutmann 1926 on the Chagga), it was not until Malinowski's *Crime and Custom in Savage Society* (1926) that anything written on law by an anthropologist achieved a wide audience and raised serious theoretical questions. With a few bold strokes Malinowski told the world his idea of what law was, why people obeyed it when they did, and why, sometimes, they did not. Malinowski was indignant about theories of primitive law like Hartland's (1924), which asserted that primitive man automatically obeyed the customs of his tribe because he was absolutely bound by tradition. Malinowski was little concerned with prohibitions and sanctions, but instead was struck by the positive inducements to conformity to be found in reciprocal obligations, complementary rights, and good reputation. He perceived the social and economic stake of the man who wished to remain in good standing among his fellows as the dynamic force behind the performance of obligations. But if the law is so much the stuff of ordinary social life that it is embodied in all binding obligations, then nothing but a full account of social relations in a society will adequately 'explain' the content and workings of its law. In a way, this is quite true, and is continuously being rediscovered.

Malinowski was dealing with the aspect of social control that resides in the mutuality and reciprocity of social obligations. There is more to social control than that, but Malinowski offered clear, new information, presented in a simple prose and illuminated with exotic Trobriand anecdotes. He burst on the world at a time when dullish debates were going on over whether there was such a thing as law at all in primitive societies. Lowie (1927) expended some print on that tiresome question, and others have since. The gist of Lowie's statement was a pleading argument that there were indeed such things as family law, property law, law of associations, and law of the state in pre-industrial societies.

There are several paradoxes in the short-term effect of Malinowski's work. *Crime and Custom* excited enormous interest outside the field of anthropology – particularly among academically minded lawyers, whose outlook was broadened considerably. It was almost certainly owing to Malinowski's influence that virtually all subsequent works of jurisprudence came to include some introductory sections or remarks on primitive law. This attention to law as a phenomenon existing outside the traditional sphere of European-style legislatures, codes, courts, and police was something new and important. But even so, many recent works on jurisprudence (Paton 1951), which include such discussions, treat the law of technologically simple societies as the historical or typological precursor of modern law – as an early stage subsequently replaced by that supposed apogee of excellence, the Western European tradition, or perhaps still better, the Anglo-American tradition. The law of pre-industrial society is not examined to see whether it operates on sociological principles that apply equally well to some aspects of social control in industrial society. On the contrary, it is treated as a phenomenon that has been superseded, rendered obsolete by later improvements. In Dennis Lloyd's *Introduction to Jurisprudence* (1965) the work of Maine, Malinowski, Hoebel, and Gluckman appears in a section on 'Custom and the Historical School,' which deals largely with the relation between custom and law. Lloyd's treatment is far more sophisticated than Paton's (1951), but it is still far from extracting any general sociological significance from the study of societies quite different from our own.

Malinowski's work, then, persuaded people outside the anthropological field that there was such a thing as law in non-industrial societies, and prepared the way for the reception of the work of Hoebel and Gluckman. But this knowledge was received only to be placed in a very narrow niche reserved essentially for exotica and historical background, rather than being understood as something that might have theoretical relevance to the present, either because of similarities or because of contrasts in systems. In a way, Malinowski's ideas suffered the common fate of many cultural innovations. When exported from anthropology and introduced into another discipline, jurisprudence, anthropological ideas were interpreted in ways that would disrupt pre-existing jurisprudential schemes as little as possible; they were selectively incorporated, but not used very creatively.

Within anthropology, the conception of law that Malinowski propounded was so broad that it was virtually indistinguishable from a study of the obligatory aspect of all social relationships. It could almost be said that by its very breadth and blurriness of conception Malinowski's view made it difficult to separate out or define as law any special provinces of study. Law was not distinguished from social control in general. Schapera (1957) has reviewed all of Malinowski's 'theories of law,' by which he means Malinowski's definitions, and concludes that anthropologists in general have rejected Malinowski's way of defining the field. Schapera (1957:153-4) lists some of the most famous definitions of other anthropologists as follows:

Some of those working in societies with constituted judicial institutions restrict the term either to 'any rule of conduct likely to be enforced by the courts' [Schapera 1938:38] or to 'the whole reservoir of rules ... on which the judges draw for their decisions' [Gluckman 1955a:164]. Wider definitions have been suggested by others, to include societies lacking courts or similar specialized agencies of enforcement. Radcliffe-Brown [1952:208,

212]... adopting Pound's definition ('social control through the systematic application of the force of politically organized society'), speaks of sanctions as legal 'when they are imposed by a constituted authority, political, military or ecclesiastic,' and adds that 'The obligations imposed on individuals in societies where there are no legal sanctions will be regarded as matters of custom or convention, but not of law.'... Hoebel [1954:28], again, says that 'A social norm is legal if its neglect or infraction is regularly met, in threat or in fact, by the application of physical force by an individual or group possessing the socially recognized privilege of so acting.'

Although differing in detail, the definitions just quoted all agree, in contrast with Malinowski, that the essential characteristic of 'law' is socially approved use of force.... The implication is that Malinowski's definition, in *Crime and Custom*, is not on the whole acceptable to his colleagues.

For all the legal, anthropological, and academic attention that *Crime and Custom* received it staked out a wider field of inquiry than anthropologists were ready to consider as an undivided whole, and pointed to sociological problems that students of jurisprudence were not prepared to consider outside the exotic Trobriand setting.

More recent formal definitions of law are as much at variance with the legal conceptions of Malinowski as are those of Schapera, Gluckman, Hoebel, and Radcliffe-Brown. Bohannan (1965) sees law as 'doubly institutionalized,' as that 'body of binding obligations ... which has been reinstitutionalized within the legal institution.' The legal institution is that body that settles disputes and counteracts flagrant abuses of social rules. For Bohannan, then, the difference between legal and other rules is that legal rules are given double legitimacy: they exist as rules in social institutions, but become law only when they are enforced by legal institutions. Pospisil (1958) defines law as 'rules or modes of conduct made obligatory by some sanction which is imposed and enforced for their violation by a controlling authority.' Bohannan, then, emphasizes legal institutions, Pospisil the potential sanctions emanating from a controlling authority. Not only do both authors obviously take into account the element of force, which Malinowski passed over lightly, but like some of their predecessors, they also stress an institutional context in which dispute settlement and law enforcement take place. The curious result of Bohannan's definition is to focus on the institutions of enforcement and repair, and to divorce these from the rules, norms, and principles that are a part of ordinary social life. Pospisil's definition does not have this effect, but its stress on authority raises problems in the analysis of legal relationships between social units where there is no supervening authority.

Pospisil (1967) has gone further in describing the internal affairs of groups, and has spoken of a multiplicity of legal systems to which individuals are subject, each system being part of the apparatus of a particular group. M. G. Smith (1966) makes an analogous argument when he asserts that corporations are the framework of law. Some anthropologists have urged the use of H. L. A. Hart's definition (1961), which combines a rule approach to obligation with a rule approach to institutions (Kuper and Kuper 1965). Hart conceives of law as a combination of primary rules of obligation with secondary rules of recognition, change, and adjudication.

Definitions of law, then, have moved from the broad and somewhat vague Malinowskian definitions that speak of the mutual rights and obligations of individuals, and of the sanctions and incentives residing in ordinary social relationships, to relatively recent specialized definitions that emphasize not only force, but also the institutional and organizational contexts of legal obligation. This is an important change because it also reflects the direction in which a good deal of research work has gone. An even more recent definition is that of Michael Barkun, a political scientist, whose writing is strongly influenced by anthropological work. He says, 'Law is that system of manipulable symbols that functions as a representation, as a model of social structure' (Barkun 1968:98). To the extent that Barkun *restricts* law to a symbolic system, I find his definition too limited; but as an addition to previous definitions it has merit. Its principal deficiency is that it does not, by itself, give a place to the organizational and action contexts in which the symbols are used. It does not face the problem of specifying the special aspects of social structure with which the law deals. However, although the formal definitions of law in anthropology have not caught up with practice, recent writings in anthropology have often been preoccupied with the ideas in law and the way they are used (Bohannan 1957, Gluckman 1965b, Moore 1958). Barkun's definition thus embodies in an extreme form one aspect of current work.

The concept of law implicit in empirical studies

This brings us to the emphases in the actual work that has been done, as opposed to those in the formal definitions so far constructed. In *Crime and Custom*, Malinowski (1926) used his Trobriand data not so much to describe legal rules themselves, but to illustrate the process by which people were constrained to adhere to rules and customs; he was not concerned with reporting the rules for their own sake. More than a decade later, by contrast, one of the landmarks in the law-anthropology field was a careful and thorough report on legal rules, Schapera's *Handbook of Tswana Law and Custom* (1938). This book is significant on several scores. Not only did it set an unprecedented standard for the detailed reporting of rules, but it did so without the slightest nod in the direction of theoretical questions, simply proceeding in a businesslike manner to describe as succinctly as possible such rules of law as were enforced by the Tswana, as well as the social organization, constitution, and court system that implemented these rules. The book's format was guided by its purpose. It was not written primarily for anthropologists, but was undertaken at the request of the Administration of the Bechuanaland Protectorate, 'to place on record, for the information and guidance of Government officials and of the Tswana themselves, the traditional and modern laws and related customs of the Tswana tribes' (p. xxv).

There have been many books like Schapera's since, particularly in the field of African law, but few match it in quality. For our present purposes it has twofold importance. First, it represents, at its best, one lawyer-like genre of description, a setting out of 'customary' rules. Second, because it was conceived and executed for applied and practical purposes, it is a type of record that is still very much in demand, and one that continues to be made in areas where the indigenous law has not heretofore been recorded in writing. One could argue, with some professional vanity, that because Schapera's work was done by an anthropologist who had completed a field study of the peoples whose law he was recording, it is superior to many other attempts to do the same thing by non-anthropologists.

In 1943, Schapera published a monograph on tribal legislation among the Tswana, and this remains the only large work on legislation in an African tribe. The subject of this monograph, like that of the *Handbook*, is of considerable practical interest. Innovation by means of legislation is a major focus of the efforts of governments all over the world today, but not nearly enough is known about legislation from a sociological point of view. There are signs in the periodical literature that anthropologists are beginning to be more interested in the subject than they have been in the past (Caplan 1967, Colson 1966, Freedman 1968). It is significant in this regard that Schapera's monograph is about to be republished.

It was not until the publication of Llewellyn and Hoebel's *The Cheyenne Way* (1941) that anthropology produced a book focused on legal cases. The authors treated individual cases as emerging from problems that required solution, the basic general task being to maintain order. They report how violations of the rules were handled, and how particular disputes were sorted out. The case material and the description of the setting in which cases arose were elicited largely from elderly informants reminiscing about the past. The book strongly affected the development of legal anthropology by its use of cases and by its application of the case-law lawyer's point of view to exotic material. The book's preoccupation with cases continues as another major trend in the field, as does its concern with techniques of keeping order. What delighted Llewellyn in the Cheyenne accounts, since he himself was an eminent professor of law, was the practice of the lawyer's art, the craft skills of the profession. He greatly admired the ingenuity with which good rules could be worked out of troublesome and difficult situations – rules that would endure and be useful in other cases. He was a specialist in the law of sales and contracts, and hence was, in his own milieu, very much aware of the relationship between commercial practices and court decisions. For Llewellyn, the 'trouble case' was an opportunity for displaying forensic skills, for making useful law out of what seemed the least promising materials. Llewellyn and Hoebel found this very skill in the Cheyennes' resolutions of dispute, and in their ways of dealing with rule-breaking. They were also struck by the policing, order-keeping techniques that were reported to have been so effective in the tribe when it assembled as a whole each summer.

Hoebel's interest in the legitimate application of force was even more evident in 1954, when he brought out an introductory textbook, *The Law of Primitive Man*. In this book, mentioned earlier, Hoebel sketched the society, culture, and law of a handful of peoples ranging in organizational complexity from the Eskimo to the Ashanti. Each description is partly cultural and partly organizational, but not systematically either. There is an occasional, but not regular, mention of cases. Each description is accompanied by a list of what Hoebel considers to be the basic jural postulates on which the legal system of each people is founded. These postulates are a rather unsystematic assortment. Hoebel does not indicate the criteria he used to decide what should be included; nor does he specifically cite his sources, though he indicates that he drew his postulates from an examination of cases. The book also includes several general essays on the nature and development of law, in which Hoebel asserts, as was indicated earlier, that the most significant change is the shift from what he considers private law (enforcement by kinsmen and associates) to public law (enforcement by government), from personal retaliation and recoupment to impersonal justice. Despite his interest in enforcement, Hoebel's treatment of law is very strongly cultural, and he emphasizes that he conceives of law as dealing with the enforceable side of a pattern of values. Very much in the Ruth Benedict vein, Hoebel assumes that each culture exemplifies a few out of the total range of possible values and styles. His treatment of law alternately emphasizes the values exemplified by enforceable rules and the nature of the agencies of enforcement; he does not integrate or reconcile the two.

In 1955 a new approach made its appearance when Gluckman published *The Judicial Process among the Barotse* (1955a), a detailed examination of the way in which the Barotse *kuta* handled cases. This was the first published book to describe the proceedings before a tribunal in a technologically simple society from the point of view of an anthropologist who had actually seen them. These were not cases recalled by informants, like those in *The Cheyenne Way* (Llewellyn and Hoebel 1941), but cases observed as they were argued over, thrashed out, and ruled on. The book was a study of the techniques of the judges in dealing with the disputes put before them, of the kinds of objectives they expressed, and of the explicit principles they sought to apply. Case after case is reported as it came up in court, some in considerable detail.

Gluckman has used his field knowledge of Barotse society to illumine cases, rather than the other way round. He describes the judicial use of general principles and rules as forming a kind of hierarchy – the most important principles being the most general and vague, and the least important rules the most specific. *The Judicial Process* is, more than anything else, Gluckman's analysis and interpretation of Barotse judicial explanation.

According to Gluckman, the Barotse judges apply the standard of the 'Reasonable Man' in assessing the behavior of parties to cases. Gluckman's critics have fixed on the Reasonable Man as if he were some sort of Piltdown hoax made up of unsuitably joined parts, and usually imply that he is a construct of the observer. Gluckman (1965a) has replied by showing that the Reasonable Man is an explicit concept in Barotse jurisprudence (Epstein (1954) has confirmed the Reasonable Man's explicit existence elsewhere), and explains the standard of the Reasonable Man largely in terms of role expectations. He acknowledges, however, that the idea has other facets as well. As I see it, the Reasonable Man is best explained not as the critics take him – as a personification of some real, average member of the society – but as a concept enunciated by Barotse judges to encompass and cope with a whole variety of awkward judicial problems and standards. He is a device, a technical tool of the judiciary, rather than an actual, invariably clear model of proper role behavior. Doubtless Gluckman is right in asserting that standard role expectations were among the resources Barotse judges could invoke to explain decisions, and that they did so in the name of the Reasonable Man. But these role expectations could hardly have been specific for all situations. The *idea* that there is a standard of reasonable behavior fills the gap. It handles awkwardly uncertain standards by treating them as nominally definite and by lumping them conceptually with ordinary role expectations. Too much print has already been expended on this subject, but it is worth noting, not only because of its historical significance, but because the very confusion in the surrounding argument conceals an important issue that is only beginning to surface, the question of the relationship among judges' *statements*, the actual *bases* of judicial decision, and *norms and practices* in ordinary social life. The question is very complex, and the distinctions between these levels must be clearly made (and have usually not been, as argument about the Reasonable Man shows) in order that analysis may go forward.

What one finds in *The Judicial Process* is an analysis of explicit Barotse judicial reasoning – what the judges said and did, the reasons they gave for what they did, and the cases that elicited these decisions. No wholly comparable study has been done since, although *The Judicial Process* itself has recently been reprinted with the addition of some retrospective comments by Gluckman.

In 1957, with the publication of Paul Bohannan's *Justice and Judgment among the Tiv*, anthropology acquired its first casebook of dispute settlement in an acephalous society. Tiv political structure was simply a lineage system, which contrasted dramatically with the structure of the centralized Barotse kingdom, and the whole legal process was very different. Moreover, Bohannan presents his ethnographic data in a form very different from Gluckman's. Bohannan distinguishes the Tiv view of their own law, 'the folk system,' from the anthropologist's analysis of it, which he calls 'the analytic system.' Bohannan's technique of unfolding the folk concepts of Tiv law is to take Tiv terms and explain them at the same time that he gets on with a description of court cases. He argues (1957:20) that the Tiv have rules of conduct, but that these rules are not thought of by the Tiv as a 'body of rules,' as a *corpus juris*. Thus he says the Tiv have 'laws' but not 'law.' Bohannan thus argues that the idea of a body of rules, the *corpus juris* Gluckman mentions in connection with the Barotse, does not exist in the folk concepts of the Tiv. The Tiv, according to him, do not think either of laws or of customs as *organized* in a body (though they have a word for 'binding rules of conduct'), but rather conceive them merely one by one, as applied in the specific social situations in which they come up.

Bohannan's contrast of 'folk' systems with 'analytic' systems is by implication a critique of Gluckman's work; and since writing the Tiv book, he has put it increasingly clearly in that form. He evidently feels that what Gluckman presented in *The Judicial Process* was too much colored by Gluckman's analysis of the Barotse system; that it was not the Barotse view of their own system, or at any rate that the two were not sufficiently distinguished. Bohannan argues that to explain the Tiv system by using the terms (i.e., vocabulary) of our own system of law does violence to Tiv ideas and folk systems. In other words, any analysis in terms other than those of the people studied imposes an alien form on the material.

There are a number of puzzling things about the emphatically terminological approach that Bohannan advocates. A fundamental question is whether certain words, *per se*, may indeed be taken to represent the basic categories of a people's thought. Is the semantic content of terms the best indication of mental classification? Are there not many mental ways of classifying ideas, only some of which are represented in the meanings of particular single words? Several words may be associated, for example. Further, one may be disposed to ask how the anthropologist chooses which words to expand on and which to disregard. There are also numerous questions about the manipulability of classifications in actual situations, and about the fact that general legal terms may encompass a variety of situations that are very tenuously related. Any anthropology student who would like to try his hand at legal analysis through the door of terminology should be assigned, as an introductory problem, the fact that in our society both marriage and the purchase of two dill pickles may be characterized as 'contracts.'

Another puzzling thing about the terminological approach is how, within it, one is to cope with those aspects of structure and order inherent in an indigenous system for which there may be no terms. For example, the grammar of a language is surely as much a part of the language and conceptual classification as its words. But among people who have not analyzed the grammar of their own language, there are commonly no terms for many grammatical categories. Most (all?) peoples distinguish between serious and trivial breaches of legal rules, but not all formalize these into named categories like 'felony' and 'misdemeanor.' When the anthropologist perceives such 'unconscious' or unexplicit order in behavior and reports it, is this part of the analytical system or inherent in the folk system? Is it imposed from the outside or merely perceived from the outside? When Gluckman tells us that Barotse judges regularly manipulate legal concepts in an ordered manner, is that order part of the Barotse folk system, the Gluckman analytic system, or both? It is interesting that when, in his conclusion, Bohannan ultimately presents the 'analytic systems' he has worked out of the Tiv materials, none of these are analyses of the Tiv substantive-terminological-legal concepts with which so much of the book is concerned. Instead, Bohannan's analytic system deals exclusively with Tiv procedural institutions.

The question of whether the study of indigenous terminology is the optimum route to the understanding of alien systems of law is distinct from the question of whether it is desirable to try as far as one can to distinguish between 'raw data' and analysis in one's writings. It is possible to have doubts about the first, as I do, without having the slightest doubt about the second, about which I have none. In Bohannan's book, the two questions have become one because of his particular method of exposition. His book also blends these two questions with a third issue: are ideas and concepts fundamental parts of legal systems? Here again, I agree wholeheartedly that they are.

In 1965 Gluckman published *The Ideas in Barotse Jurisprudence* (1965b), a record of the Storrs lectures that Gluckman delivered at the Yale Law School. Although this book takes up the theme of legal ideas, it adopts a point of departure quite different from Bohannan's, perhaps in part because the lectures were addressed to an audience of lawyers. Gluckman outlines such specific and conventional legal topics as treason, succession and inheritance, rights in land, marriage and affiliation, injury and responsibility, debt and other quite concrete common social circumstances, and then proceeds to untie the relevant package of related Barotse concepts. Characteristically, he uses the dichotomous model of tribal as against more differentiated societies, and seeks to formulate generalizations about how the ideas in Barotse jurisprudence are related to the fact that the Barotse are a tribal society, operating within the limitations of a relatively simple technology. I find the dichotomous model less satisfactory than the more complex morphological series that Gluckman also uses on occasion. But the contribution of the book lies in the fact that Gluckman seeks to relate the recurrent ideas in Barotse substantive law to the circumstances of Barotse life. It is a bold attempt to relate law to society on a broad canvas, a scholarly speculation on a grand scale. He plucks parallel examples from other societies here and there. His objective is to formulate generalizations from the Barotse material that will hold in other places and other times, given similar fundamental social circumstances. The extended testing of the hypotheses suggested in *The Ideas in Barotse Jurisprudence*, the detailed comparison of the legal norms, ideas, and social processes of many other societies, remains to be done. I would guess that when these comparisons are made, the dichotomous model will give way to a much more complex typology. But the stimulus value of such a broad formulation of problems is inestimable. It is a vigorous attempt to relate substantive rules and ideas to the kinds of social relationships that exist in a particular sort of society. Many people have worked on one or another aspect of the relationship between legal procedures and their socio-political settings, but few have attempted anything of the kind with substantive law. Gluckman's is a pioneering effort.

Another important theme in law and anthropology has been the process of dispute settlement itself. In *Social Control in an African Society* (1963) P. H. Gulliver describes the indigenous ways of settling disputes among the Arusha, a Masai tribe living on Mount Meru in Tanzania. The Arusha were originally an acephalous people organized in patrilineages, age-grades, and localities. Their indigenous legal system did not have judges, though the government has introduced a system of courts. Gulliver's study deals principally with the settlement of disputes outside the courts. The parties customarily argue out their cases at public meetings, each party appearing with a flock of supporters and locally eminent spokesmen, who participate actively in the settlement of cases. Partisanship on one side or the other generally depends on previous social ties rather than on the merits of the case, and the outcome of a dispute has much to do with the quality and quantity of support a man can muster. Gulliver explains in detail the organizational basis of Arusha society on which the composition of these dispute palavers depended, and also describes a substantial number of the cases he heard. He asserts that norms are of negligible importance in the settlement of Arusha disputes, and that nowhere in Arusha proceedings did he find any sign of the 'reasonable man.' He does indicate that norms are continuously cited in argument in the settlement process, but he concludes that the relative 'strength' of the parties, rather than the norms, determines the outcome.

Gulliver's conclusion contrasts the Arusha dispute settlement process with that of the Barotse. The Arusha had no judges, and settled disputes on the basis of the relative social strength of the two parties, demonstrated through social action at the moots and assemblies. In contrast, the Barotse had judges, who were supposed to decide disputes on the basis of norms. From these two processes of dispute settlement, Gulliver constructs a typological continuum, with the Arusha type ('political') near one end, the Barotse type ('judicial') near the other, and most other peoples somewhere in between. Some of Gulliver's theoretical conclusions about the Arusha depend heavily on his inferences about the place of norms in those decision-making processes that take place in bargaining situations. My own feeling is that his model has simplified the place and nature of norms. Even the most 'impartial' judicial action can be understood as a process of selection among norms to rationalize a decision made at least partly on other bases, rather than as a simple 'application' of norms. The decision-making process is a complex one, and in bargaining processes it is doubly complex. Norms are sometimes thought of as a simple schedule of quite specific rules, without internal conflicts or alternative applications and Gulliver seems to treat them so; however, they lose all such appearance and are seen to function quite differently when one observes them invoked as counters in legal argument, or as explanations rather than determinants of judicial decision. These reservations notwithstanding, it must be said that not only· has Gulliver considerably enlarged the range of ethnographic knowledge of legal processes with his Arusha book, but he has also, as can readily be seen, raised fundamental questions about the analysis of dispute settlements.

These writers – Malinowski, Schapera, Hoebel, Gluckman, Bohannan, and Gulliver – are by no means the only anthropologists who have written books on law. Some other substantial works of the last decades, though not commented on here, appear in the Bibliography. But I have discussed these six at length because of the importance of their work, and because their work encompasses the principal types of description, research, argument, and construction of hypotheses that have been produced. It is perhaps worth noting that although all six writers tend to deal with legal procedures in terms of their socio-political contexts, each approaches substantive law in a different way. Malinowski approaches it piecemeal as an aspect of social relations. Schapera treats it as a straightforward set of rules, enforced by courts. Hoebel tries to abstract a pattern of values, embodying them in 'jural postulates.' Gluckman deals with the ideas in Barotse law as expressions of a pre-industrial way of life, dominated by the need to maintain multiplex relations and certain status relations. Bohannan does not find any analogous overall pattern in Tiv substantive law, but instead seeks to identify its principal legal perceptual categories, which he assumes to be encapsulated in particular terms. Gulliver goes to the point of arguing that norms have almost no effect on the outcome of Arusha disputes, and he explicitly concentrates on procedure.

The varied approaches of these six authors testify to the grave difficulties attending any effort to characterize substantive rules in a comprehensive and systematic manner. There is, in fact, a serious question about whether substantive rules can be, or ever need be, assumed to form a single system of inter-related parts. For example, as I indicated earlier, Bohannan seems to think that Gluckman has presented Barotse law as if it were 'organized' into a single system, and counters by saying that the Tiv have no such systematic notion, hence no 'corpus juris,' and hence no idea of 'law,' only that of 'laws.' As I see it, Gluckman was simply describing how Barotse judges used the whole body of legal rules and principles known to them as a resource for decision-making. In doing so, they invoked principles of varying degrees of generality. That these levels may be ordered into hierarchy according to the criterion of generality does not, to me, suggest a rigid 'organization' of all of Barotse substantive law, but instead makes explicit one regular aspect of the process of Barotse judicial explanation. In fact, none of these writers, neither Hoebel, nor Gluckman, nor Bohannan, has presented substantive law as a system. Instead, each has taken what he considers to be the most important consistent theme in culture and society, and has traced signs of that theme through some substantive rules. For Hoebel the unifying theme is one of values, for Bohannan one of perceptual categories, and for Gluckman the system of social relations in a technologically simple society.

Most of the scholarly literature of the past few years addresses itself to only limited aspects of these enormous problems. And although some shifts of emphasis may be discerned, the effect of this earlier work is everywhere evident – not surprisingly since all the above writers except Malinowski are still professionally active. This very situation gives one a sense of how recently interest in law has developed within anthropology as a whole.

Current literature

Some techniques of study

Cases. The argument that case study is the best field technique for the investigation of dispute settlement, legal rules, and legal concepts is presented by A. L. Epstein in 'The Case Method in the Field of Law' (1967). In this paper, Epstein identifies what he considers to be the universal characteristics of law and legal systems, i.e., what he considers to be the body of information accessible through law cases. He begins with rules, concepts, and categories, and discusses the merits of using cases rather than informants to discover what these are. He then considers the universality of dispute in human society, and by implication the concomitant universality of procedural means through which grievances can be legitimately aired and disputes properly conducted. Epstein divides the resolution of dispute into three phases: the *inquiry* into guilt or responsibility for a particular event; the process of *adjudication* between conflicting claims; and the modes of *redress* and enforcement available when a breach has been established or assumed. He ends by suggesting very briefly that the sequence of events called a case, although it may be isolated for certain analytical purposes, must be considered in its social matrix if one is to fully understand its place in the social process. Although Epstein touches on this last, he concentrates on the general anatomy of law and dispute settlement rather than on enumerating the vast potentialities for research that are opened by using the study of law cases as a standard field technique.

Epstein's concluding remarks clearly allude to a theme common in certain schools of social anthropology today. In his introduction to *The Craft of Social Anthropology* (1967) Gluckman hails the extended case method as a new tool in social anthropology. He says (p. xv): 'This new kind of analysis treats each case as a stage in an on-going process of social relations between specific persons and groups in a social system and culture.' Epstein's "Case Method" oscillates between seeing law cases as one kind of case material to which the extended case method may be applied, and seeing law cases as one way to study the ideas, values, and basic premises of a society.

Comparisons. Since so many students of law vigorously and interminably contend that the field is riddled with terminological and conceptual ethnocentrism, it is refreshing to find van Velsen (1969:137) arguing that most writers on African law, with or without legal training, 'have an imperfect understanding of their own legal system, with which, explicitly or implicitly, they tend to compare African legal systems.' His paper, 'Procedural Informality, Reconciliation, and False Comparisons' (1969), describes what he regards as two prevalent pieces of mythology about African as compared with Anglo-European law: the notion that traditional African tribunals have a very informal procedure in which the taking of evidence is not restricted by the kind of limiting rules that apply in Anglo-American courts; and the notion that reconciliation is a more significant objective of African courts than the application of rules of law, and that the reverse is true in Anglo-American courts. Van Velsen contends that false comparisons are made between Anglo-American high courts and rural African tribunals rather than between the comparable English lay magistrates' courts or American small-claims courts and their African counterparts. Moreover, he argues that more attention should be given to European pre-trial reconciliation procedures, and to determining whether reconciliation is indeed as prominent a feature of African judicial process as it is supposed to be.

Van Velsen's is a brief paper, and more a number of suggestions than a fully supported argument; but it sounds a note that will doubtless be heard again in other forms. There is a paucity of sociological data on Anglo-American law (see Skolnick 1965), and anthropologists have barely begun to tackle the parts of the problem in industrial society that are amenable to their techniques of study. Tentative comparative generalizations are essential for the progress of legal anthropology, even though these generalizations are almost certain to be revised as more and more information becomes available. Knowing the extensive range of other social phenomena in non-industrialized societies, we may expect that further research will eventually enable us to speak in terms of numerous types of legal systems, rather than purely in terms of the gross contrasts that now seem to distinguish present urban-national Anglo-American-European systems from what Gluckman calls 'tribal' systems.

In one useful comparative paper, M. G. Smith (1965b) has had a look at some of the variations in the legal theory of corporations. He has attempted to characterize the Muslim, French, and British traditions, and from the theories and ideologies embodied in them to come to some conclusions about the legal approach of the colonial powers to dealing with indigenous African corporate units. Since this is a swift and very general review of a very large subject, it touches on more subjects than it can cope with adequately; but Smith's argument for the importance of a historical analysis of legal institutions is persuasive, as is his stress on the significance of legal procedures.

Illuminating comparisons are also possible within a single system or region. Some of the complications inherent in the not uncommon situation of a multiplicity of tribunals are described in R. E. S. Tanner's 'The Selective Use of Legal Systems in East Africa' (1966). Tanner speaks of three legal systems operative in that area. The 'paper system' includes the courts of the resident magistrates and above, in which the magistrate or judge has had legal training and deals with judicial matters in terms of statutes and a written record. The 'impressionistic system' includes the courts instituted by government and presided over by magistrates who have had some legal training but are not members of the legal profession. These men apply both statutory law and customary law, but their reliance on written materials is more limited than that of the 'paper system' judiciary. They make summaries of the evidence and reasoning rather than keeping full verbatim records. They are in touch with the paper system, and also with the third set of legal processes. Tanner describes this third system as having 'no formal structure,' but I doubt that he means this in a sociological sense. Rather, he seems to mean that the moots and meetings of family heads and of neighbors do not take place in a uniformly prescribed way, but adjust their procedure and membership according to the importance of the case or of the litigants. The article discusses, in general terms, the various conditions under which one system is used rather than another.

Tanner's choice of terms is not altogether a happy one, since, sociologically speaking, order and structure exist on all three levels. The important differences are not attributable either to the degree of reliance on written documents or to the rigidity or formality of certain procedures, but rather to the social context in which these tribunals operate, the social units or levels to which they are attached, the kinds of cases they handle, the social orientation of those who play judicial roles, and so on. But Tanner's description has raised an important point. Where varieties of techniques are available for the resolution of dispute (as there would seem to be in most societies), it is important to discover the how and why of alternative choices. There is room for a great deal more detailed research, and need for the assembling of adequate statistical data on this problem. It is very important both for the purposes of sociological analysis and for the practical information of legislators and administrators. Legal-anthropological-sociological research of this kind is as much needed in the highly industrialized countries of the world as it is in the young nations.

Rules. Goldschmidt (1967) has written a book on the law of the Sebei of Eastern Uganda, and introduces it with his characteristic candor by indicating that he considers it not merely a descriptive record, but a contribution to the general theory of jurisprudence. But he also indicates that he has not reviewed the literature on the theory of primitive law, nor does he attempt comparisons with any other societies. Moreover, he did not observe any legal action from beginning to end, nor was any case narrated to him in full detail. The core of the book consists of a statement of legal rules as abstracted by the author, interspersed with terse, illustrative accounts of specific disputes and their outcome. Goldschmidt does not treat his task as a study of the sociological context of law; his immediate objective is rather the discovery of rules, illustrated by cases in which they were applied.

Goldschmidt's concluding chapters attempt to draw together all of the rules he has set forth, on the inference that they are governed by three basic principles. He calls the result 'the metaphysical infrastructure of Sebei legal behavior.' The three principles have to do with general Sebei attitudes toward kinship, property, and the transmutability of all social relations into pecuniary terms; the last joins the first two into a single system. Of course, Gluckman, following Sir Henry Maine and E. E. Evans-Pritchard, had said in *The Judicial Process* (1955a) that things are links in institutionalized relationships between persons, an insight he further developed in *Barotse Jurisprudence* (1965b). Goldschmidt, without reviewing or citing the literature, is thus making at least one contribution to the general theory of jurisprudence that seems to have been made before. His comments on changes in Sebei legal rules that are unaccompanied by changes on what he calls the 'ideational level' are more novel, and they present an interesting problem in simultaneous continuity and change. The descriptive core of the book – the rules illustrated by cases – is an addition to our ethnographic knowledge.

The prevention and settlement of dispute

Legal institutions as alternatives to fighting. Bohannan's (1967) introduction to his recently published collection of readings on law and warfare takes the exposition of his theoretical position a step further. He speaks of societies racked by conflicts, and of others that have 'solved' their conflicts and replaced them with the rule of law. He thus characterizes a difference between feuding societies and our own. Negotiation and bargaining seem to have no place in Bohannan's scheme. 'There are basically two forms of conflict resolution: administered rules and fighting.' The readings in the book are selected to illustrate this duality. Part I is devoted to a few definitions of law by Redfield, Pospisil and Bohannan himself. Part II is entitled 'The Ethnography of Law: the Judicial Process.' And Part III considers 'Feuds, Raids, and Wars.' Bohannan feels that 'the next great step in legal institutions *must* be in the field of international law and other bicentric power situations,' and speaks of the world's need for a new 'code of aggression' (Bohannan 1967:xii).

In this context Bohannan is treating law as a solution to social problems – essentially, as a means of peacefully resolving conflicts of interest and as a system for the maintenance of social peace and order. What is interesting about this, and about Bohannan's decision to reprint his own article on 'The Differing Realms of the Law' (1965), is that it emphasizes a fundamental duality in his approach to the subject of law. On the one hand, he defines law in terms of *institutions* that settle disputes and 'counteract' gross abuses of norms; and on the other hand, he emphasizes *perception*, cognition, 'key concepts,' and ideas as the fundamental basis of law (cf. Bohannan 1957, 1965, 1967). This pull in two directions, drawing toward an institutional approach on one side and a cognitive approach on the other, is somewhat like the split one sees between Hoebel's attention to the development of 'public centralized institutions of law enforcement' and his notion of 'jural postulates' (Hoebel 1954). It is a duality that runs deep in American anthropology. By contrast, when Gluckman (1965b) talks about legal ideas, he is trying to show how particular concepts can be explained in terms of their institutional setting. He is not treating the ideas as if they were a system of cognitive categories or value-laden principles that in themselves may give fundamental shape to the social system; rather, he assumes that the legal ideas and categories are expressions of the social and historical settings in which they are found. He gives an analytic priority to institutions and connects them with ideas, whereas Hoebel and Bohannan do not make any similar attempt to fit together the framework of ideas and the framework of institutions.

A new book that seeks to reconcile these two frames of reference is Michael Barkun's *Law without Sanctions* (1968). The title will at once remind anthropologists of the anthology *Tribes without Rulers*, which Barkun has studied carefully. His argument, following that of Masters (1964), asserts that there are important parallels between order in stateless societies and international order. Barkun further contends that these parallels affect the definition and analysis of legal systems in general. He is a political scientist, but his argument draws heavily on anthropological data and ideas. Interpreting law as founded more on consensus than on force, he defines the consensus for 'conflict management' as including not only shared procedures but shared perceptual categories. His definition of law as a system of manipulable symbols that functions as a model of social structure has already been mentioned.

For all Barkun's formal emphasis on law as a set of interrelated symbols, he ultimately concedes that 'legal systems have *some* empirical referents' (1968:151), and goes on to say that law is a means of both conceptualizing and *managing* the social environment. His discussion thus goes full circle – from social relationships to ideas about social relationships and back again to empirical referents and management, not just to 'representations' of the social environment. A *déformation professionel* of certain academics preoccupied with international affairs would seem to be the regular sifting out of a few optimistic conclusions from their convictions about the effectiveness of common concepts in the absence of common political organization. Optimism notwithstanding, Barkun's is a very up-to-the-minute account; and it is particularly stimulating in its repeated and creative use of the distinction between the symbolic manifestations of law and the behavioral referents of law. It is a book to be read – and argued with – but decidedly to be taken seriously.

Non-'legal' institutions as a means of airing legal controversy. Legal institutions as a vehicle for the expression of other interests. Aubert (1963) has argued that the legal process involves the transformation of dyadic relationships into triadic ones. Once a dispute is at a point where it is not going to be settled between the parties but is going to involve others, the question of which 'others' may have important effects not only on procedure, but on outcome; it also may affect the breadth of significance of the dispute. To the extent that recourse to a particular mode of settlement involves others, it may also involve the personal interests of those others, or the interests associated with their position.

Primitive peoples often deal with erupting hostilities by translating them into sorcery or witchcraft terms, describing them and resolving them symbolically in terms of the spirit world. If this process involves assembling a group of people and carrying out a public investigation, explanation, and resolution, what takes place often resembles a legal hearing. Social events that get out of hand resemble manifestations of the spirit world in that techniques must be prescribed and applied to bring the untamed under control. Accordingly, Audrey Butt (1965–6) describes 'The Shaman's Legal Role' among the Akawaio, a Carib-speaking people in the Guiana Highlands. The Akawaio live in autonomous villages and joint-family settlements, each recognizing a leader; but leadership is a matter of persuasion and influence, not coercion. The redress of grievances and the settlement of dispute are largely in the hands of the parties concerned, though gossip and scandal play their part in affecting the outcome. The only kind of public meeting over a dispute is a shamanistic séance to discover the cause of sickness or death. Butt describes a series of cases to show how, in the course of these séances, the shaman attributes the cause of an illness to various forms of interpersonal hostility or incorrect behavior. The séance openly airs disputes of which all the persons present are aware, and adds public social pressure to other efforts to resolve disputes or limit 'anti-social' behavior. The basic occasion for this action among the Akawaio is always a medical inquiry in form but a dispute in substance.

Disputes may also be transformed by absorbing confrontations between the individual members of competing political units into the general, long-term competition between the political entities. Feuding is the classic example, but there are others. Beidelman (1966–7) describes the use of locally run government courts in the Ukaguru chiefdoms of Tanzania, and shows how the judgments of these courts were used to further Kaguru political aims at the expense of four minority tribal groups living in the same area. Political and judicial roles were somewhat confused: a vigilante Kaguru group apprehended people and brought them to court, sometimes for violations of law, and sometimes for violations of its own regulations. Beidelman shows, through the description of 22 law cases involving non-Kaguru and Kaguru, that members of the minority tribes were regularly dealt with much more peremptorily and severely than Kaguru. In some cases, the vindictiveness of the Kaguru against the members of minority tribes was mitigated by the intervention of a Kaguru patron, or by special relationships between the defendant and the Kaguru headmen or court holders, but without this aid a non-Kaguru evidently did not stand a chance against a Kaguru in court. Beidelman cites the Kaguru situation to show the divergence between the declared aims of the government policy of indirect rule and the effect of that policy at the local level. However deplorable this use of the courts may be, it is difficult to imagine a practical policy that would have prevented Kaguru political dominance from asserting itself in some form, since there are 48,000 Kaguru and barely 6000 non-Kaguru.

The use of courts and other processes of dispute settlement in the struggle for political power is not unusual. Barnes (1961) discussed this use as it occurred among the Plateau Tonga and the Ngoni. Nader (1965a) attributes differences in dispute settlement procedures in part to differences in political structure. Gulliver (1963) has made the political settlement one of his two basic types of dispute settlement. Law cases that involve political issues, and settlements that depend on political factors, are easy to find in industrialized societies, as well as agricultural ones.

Accepting bribes, of course, is another classic way for a judge to use his office for ends other than the simple settlement of disputes. Ottenberg (1967) examines the question of bribery and corruption in local government in southern Nigeria. He treats it as a social phenomenon, not as a moral matter. Using M. G. Smith's definition of corruption as 'the use of public office or authority for private advantage and gain,' Ottenberg develops the argument that corruption is the natural result of the interaction of two political systems in a society, the consequence of contact between two quite different political styles. He sees as inevitable in countries undergoing change a considerable discrepancy between what is legal and what is actually done in the way of political behavior. He emphasizes that in Nigeria bribery brings relations with strangers into line with traditional patterns of gift-giving and reciprocity standard among kinsmen and familiars. He argues that bribery is thus in certain social circumstances the guarantor and regulator of secure relations between strangers. But having pursued that line of argument, Ottenberg asks whether corruption is not universal, existing in all societies but varying in form.

Some of the questions examined in Ottenberg's paper have to do with different social or cultural *views* of what is proper behavior, and some have to do with the *objective existence* of the phenomenon of the use of office for personal gain. It follows that if there are two distinct political styles in contact, persons committed to one will think that people committed to the other are behaving improperly. This is certainly likely. But the meaning of such culturally or socially determined moral judgments is distinct from the question of whether there is regular personal exploitation of political office or authority. These may be two very different matters. Had the distinction between cultural attitudes and objective behavioral phenomena been maintained throughout the paper, the discussion would have been clearer. As it is, Ottenberg does not always explain which he is discussing. He has, however, made some interesting comments on a practical problem that has considerable analytic significance.

Inheritance and the sorting of competing claims. There are certain competing claims that regularly come to a head through an event that is not in itself part of a dispute. A redistribution of property, positions, or rights may be necessitated by events like a death, a marriage, the accession of a new officeholder, or the moving of settlers to new lands. Competing claims like these may be handled institutionally by a meeting of claimants and others to work out an allocation of rights. Unlike the procedures mentioned earlier, these meetings do not occur because of some existing dispute, but the claims they concern inherently involve the kind of competition that is likely to boil up into a confrontation and a fight. This kind of event has received a great deal of attention in anthropology. But it has seldom, if at all, been treated as a topic related to processes of dispute settlement and mechanisms of dispute prevention and control. It certainly merits this treatment.

A common social institution of this kind is the meeting of kin to arrange the distribution of a decedent's property. Some societies have an explicit set of rules governing how this is to be done, who are to be the primary recipients of property and prerogatives, and who are to be the contingent heirs. But in other societies the matter of distribution may be mostly left to the discretion of specific surviving kin. Shepardson and Hammond (1966) have examined Navaho inheritance patterns. Having been told by one informant that 'every family does it differently,' they tried to discover what variables affected the decision. The paper mentions a few cases, but does not report any figures on the patterns of distribution, so that the paper is essentially a description of the variables that may affect each case, and a discussion of those aspects of Navaho life that are assumed by the authors to militate against more rigidly formulated rules of inheritance. Shepardson and Hammond see the Navaho inheritance pattern as one that tends to disperse rather than preserve intact the assets of any decedent, and they relate this dispersal to other economic conditions. Their approach is to rationalize Navaho inheritance in terms of present Navaho social and economic organization, and then show how the two fit together.

If anyone ever doubted the intimate links between inheritance and social structure, Goody's *Death, Property, and the Ancestors* (1962) has surely removed this doubt. But to study the rules by which the property and statuses of dead persons *should be* distributed in a particular society according to expressed local norms, and the even greater number of ways in which these holdings *are* actually distributed, may be more than an exercise demonstrating congruence between institutions. Analytically, the study of inheritance can include variation and change as often as stability.

Since inheritance is one way to maintain social continuities, inheritance practices in a changing society are likely to reflect the extent to which continuities are in fact perpetuated by this means, as well as the margin of change or variation accommodated. M. G. Smith (1965a) has raised these questions of interpretation in the very complex setting of Hausa society. He describes how indigenous Hausa rules, Maliki Moslem law, and colonial Nigerian statutes and ordinances have interwoven, so that the Hausa actually practice many modes of inheritance and succession at the same time. If one recognizes the elements that have produced these variations during the last century and a half, one is forced to consider Hausa inheritance practice as expressing the relation between continuity and change. Smith argues that Hausa society is in a state of moving equilibrium, and that its inheritance laws reflect that structural condition.

The contention that legal norms should be looked at in a historical perspective is extremely important for the understanding of legal institutions – and, by implication, important for the study of other norms and institutions. This kind of investigation is not possible everywhere; but even where it is not possible to reconstruct the past, an awareness of the past's importance is a safeguard against the most simplistic, casual explanations, which take simultaneity in time as certain evidence of 'functional' or 'causal' connection. Laws of inheritance that appear to be reproducing a social situation from generation to generation may in fact be accommodating changes that are not acknowledged as such. Declarations that there has been continuity of legal norms over the generations are not necessarily an indication that such as been historically the case. The past may be formally invoked to legitimize the present; yet actual practices may be only selectively perpetuated, and change may be accommodated under the cloak of ancestral custom.

Certain papers in the Derrett (1965) volume on inheritance and succession in Nigeria – particularly those of Ottenberg on the Afikpo Ibo, Harris on the Mbembe, and P. C. Lloyd on the Yoruba – are solid descriptive essays on the way in which inheritance and succession reflect basic social relationships, and in some cases accommodate changing conditions. Ottenberg suggests a typology of systems of inheritance and succession based on the extent to which the two reflect prescribed full role-succession, and conversely on the extent to which succession and inheritance are separable and not 'automatic.' Harris describes how the Mbembe all express the wish that movable goods were inherited agnatically, but continue to pass them on matrilineally, as they do land, despite conditions of land shortage. Like Colson (1966), Harris describes the operating context of the rules, and gives statistical data on the ways in which men acquire land. Lloyd's paper is a brief description of the organizational background and rules relating to the Yoruba concept of family property. He has expanded on this subject elsewhere, and has also produced a very detailed and useful volume on Yoruba land law (P. C. Lloyd 1962). But the paper in the Derrett collection that attempts to draw together the largest theoretical implications of laws of inheritance and succession is that of M. G. Smith (1965a), whose emphasis on historical depth provides a dimension that complicates the facts but clarifies the analytical issues.

Legal norms and social change

Theoretical questions

Classic discussions in jurisprudence and sociology sometimes oppose the Austinian imperative concept of law to one or another version of a consensus theory. The consensus theory suggests in some form that law resides essentially in the minds and practices of people in a society, rather than in the compulsion imposed by statutes and 'commands of the sovereign.' Since anthropologists have, on the whole, operated in societies where written law is minimal or non-existent, they have not been troubled by any lack of congruence between statutes and practice, and are seldom concerned with law as the command of a sovereign. Pospisil (1958) is the only anthropologist who has strongly emphasized the authoritative element in law, and Schapera (1943) is the only one to have dealt at all extensively with legislation. Anthropologists have coped with the difference between stated norms and observed practice by absorbing both into ideal–real or multiple norm models.

Many lawyers and law professors view law as an instrument for controlling society and directing social change, but most anthropologists are concerned with law as a reflection of a particular social order. This difference in perspective has had considerable effect. An article that describes some of these classic dilemmas is Clifford-Vaughan and Scotford-Norton's 'Legal Norms and Social Order: Petrazycki, Pareto, Durkheim' (1967). It is revealing, though a very general discussion, because it touches on all of these questions rather unselfconsciously. In particular, it describes Petrazycki's view that law is both a prescriptive and descriptive device, i.e., that norms both reflect and direct social organization.

As anthropology becomes more preoccupied with the insights that the study of society over time can give it, we may expect that law will be considered more often in this complex double image; and we may come to know more of the conditions that determine when law reflects and when it directs. We may expect not only extended case studies of the kind that Epstein (1967) calls for, but more studies of legal norms and rules in changing circumstances. One of the most important recent papers on law, I think, is written along these lines: Elizabeth Colson's 'Land Law and Land Holdings among the Valley Tonga of Zambia' (1966). Colson confines herself to the evidence, and does not pursue the considerable theoretical implications of what she has described. She shows that even though three Valley Tonga villages experienced fundamental changes in the pattern of land tenure when they were moved from their traditional area to a new one because of the construction of the Kariba Dam, they did not recognize any change in their land law. Furthermore, at none of the times she studied the Tonga could the system of land tenure be regarded as a 'stable equilibrium based on the functioning of the land rules.' Rather, the land tenure system was always unstable, changing with land conditions, the extent of exhausted land, the amount of fallow, etc. Nevertheless, whether subjected to gradually changing land conditions or to the sudden changes caused by the dam, the Valley Tonga did not alter one whit the legal rules governing land tenure.

The legal rules of tenure in the Tonga situation had to do with the acquisition and use of land. They bestowed different rights depending on the mode of acquisition – whether through kin (maternal or paternal), through use, as in the case of previously unoccupied bush land. As one might expect, when Colson examined figures for two years before and for five years after the population had been moved, she found that the proportion of land acquired from kin had shrunk dramatically from one period to the other, and that the land acquired by cultivating open bush had increased enormously. The system of 'norms' could accommodate this change without itself changing. The story Colson does not tell at length, but alludes to briefly and tantalizingly, is that having to do with why the new lands after the move were treated as bush lands under the old rules, though headmen, chiefs, and administrators had argued that *they* should be permitted to distribute the land. The construction that the old legal rules relating to bush land should apply to new territory, rather than some scheme of distribution through officials, would seem to indicate that there were political implications in maintaining the traditional legal rules and not permitting innovation in modes of land allocation.

Whereas Colson's paper deals with a socio-economic change from which certain legal rules emerged unchanged, Caplan (1967) has written a paper describing the socio-economic changes that resulted from the alteration of legal rules. He traces the effects of government land legislation and other circumstances on the status of local headmen in the Limbuan region of Nepal. In the eighteenth century local headmen had granted land to immigrant settlers; in the nineteenth century the status of these lands was changed, so that they were held directly from the state and not through local headmen. At present, many headmen are no better off than their followers, and a group of Limbu, grown affluent through military service, have usurped most of the power and influence of the Limbu headmen by buying control over extensive lands through the purchases of mortgages.

Caplan's very modest conclusion is that factors outside the small-scale social arena normally studied by anthropologists must be taken into account to explain local circumstances. He is certainly right about this. The historical material in his paper, however, has other interesting implications. It touches on, but does not analyze, questions relating to the way in which legislation affects political control and the extent to which the legislative power is used to this end in different kinds of polities. Caplan's material implies that local political power in the Limbuan region is closely connected with control of land. It would appear that there were at various periods two avenues to that control, one administrative, the other economic. Looking at the material as a problem in the social setting of law (though this was not Caplan's focus) opens many theoretical issues about the relationship between the respective rules of law relating to administrative and to economic control of property. Gluckman's (1965b, 1969) distinction between estates of administration and estates of production in land can be effectively extended and exploited in analyzing this kind of material. Questions about the circumstances under which effective political power relates to legal rules affecting one or the other might be very illuminating if answered in a comparative framework.

Questions of policy

Land reform. Surely one of the most chewed-over questions of policy affecting the primarily agricultural parts of the world is that of the

246

redistribution of land and changes in the land law. From the UN down, there has been a constant search for viable ways of improving present landholding systems to make them more productive – and in some places less politically explosive. Legislation is the most commonly considered technique for making these changes. There is an enormous literature on this subject, and more books and papers are constantly appearing (Aktan 1966, Apthorpe 1964, Blok 1966, Feder 1967, Ruillière 1966, Simpson 1967, Thambyahpillai 1966). Anthropologists may not have much of a hand in making the policy decisions that will determine political attempts to deal with the problem, but they will doubtless have many opportunities to study a subject they have somewhat neglected: the legislative introduction, and the consequences, of planned change. On the whole, applied anthropology has most committed itself to examining these matters; but the more academically and theoretically minded may well find research problems in it during the years to come, especially when there are more and more attempts to produce planned change among the very peoples that anthropologists have studied in the past.

Rosenberg's 'Maori Land Tenure and Land Use' (1966) reviews the question of whether legislation originally designed to protect the indigenous Maori land-tenure systems from exploitation is now interfering with Maori economic development. Rosenberg argues that complete security of communal land tenure may not be the optimum arrangement for economic development, since it prevents the mortgaging of land and hence prevents Maori from gaining the capital needed for development. He examines the two alternatives of individualizing land tenure and incorporating the joint owners, and favors the second. For anthropologists interested in law, the attempts at handling such practical problems provide the closest thing to a laboratory experiment available in real social action. Rosenberg's article is not a before-and-after study like Colson's (1966), but rather a prelegislative recommendation for a particular policy.

Reform of family law. Freedman's 'Chinese Family Law in Singapore: the Rout of Custom' (1968) touches on two fundamental matters: the complexities of law in plural societies and the uses of culturally and politically founded models of the family in judicial and legislative action. In the colonial period the Chinese in Singapore were not considered indigenes, and were hence considered to be subject to English law, modified to accommodate certain features of their institutional life. Freedman demonstrates the curious consequences of combining an English family model and an imprecisely known Chinese family model in deciding court cases. Judges recognized the structure of the Chinese family to some extent, but here and there they applied English law to it. The resulting mélange was neither English nor Chinese. Polygamy, for example, was recognized as one of the facts of Chinese life; but by some curious application of British ideas of equality, concubines and secondary wives had the same legal status as major wives. Freedman details the comic oddities that ensued from this vaguely defined attempt to apply the family law of England to the Chinese family.

Complicating new elements are added to an already knotty subject when Freedman explains that two years after Singapore became self-governing, it passed a piece of legislation called 'The Women's Charter,' which was supposed to give women instantaneous equality with men in all (legislatable) matters. The Charter proposed a sort of ideological redesigning of the family. Freedman reviews the provisions of the statute, and argues that it is essentially 'English law justified by the principles of Asian socialism' He is understandably skeptical about whether this attempt to create a new form of the family by legislation will succeed, and indicates what is known of the Charter's effect since its passage.

Freedman's article is stimulating not only because of the peculiarities of the Singapore situation, but because that very situation suggests a research problem of wide current application: the study of the preconceived models of society on which judicial and legislative action are founded. Attempts to remold society through legislation presume ideas of what society is, how it works, how it can be changed, and what it should be. Although judicial innovation and legislation by no means always have the intended effects, the models on which they are based imply a way of looking at social life, and a 'folk' sociology of change implicit in legislation, that may be a way of finding out more about the relationship of ideas to social action.

Buxbaum (1968b), like Freedman, has written on Chinese family law in a common-law setting, but he extends the comparison, discussing Chinese law in all of Malaysia. He has also edited a volume (Buxbaum 1968a) that includes this and several other papers, all presented at a 1964 conference on family law and customary law in Asia. Most of the papers are not sociological studies, but descriptions of legal rules; many describe statutory enactments that have sought to codify or change the customary law of the family. Some of these papers are interesting sociological documents in themselves. For example, S. Takdir Alisjabbana, writing on 'Customary Law and Modernization in Indonesia,' rejects customary law out of hand as archaic and backward, and looks to modernizing legislation to stimulate and guide social growth. This attitude toward legislation as an almost magical instrument of rapid reform is one characteristic sector of thought in many countries, developing and industrialized, and as indicated above, is itself a readymade field for investigation.

The definition of group membership. In plural societies in which different customary laws apply to the affairs of different corporate groups or social categories, and in societies in which certain groups are singled out for preferential or discriminatory treatment, one must define what constitutes membership in a group. This is a legal problem very closely tied to a sociological one. Galanter (1967) discusses it with relation to the 'scheduled castes, tribes, and backward classes of Indian society.' Indian legislation has authorized the government to bestow special benefits and preferences on persons belonging to these groups. Peck (1967) deals with Philippine legislation that restricts the privilege of conducting retail trade to citizens, thus discriminating against local Chinese merchants. Derrett (1968b) discusses the judicial difficulties in determining whether a person is or is not a Hindu for the purpose of applying a law. In the world of multitribal and other plural societies, group and category membership will frequently crop up as a legal problem with policy significance. Cases and legislation involving this issue cannot help but be loaded with information and insights into changing facets of social structure. Decisions in 'conflict of laws' cases are always policy decisions at bottom.

The codification of customary law. In recent years there has been a running battle in some of the developing countries over the extent to which customary law should be reformed or rejected, or if preserved, by what means it should be recorded and standardized. A number of countries, having decided that customary law should be written down, have started official schemes for doing so. A great impetus has also come from academic quarters. In 1959 Professor A. N. Allott, at the School of Oriental and African Studies of the University of London, established the Restatement of African Law Project with support from the Nuffield Foundation. This project is still in full swing ten years later, pursuing the enormous task of trying to set down in writing the customary laws of African peoples. Allott himself is a veritable factory of papers on the project and its implications and on the future of customary laws in Africa (Allott 1966, 1967a, 1967b). He clearly feels that the project is contributing to the acceleration of an evolutionary process: 'The trend towards crystallization and abstraction of legal rules in Africa is merely part of a universal movement in legal history, which has equally affected European systems of law in the course of their evolution' (1967b:13). With great charm and accuracy, he says that customary law appearing in quasi-statutory and precise form is 'processed law,' which 'like processed cheese ... has got quite a different flavour and appearance from the original article' (1967b:5). It remains to be seen whether this transformation of form will have the effect of changing more than the form. It might, for example, restrict the adaptability of customary law to rapidly changing social conditions. If so, it might have the effect, not of accelerating legal development, but of slowing it up. The Restatement program gathers its information on customary law by using such written materials as exist, and by assembling law panels where hypothetical cases are put to knowledgeable persons, who are asked what the governing rules are. Allott is well aware of the objections by anthropologists that law is incomprehensible outside of its social context, and hence that it cannot be fully investigated except by means of fieldwork. But he replies that he is working on an applied problem with clear time limits: and that of the practical alternatives, the Restatement is the best course available. He rejects Bohannan's argument that one cannot give a satisfactory account of the customary law unless one uses indigenous terms, and seeks to set out the general requirements of a legal terminology – most of them quite pragmatic, such as precision, convenience, and conformity with prior usage. But he also acknowledges that on occasion there can be very difficult problems of translation.

Conferences and collections of papers

Books of papers given at interdisciplinary conferences are beginning to abound. Lawyers can be found talking about social contexts, and anthropologists about legal rules. Papers on wildly different kinds of society appear in the same volume, having in common only that they have to do with the law of the family, or that the peoples they concern are found on the same continent. They are not often linked by analytical problems, but rather by geographical areas or by topic (land, family, inheritance, etc.). I usually find it dizzying to read such books of papers through, and I wonder if it is some personal incapacity, or whether they were not meant to be read through, but rather to be sampled from time to time according to interest; which seems more sensible, whatever was intended. Some of them seem to have been assembled without any thought of possible readers.

Mixed assortments of papers, like boxes of filled chocolates, are bound to contain some one does not want. It does not take much practice to distinguish the caramels from the violet creams among conference papers. When the subject discussed is 'What are the rules of law?' rather than 'What is the relationship between those rules and their social milieu?' the writer (whether anthropologist or lawyer) has moved away from the central analytic concerns of social anthropology. Yet such rules are an essential part of any thorough ethnographic description. Is all law then anthropology? Surely all law is the raw material for anthropological analysis; but descriptions of laws as such, important, interesting, and numerous as they are, are not pieces of sociological analysis.

Some articles appearing in collections of papers have been mentioned in various parts of this review of recent literature, but it may be useful to describe a few of the collections themselves, since the subjects on which conferences are held and books organized are some indications of the locus of current activity.

Two groups of papers published earlier than the past two years should be noted: Nader's *Ethnography of Law* (1965b), and Kuper and Kuper's *African Law* (1965). Both contain more papers by anthropologists than most such assemblages of legal essays, and each has an introductory essay of theoretical interest. Nader's introduction is a brief general review of the literature in the law-anthropology field. The Kupers' introduction discusses general subjects of the papers in their volume: the diversity of indigenous legal systems in African societies, the complexities of law in colonial plural societies, and the problems inherent in the attempts of the new national governments of Africa to use law to unify and shape society. The inescapability of the very complex historical dimension, and the perpetual presence of change, is the most pervasive theme in the book.

A more recent book of papers, which displays a staggering amount of specialized erudition, is Anderson's *Family Law in Asia and Africa* (1968). The book contains 14 lecture papers by members of the School of Oriental and African Studies and some guests. Their societal subjects are very diverse, and scarcely connected. All the papers deal with matters that would interest an anthropologist, but most are more legal than sociological in approach. I have already discussed Freedman's paper in this volume.

Another recent collection is Buxbaum's *Family Law and Customary Law in Asia* (1968a). Unfortunately, its essays are even more removed from any sociological orientation than those in the Anderson volume. Buxbaum's introduction, however, discusses customary law in the developing countries in terms of Weber's classifications, pointing out some of the shortcomings of Weber's types but using them with modifications. Buxbaum pleads for the organic growth of law from traditional institutions toward modernization, and speaks against the wholesale importation of inappropriate alien legislation, however 'modern.' Buxbaum also edited an issue of the *Journal of Asian and African Studies* that has now appeared in book form (Buxbaum 1967a, 1967b). A number of papers in that volume have been mentioned here; with the exception of Ottenberg's (1967), most are not particularly sociological in approach. Buxbaum introduces them as dealing with various aspects of law in 'modernizing' countries. In short, they are only tenuously linked with each other, dealing with such varied problems as the publicizing of legislation, bribery and corruption, mediation and conciliation procedures, and legally defined group membership.

Max Gluckman's *Ideas and Procedures in African Customary Law* (1969) is a really thoroughgoing editorial attempt to put out a book of legal conference papers and pull it together with a lengthy introduction that combines material from the conference discussions with material from the papers and tries to set them out in some meaningful relationship. The 78-page introduction by

Allott, Epstein, and Gluckman discusses courts, procedures, and the problems of research, as well as some conceptions used in African substantive law. Its style suffers a bit from committee production, and somewhat from having combined small pieces of such a vast number of things. However uneven, it is a worthy attempt at a difficult task that too many conference editors avoid. Half the people at the Addis Ababa meeting (where the papers were originally presented) were lawyers; the remainder were predominantly anthropologists, and there were a few persons from other disciplines. The papers are mainly descriptions of legal rules and practices rather than sociological treatments. Since it is almost impossible to make generalizations about so vast and varied a geographical unit as Africa, the introductory discussion attempts to settle on some classifications of data and to define some general problems into which the minutiae of the papers fit: the concept of legal personality in African law; the question of whether one can work out a fairly simple, comprehensive classification of modes of inheritance and succession; and the classification of rights in land, is particularly the different participants' views of Gluckman's ideas about the hierarchies of estates of administration that lie above a basic estate of production. There is also some discussion of marriage and divorce, liability and responsibility for injuries, and the indigenous African law of contract. As in all such collections, the papers are uneven in quality; but they are bound to be much more meaningful to any reader by having been presented in a general framework.

Future developments

Future law studies in anthropology are likely to place more emphasis on the development of cases and on the development of legal rules and procedural practices through *time*. This is partly because of the analytic problems that are thrust upon anthropology by a rapidly changing world. It is also partly because it is the obvious next step after the kind of ethnographic work that has already been done. The foundation from which the field is proceeding consists essentially of two elements: abstracted models of systems of social relationships (called variously social structures or institutions), and the abstracted rules and ideas that are the framework of these models. In law, as in other fields, these abstractions or generalizations are now in the process of being broken down into their social action components. Generalizations about law, and about the rules, ideas, and procedures of dispute settlement have often been abstracted from case materials in the past. These case materials as well as the kind of generalization they were used to generate are now likely to be reset in the social nexus from which they arose. Cases will be considered in greater detail, as microcosms of dynamic interaction, and also as a part of both short- and long-term processes of institutional continuity and change.

Although the dimension of time was by no means absent from the works of the six principal writers described in the introduction to this review, they were mostly occupied with generalizing about the operation of a particular institutional system at a particular moment, the period of fieldwork. In 1967, Gluckman, speaking retrospectively in the new edition of his *Judicial Process among the Barotse*, said that in it he had approached each case as an isolated incident before a court; but that he now considered that the next step must be the intensive study of processes of social control in a limited area of social life viewed over a period of time. This emphasis on detailed, temporally extended case studies also implies a focus on processes of change. We are likely to see more historical investigations of institutional change over periods of varying length. In the past, with the notable exception of Schapera (1943), anthropologists gave little attention to legislation. The preoccupations of the developing world and of the current periodical literature indicate that this is not likely to continue. Legislation will not long be ignored in a field concentrating on change and having a geographical bias toward the newly independent countries. And once legislation comes firmly within the purview of the legal anthropologists, they are likely to open the vast legal avenues to the study of political systems, instead of confining themselves to dispute settlements, rules, and ideas.

Just as attention to the dimension of time is bound to increase the number of analytic problems perceived, just so are problems likely to be opened by the current attitude toward the collection of detailed quantitative data. For example, it is important to know not only what the rules are concerning the transfer of land, but also how often it is actually transferred. Legal rules must be understood outside the dispute situation in the setting of practices in ordinary life. The studies published in the past sometimes gave 'figures on the number of cases of particular kinds that came before the courts or other dispute-resolving bodies, but why some kinds of matters are more often in dispute than others has not been gone into at all deeply; nor do we know between what sorts of people and in what sorts of situations these disputes are likely to arise. The opposite situation is equally unexplored: what kinds of matters and social situations do not produce dispute? In some social contexts the incidence of dispute may indicate the points of serious tension in the social fabric. In others deep conflict may not come out in this form, and disputes may be no more than the occasional eruption in a legal forum of ordinary orderly competition. Much more needs to be known about these questions.

As for legal concepts, some discussions in the past have focused on deciding whether to look on them as cognitive categories that shape behavior, or whether to look on them as abstract reflections of social and technological conditions. Surely legal ideas can be both or either at the same time. But there is a third component that changes the significance of the first two: the way in which allusions to these legal ideas and legal norms are used and manipulated in particular social situations to legitimate or discredit behavior, to affect social relationships, and to communicate all manner of messages. Legal ideas, principles, and rules together are used in many ways in social life. They cannot be thought of simply as unambiguously defining prescribed and proscribed behavior. An important use of these ideas, well recognized by lawyers in their daily work but mostly ignored by anthropologists, is the operation of legal concepts as a manipulable, value-laden language and conceptual framework within which behavior may be described or classified for any number of instrumental purposes. Not only case studies and institutional studies extended in time, but case studies and historical studies expanded in *conception* will increase our knowledge of the relationship between the institutional frameworks, the frameworks of discussion, argument, and conception, and the level of action.

To summarize: the classical task of legal anthropology has been to understand the relationship between law and society. The general goal in the past has been to identify the kinds of societies in which certain legal institutions appear, and to examine the kinds of legal procedures, norms, principles, rules and concepts that are found under given social conditions. These interests continue. But a shift that is now under way in some quarters is partly a shift in method, partly a shift in problem. There is a new emphasis on sequences of events – on legal transactions, disputes, and rules seen in the dimension of time. Case studies of this kind bring the minutiae of social interaction into focus and thereby reveal certain general processes in detail, whereas historical studies illustrate large-scale continuities and changes. In this context legislation appears as one of a number of forms of structural innovation. In the future, law and legal institutions are likely to be analyzed simultaneously from a long-term historical perspective, and from the perspective of individual-centered, short-term, choice-making, instrumental action and interaction. Cases already epitomize this duality and its concomitant unity. When both of these levels are given further attention, and when quantitative data are assembled, anthropologists may hope to understand more about the way in which legal institutions, rules, and ideas function as part of the framework within which ongoing social life is carried on, and how the processes of social life affect that very framework.

Bibliography

Atkan, R. (1966), 'Problems of land reform in Turkey,' *Middle East J.*, 20 (3):317–34.

Alisjabbana, S. Takdir (1968), 'Customary law and modernisation in Indonesia,' in Buxbaum (1968a).

Alliot, M. (1967), 'Problems of the unification of African Laws' (in French; English summary), *J. Afr. Law*, 11 (2):86–98.

Allott, A. N. (1966), 'The codification of the law of civil wrongs in commonlaw African countries' (German summary), *Sociologus*, n.f., 16 (2):101–22.

Allott, A. N. (1967a), 'Law in the new Africa,' *Afr. Aff.*, 66 (262):55–63.

Allott, A. N. (1967b), 'Law and social anthropology, with special reference to African laws' (German summary), *Sociologus*, n.f., 17(1):1–19.

Anderson, J. (1968), *Family Law in Asia and Africa*, London, Allen & Unwin.

Apthorpe, R. O. (1964), 'Opium of the state – some remarks on the law and society in Nigeria,' *Nigerian J. Econ. and Soc. Stud.*, 6:139–53.

Apthorpe, R. O. (1966), 'A survey of land settlement schemes and rural development in East Africa', *E. Afr. Inst. Soc. Res. Conf.*, January, E, 786–810.

Aubert, V. (1963), 'Researches in the sociology of law,' *Am. Behav. Scientist*, 18:16–20.

Bailey, F. G. (1960), *Tribe, Caste, and Nation*, Manchester University Press.

Balandier, G. (1970), *Political Anthropology* (tr., A. M. Sheridan Smith, 1967), New York, Vintage Books, Random House.

Banton, M. P. (1964), *The Policeman in the Community*, London, Tavistock.

Barkun, M. (1968), *Law without Sanctions*, New Haven and London, Yale University Press.

Barnes, J. A. (1961), 'Law as politically active: an anthropological view,' in G. Sawer (ed.), *Studies in the Sociology of Law*, Canberra, Australian National University.

Barnes, J. A. (1962), 'African models in the New Guinea highlands,' *Man*, 62:5–9.

Barnes, J. A. (1969), 'The politics of law,' in M. Douglas and P. Kaberry (eds), *Man in Africa*, London, Tavistock.

Barth, F. (1966), *Models of Social Organization*, Royal Anthropological Institute, London, Occasional Paper no. 23.

Barton, R. F. (1919), *Ifugao Law*, Berkeley, University of California Press.

Beattie, J. (1957), 'Informal judicial activity in Bunyoro,' *J. Afr. Admin.*, 9:188–96.

Beidelman, T. O. (1961), 'Kaguru justice and the concept of legal fictions,' *J. Afr. Law*, 5 (1):5–20.

Beidelman, T. O. (1966–7), 'Intertribal tensions in some local government courts in colonial Tanganyika,' *J. Afr. Law*, 10 (2):118–30; 11 (1):27–45.

Bibliography of African Law, published annually in the spring number of *Journal of African Law*, official organ of the International African Law Association, London, Butterworth.

Bienen, H. (1967), *Tanzania, Party Transformation and Economic Development*, Princeton University Press.

Blok, A. (1966), 'Land reform in a west Sicilian latifondo village: the persistence of a feudal structure,' *Anthropol. Quart.*, 39 (1):1–16.

Bohannan, P. J. (1957), *Justice and Judgment among the Tiv*, London, Oxford University Press for International African Institute.

Bohannan, P. J. (1963), *Social Anthropology*, New York, Holt, Rinehart & Winston.

Bohannan, P. J. (1965), 'The differing realms of the law,' in Nader (1965b).

Bohannan, P. J. (ed.) (1967), *Law and Warfare: Studies in the Anthropology of Conflict*, New York, Natural History Press.

Brown, D. (1966), 'The award of compensation in criminal cases in East Africa,' *J. Afr. Law*, 10 (1):33–9.

Butt, A. (1965–6), 'The shaman's legal role among the Akawaio,' *Rev. do Mus. Paulista*, n.s., 16:151–86.

Buxbaum, D.C. (1967a), 'Introduction to a special issue on traditional and modern legal institutions in Asia and Africa,' *J. Asian and Afr. Stud.*, 2 (1–2):1–8.

Buxbaum, D.C. (ed.) (1967b), *Traditional and Modern Legal Institutions in Asia and Africa*, The Hague, Martinus Nijhoff.

Buxbaum, D.C. (ed.) (1968a), *Family Law and Customary Law in Asia*, The Hague, Martinus Nijhoff.

Buxbaum, D. C. (ed.) (1968b), 'Chinese family law in a common-law setting: a note on the institutional environment and the substantive family law of the Chinese in Singapore and Malaysia,' in Buxbaum (1968a).

Caplan, L. (1967), 'Some political consequences of state land policy in East Nepal,' *Man*, 1 (2):185–90.

Cardozo, B. N. (1963), *The Growth of the Law* (12th printing), New Haven, Yale University Press (1st ed. 1924).

Carlston, K. S. (1968), *Social Theory and African Tribal Organization: the Development of Socio-legal Theory*, Urbana and London, University of Illinois Press.

Chambliss, W. J. and Seidman, R. (1971), *Law, Order and Power,* Reading, Massachusetts, Addison-Wesley.

Clifford-Vaughan, M. and Scotford-Norton, M. (1967), 'Legal norms and social order: Petrazycki, Pareto, Durkheim,' *Brit. J. Sociol.*, 18 (3):269–77.

Cochrane, G. (1971), *Development Anthropology*, New York, Oxford University Press.

Cohen, Y. A. (1964), *The Transition from Childhood to Adolescence*, Chicago, Aldine Press.

Colson, E. (1951), 'The Plateau Tonga of Northern Rhodesia,' in E. Colson and M. Gluckman (eds), *Seven Tribes of British Central Africa*, Manchester University Press.

Colson, E. (1966), 'Land law and land holdings among the Valley Tonga of Zambia,' *Southwest. J. Anthropol.*, 22 (1):1–8.

Cory, H. (1953), *Sukuma Law and Custom*, London, Oxford University Press for International African Institute.

Derrett, J. D. M. (ed.) (1965), *Studies in the Law of Succession in Nigeria*, London, Oxford University Press.

Derrett, J. D. M. (1968a), 'A juridical fabrication of early British India: the Mahanirvana-tantra,' *Z. vergl. Rechtswiss.*, 69 (2):138–81.

Derrett, J. D. M. (1968b), 'Hindu: a definition wanted for the purpose of applying a personal law,' Z. vergl. Rechtswiss., 70 (1):110–28.

Diamond, A. S. (1935), Primitive Law, London, Watts.

Diamond, A. S. (1951), The Evolution of Law and Order, London, Watts.

Diamond, A. S. (1965), The Comparative Study of Primitive Law, London, Athlone Press.

Djamour, J. (1966), The Muslim Matrimonial Court in Singapore, London School of Economics Monographs on Social Anthropology, no. 31.

Driberg, J. H. (1923), The Lango, London, Unwin.

Dror, Y. (1968), 'Law and social change,' in R. J. Simon (ed.), The Sociology of Law, San Francisco, Chandler.

Dundas, C. (1924; 1968), Kilimanjaro and its People (1st ed., 1924), London, Cass.

Durkheim, E. (1912; 1961), The Elementary Forms of the Religious Life, trans. Joseph Ward Swain, London, 1915. Republished 1961, New York, Collier.

Durkheim, E. (1933), The Division of Labor in Society (tr., G. Simpson), Chicago, Free Press (1st ed. as De la division du travail social, Paris, Alcan, 1893; 2nd ed., N.Y., Macmillan, 1960).

Easton, D. (1959), 'Political anthropology,' in B. Siegel (ed.), Biennial Review of Anthropology, Stanford University Press.

Eggan, F. (1965), 'Some reflections on comparative method in anthropology,' in M. E. Spiro (ed.), Context and Meaning in Cultural Anthropology, New York, Free Press.

Elias, T. O. (1956), The Nature of African Customary Law, Manchester University Press.

Epstein, A. L. (1953), The Administration of Justice and the Urban African, London, HMSO.

Epstein, A. L. (1954), Judicial Techniques and the Judicial Process: a Study in African Customary Law, Manchester University Press.

Epstein, A. L. (1967), 'The case method in the field of law,' in A. L. Epstein (ed.), The Craft of Social Anthropology, London, Tavistock.

Etzioni, A. (1961), Complex Organisations, New York, Free Press.

Evans-Pritchard, E. E. (1940), The Nuer, Oxford, Clarendon Press.

Fallers, L. A. (1960), 'Homicide and suicide in Busoga,' in P. J. Bohannan (ed.), African Homicide and Suicide, Princeton University Press.

Fallers, L. A. (1962), 'Customary law and the new African states,' Law and Contemporary Problems, 27 (4):605–31.

Fallers, L. A. (1969), Law without Precedent, University of Chicago Press.

Feder, E. (1967), 'Land reform: a twentieth-century world issue,' Amer. latina, 10 (1):96–135.

Firth, R. (1964), Essays on Social Organization and Values, London, Athlone Press.

Fortes, M. (1945), The Dynamics of Clanship among the Tallensi, London, Oxford University Press for International African Institute.

Fortes, M. (1949), The Web of Kinship among the Tallensi, London, Oxford University Press for International African Institute.

Fortes, M. (1959), 'Descent, filiation and affinity,' Man, 59 (309):193–7.

Freedman, M. (1968), 'Chinese family law in Singapore: the rout of custom,' in J. N. D. Anderson (ed.), Family Law in Asia and Africa, London, Allen & Unwin.

Friedman, L. and Macaulay, S. (eds) (1969), Law and the Behavioral Sciences, New York, Bobbs-Merrill.

Galanter, M. (1967), 'Group membership and group preferences in India,' in Buxbaum (1967b).

Garbett, G. K. (1970), 'The analysis of social situations,' Man, 5 (2):214–27.

Gearing, F. (1967), 'Sovereignties and jural communities in political evolution,' Proc. Am. Ethnol. Soc., 111–19.

Gibbs, J. L. (1962), 'Poro values and courtroom procedures in a Kpelle chiefdom,' Southwest. J. Anthropol., 18:341–9.

Gibbs, J. L. (1963), 'The Kpelle moot: a therapeutic model for the informal settlement of disputes,' *Africa* 33:1–11.

Gluckman, M. (1955a), *The Judicial Process among the Barotse of Northern Rhodesia* (2nd ed., 1967), Manchester University Press.

Gluckman, M. (1955b), *Custom and Conflict in Africa*, Oxford, Blackwell.

Gluckman, M. (1965a), 'Reasonableness and responsibility in the law of segmentary societies,' in H. and L. Kuper (eds) (1965).

Gluckman, M. (1965b), *The Ideas in Barotse Jurisprudence*, New Haven, Yale University Press.

Gluckman, M. (1965c), *Politics, Law and Ritual in Tribal Society*, Chicago, Aldine Press.

Gluckman, M. (1967), 'Introduction' in A. L. Epstein (ed.), *The Craft of Social Anthropology*, London, Tavistock.

Gluckman, M. (1968), 'The utility of the equilibrium model in the study of social change,' *Am. Anthropol.*, 70:219–37.

Gluckman, M. (ed.) (1969), *Ideas and Procedures in African Customary Law*, London, Oxford University Press for International African Institute.

Goldschmidt, W. (1967), *Sebei Law*, Berkeley and Los Angeles, University of California Press.

Goody, J. (1962), *Death, Property, and the Ancestors*, Stanford University Press.

Gulliver, P. H. (1955), *The Family Herds*, London, Routledge & Kegan Paul.

Gulliver, P. H. (1958), *Land Tenure and Social Change among the Nyakyusa*, Kampala, East African Institute of Social Research.

Gulliver, P. H. (1963), *Social Control in an African Society*, London, Routledge & Kegan Paul.

Gulliver, P. H. (1969), 'Dispute settlement without courts: the Ndendeuli of southern Tanzania,' in L. Nader (ed.), *Law in Culture and Society*, Chicago, Aldine Press.

Gutmann, B. (1926), *Das Recht der Dschagga*, Munich, C. H. Beck (English tr., A. M. Nagler, *Human Relations Area Files*, New Haven, Yale University Press).

Hailey, Lord (1938), *An African Survey*, London, Oxford University Press.

Harding, A. (1966), *A Social History of English Law*, Baltimore, Penguin Books.

Harris, R. (1965a), *The Political Organization of the Mbembe, Nigeria*, London, Ministry of Overseas Development, HMSO.

Harris, R. (1965b), 'Intestate succession among the Mbembe of southeastern Nigeria,' in Derrett (1965).

Hart, H. L. A. (1961), *The Concept of Law*, Oxford, Clarendon Press.

Hartland, S. (1924), *Primitive Law*, London, Methuen.

Hayley, T. T. (1947), *The Anatomy of Lango Religion and Groups*, Cambridge University Press.

Hoebel, E. A. (1954), *The Law of Primitive Man*, Cambridge, Mass., Harvard University Press.

Hoebel, E. A. (1968), 'The character of Keresan pueblo law,' *Proc. Am. Philos. Soc.*, 112 (3).

Hohfeld, W. N. (1923), *Fundamental Legal Conceptions as Applied in Judicial Reasoning and Other Essays*, W. W. Cook (ed.), New Haven, Yale University Press.

Hohfeld, W. N. (1919; 1964), *Fundamental Legal Conceptions*, New Haven, Yale University Press (1st printing 1919).

Holmes, O. W. (1881), *The Common Law*, Boston, Little, Brown.

Howell, P. P. (1954), *A Manual of Nuer Law*, London, Oxford University Press for International African Institute.

Johnston, H. H. (1886), *The Kilimanjaro Expedition*, London. Kegan Paul, Trench.

Johnston, P. H. (1953), 'Chagga constitutional development,' *J. Afr. Admin.* 5 (3):134–40.

Kinyon, S. V. (1971), *Law Study and Law Examinations in a Nutshell*, St Paul, West Publishing Co.

Kopytoff, I. (1964), 'Family and lineage among the Suku of the Congo,' in R. B. Gray and P. H. Gulliver (eds), *The Family Estate in Africa*, London, Routledge & Kegan Paul.

Krader, L. (ed.) (1967), *Anthropology and Early Law: Selected from the Writings of Paul Vinogradoff, Frederic W. Maitland, Frederick Pollock, Maxim Kovalevsky, Rudolf Huebner, Frederic Seebohm*, New York and London, Basic Books.

Kuper, H. (1961), *An African Aristocracy*, London, Oxford University Press.

Kuper, H. and Kuper, L. (eds) (1965), *African Law: Adaptation and Development*, Berkeley and Los Angeles, University of California Press.

La Fontaine, J. (1960), 'Homicide and suicide among the Gisu,' in P. J. Bohannan (ed.), *African Homicide and Suicide*, Princeton University Press.

Langness, L. L. (1964), 'Some problems in the conceptualization of highlands social structures,' in J. B. Watson (ed.), special issue, *Am. Anthropol.*, 66 (4):2:162–82.

Lawrence, J. C. D. (1957), *The Iteso*, London, Oxford University Press.

Leach, E. R. (1954), *Political Systems of Highland Burma*, London, Bell.

Leach, E. R. (1961), *Rethinking Anthropology*, London, Athlone Press.

Leach, E. R. (1962), 'On certain unconsidered aspects of double descent systems,' *Man*, 62:130–4.

Leakey, L. S. B. (1952), *Mau Mau and the Kikuyu*, London, Methuen.

Lévi-Strauss, C. (1955), *Tristes Tropiques*, Paris, Plon (English tr., J. Russell, New York, Atheneum, 1967).

Lévi-Strauss, C. (1958; 1963), *Structural Anthropology*, trans. C. Jacobsen and Brooke G. Schoepf. Reprinted 1963, New York, Basic Books.

Lewis, I. M. (1965), 'Problems in the comparative study of unilineal descent,' in *The Relevance of Models for Social Anthropology*, A.S.A. Monographs no. I, M. Banton (ed.), London, Tavistock.

Liebenow, J. G. (1958), 'Tribalism, traditionalism, and modernism in Chagga local government,' *J. Afr. Admin.*, 10 (2): 71–82.

Liebesny, H. J. (1967), 'Stability and change in Islamic law,' *Middle East J.*, 21 (1): 16–34.

Lindblom, C. E. (1959), 'The science of muddling through,' *Public Admin. Rev.*, 19.

Litwak, E. and Meyer, H. J. (1966), 'A balance theory of coordination between bureaucratic organizations and community primary groups,' *Admin. Sci. Quart.*, 31; reprinted in Friedman and Macaulay (1969).

Llewellyn, K. N. and Hoebel, E. A. (1941), *The Cheyenne Way*, Norman, University of Oklahoma Press.

Lloyd, D. (1964), *The Idea of Law*, Baltimore, Penguin Books.

Lloyd, D. (ed.) (1965), *Introduction to Jurisprudence*, London, Stevens.

Lloyd, P. C. (1962), *Yoruba Land Law*, London, Oxford University Press for Nigerian Institute of Social and Economic Research.

Lloyd, P. C. (1965), 'Yoruba inheritance and succession,' in Derrett (1965).

Lowie, R. H. (1920), *Primitive Society*, New York, Boni & Liveright.

Lowie, R. H. (1927), 'Anthropology and law,' in W. F. Ogburn and A. Goldenweiser (eds), *The Social Sciences*, Cambridge University Press.

Lupton, T. and Cunnison, S. (1964), 'Workshop behaviour,' in M. Gluckman (ed.), *Closed Systems and Open Minds*, Chicago, Aldine Press.

Macaulay, S. (1963), 'Non-contractual relations in business: a preliminary study,' *Am. Sociol. R.*, 55; reprinted in Friedman and Macaulay (1969).

Maine, H. S. (1861), *Ancient Law*, London, Murray.

Mair, L. P. (1934), *An African People in the Twentieth Century*, London, G. Routledge.

Malinowski, B. (1926), *Crime and Custom in Savage Society*, London, Kegan Paul.

Malinowski, B. (1935), *Coral Gardens and their Magic*, London, Allen & Unwin.

Mangin, E. (1921), *Les Mossi*, Paris, Augustin Challamel (tr., in *Human Relations Area Files*, New Haven, Yale University Press).

Masters, R. D. (1964), 'World politics as a primitive political system,' *World Politics*, 16:595–619.

Mayer, A. C. (1966), 'The significance of quasi-groups in the study of complex societies,' in M. Banton (ed.), *The Social Anthropology of Complex Societies*, London, Tavistock.

Meek, C. K. (1937), *Law and Authority in a Nigerian Tribe*, London, Oxford University Press.

Meggitt, M. (1965), *The Lineage System of the Mae Enga of New Guinea*, Edinburgh, Oliver & Boyd.

Middleton, J. and Tait, D. (eds) (1958), *Tribes without Rulers*, London, Routledge & Kegan Paul.

Mitchell, J. C. (1964), Foreword to J. van Velsen, *The Politics of Kinship*, Manchester University Press.

Mitchell, J. C. (*et al.* 1969), *Social Networks in Urban Situations*, Manchester University Press.

Moore, D. C. (1976), *The Politics of Deference*, Hassocks, Harvester Press.

Moore, S. F. (1958), *Power and Property in Inca Peru*, New York, Columbia University Press.

Moore, S. F. (1965), 'Comment on Cohen,' *Am. Anthropol.*, 67:748–51.

Moore, S. F. (1969), 'Law and anthropology,' in B. J. Siegel (ed.), *Biennial Review of Anthropology*, Stanford University Press.

Moore, S. F. (1970), 'Politics, procedures and norms in changing Chagga law,' *Africa*, 40 (4):321–44.

Morgan, L. H. (1877), *Ancient Society*, republished New York, Meridian Books, 1963.

Murdock, G. P. (1949), *Social Structure*, New York, Macmillan.

Murphy, R. F. (1971), *The Dialectics of Social Life*, New York, Basic Books.

Nadel, S. F. (1947), *The Nuba*, London, Oxford University Press.

Nadel, S. F. (1957), *The Theory of Social Structure*, London, Cohen & West.

Nader, L. (1965a), 'Choices in legal procedure: Shia Moslem and Mexican Zapotec,' *Am. Anthropol.*, 67 (2):394–9.

Nader, L. (ed.) (1965b), *The Ethnography of Law*, supplement to *Am. Anthropol.*, 67 (2):3–32.

Nader, L. (ed.) (1969), *Law in Culture and Society*, Chicago, Aldine Press.

Nader, L., Koch, K. F. and Cox, B. (1966), 'The ethnography of law: a bibliographical survey,' *Current Anthropol.*, June:267–94.

Needham, R. (1963), Introduction to E. Durkheim and M. Mauss, *Primitive Classification*, University of Chicago Press.

Needham, R. (1975), 'Polythetic classification: convergence and consequence, *Man*, 10 (3):349–69.

Ottenberg, S. (1965), 'Inheritance and succession in Afikpo,' in Derrett (1965).

Ottenberg, S. (1967), 'Local government and the law in southern Nigeria,' *J. Asian and Afr. Stud.*, 2 (1–2):26–43.

Pacques, V. (1954), *Les Bambara*, Paris, Presses Universitaires de France (tr., *Human Relations Area Files*, New Haven, Yale University Press).

Paine, R. (1969), 'In search of friendship: an exploratory analysis in "middle class" culture,' *Man*, 4 (4):505–24.

Paine, R. (1974), *Second Thoughts about Barth's Models*, London, Royal Anthropological Institute, Occasional Paper no. 32.

Paton, G. W. (1951), *Jurisprudence*, London, Oxford University Press.

Peck, C. J. (1967), 'Nationalism, "race," and developments in the Philippine law of citizenship,' in Buxbaum (1967b).

Penwill, D. J. (1951), *Kamba Customary Law*, London, Macmillan.

Peristiany, J. G. (1939), *The Social Institutions of the Kipsigis*, London, G. Routledge.

Peters, E. L. (1963), 'No time for the supernatural', a review of P. Bohannan's *Social Anthropology*, *New Society*, 19 December.

Peters, E. L. (1967), 'Some structural aspects of the feud among the camel-herding Bedouin of Cyrenaica,' *Africa*, 37 (2):261–82.

Pospisil, L. (1958), *Kapauku Papuans and their Law*, New Haven, Yale University Press.

Pospisil, L. (1963), *Kapauku Papuan Economy*, New Haven, Yale University Publications in Anthropology, no. 67.

Pospisil, L. (1967), 'Legal levels and multiplicity of legal systems in human societies,' *J. Conflict Resolution*, 11 (1):2–26.

Pospisil, L. (1971), *Anthropology of Law*, New York, Harper & Row.

Pound, R. (1921; 1963), *The Spirit of the Common Law*, Boston, Beacon Press (reprinted 1963).

Pound, R. (1942) *Social Control through Law*, New Haven, Yale University Press.

Pound, R. (1965), 'Contemporary juristic theory,' in D. Lloyd (ed.), *Introduction to Jurisprudence*, London, Stevens.

Radcliffe-Brown, A. R. (1952), *Structure and Function in Primitive Society*, London, Cohen & West.

Rattray, R. S. (1929), *Ashanti Law and Constitution*, Oxford, Clarendon Press.

Raum, O. F. (1965), 'German East Africa: changes in African life under German administration 1892–1914,' in V. Harlow and E. M. Chilver (eds), *History of East Africa*, Oxford, Clarendon Press.

Rheinstein, M. (1954), Introduction to M. Weber, *Law in Economy and Society*, New York, Simon & Schuster.

Roscoe, J. (1911), *The Baganda*, London, Macmillan.

Rosenberg, G. (1966), 'Maori land tenure and land use: a planner's point of view,' *J. Polynes. Soc*, 75 (2):210–22.

Rudolph, L. I. and Rudolph, S. H. (1965), 'Barristers and Brahmans in India: legal cultures and social change,' *Comp. Stud. Soc. Hist.*, 8 (1):24–49.

Ruillière, G. (1966), 'Land reform: the great challenge of the XXth century,' *Civilisations*, 16 (4):442–59.

Sahlins, M. (1961), 'The segmentary lineage: an organization for predatory expansion,' *Am. Anthropol.*, 63 (2):322–45.

Sahlins, M. (1965), 'On the ideology and composition of descent groups,' *Man*, 65:104–7.

Schapera, I. (1938), *A Handbook of Tswana Law and Custom*, London, Oxford University Press for International African Institute.

Schapera, I. (1943), *Tribal Legislation among the Tswana of the Bechuanaland Protectorate*, London, London School of Economics Monographs in Social Anthropology no. 9. Revised and reprinted 1970 as *Tribal Innovators*.

Schapera, I. (1956), *Government and Politics in Tribal Societies*, London, Watts (2nd ed., 1967, New York, Schocken Books).

Schapera, I. (1957), 'Malinowski's theories of law,' in R. Firth (ed.), *Man and Culture*, London, Routledge & Kegan Paul.

Schapera, I. (1970), *Tribal Innovators*, London, Athlone Press (rev. 1943 ed.).

Scheffler, H. (1965), *Choiseul Island Social Structure*, Berkeley, University of California Press.

Schiller, A. A. (1965), 'Law,' in R. A. Lystad (ed.), *The African World*, London, Pall Mall Press.

Schubert, G. (1964), *Judicial Behavior: a Reader in Theory and Research*, Chicago, Rand-McNally.

Schwartz, R. D. and Miller, J. C. (1964), 'Legal evolution and societal complexity,' *Am. J. Sociol.*, 70:159–69.

Seavey, W. A. (1942; 1963), 'Principles of torts,' *Harvard Law Rev.*, 1942; reprinted in R. D. Benson (ed.), *Landmarks of Law*, Boston, Beacon Press, 1963.

Selznick, P. (1959), 'The sociology of law,' in R. K. Merton and L. S. Cottrell (eds), *Sociology Today*, New York, Basic Books.

Shack, W. A. (1967), 'On Gurage social structure and African political theory,' *J. Ethiop. Stud.*, 5 (2):89–101.

Shepardson, M. and Hammond, B. (1966), 'Navajo inheritance patterns: random or regular?,' *Ethnology*, 5 (1):87–96.

Shiga, A. (1967), 'Some remarks on the judicial system in China: historical development and characteristics,' *J. Asian and Afr. Stud.*, 2 (1–2):44–53.

Simpson, R. (1967), 'New land law in Malawi,' *J. Admin. Overseas*, 6 (4):221–8.

Skolnick, J. H. (1965), 'The sociology of law in America: overview and trends,' *Law and Society* (supplement to *Social Problems*):4–39.

Smith, E. W. and Dale, A. M. (1920), *The Ila-speaking Peoples of Northern Rhodesia*, London, Macmillan.

Smith, M. G. (1956), 'On segmentary lineage systems,' *J. Royal Anthropol. Inst.*, 86 (2):39–80.

Smith, M. G. (1965a), 'Hausa inheritance and succession,' in Derrett (1965).

Smith, M. G. (1965b), 'The sociological framework of law,' in H. and L. Kuper (1965).

Smith, M. G. (1966), 'A structural approach to comparative politics,' in D. Easton (ed.), *Varieties of Political Theory*, Englewood Cliffs, Prentice-Hall.

Smith, M. G. (1974), *Corporations and Society*, London, Duckworth.

Southwold, M. (1965), 'The Ganda of Uganda,' in J. L. Gibbs (ed.), *Peoples of Africa*, New York, Holt, Rinehart & Winston.

Stahl, K. (1964), *History of the Chagga People of Kilimanjaro*, The Hague, Mouton.

Tanner, R. E. S. (1966), 'The selective use of legal systems in East Africa,' *E. Afr. Inst. Soc. Res. Conf.*, January, E, 966–77.

Thambyahpillai, G. (1966), 'The right to private property and problems of land reform,' *Int. Soc. Sci. J.*, 18 (1):69–80.

Turner, V. W. (1957), *Schism and Continuity in an African Society*, Manchester University Press.

Turner, V. W. (1967), 'Aspects of Saora ritual and shamanism: an approach to the data of ritual,' in A. L. Epstein (ed.), *The Craft of Social Anthropology*, London, Tavistock.

Turner, V. W. (1969), *The Ritual Process: Structure and Anti-structure*, Chicago, Aldine Press.

Turner, V. W. (1975), 'Symbolic studies,' in B. J. Siegel (ed.), *Biennial Review of Anthropology*, Stanford University Press.

van Velsen, J. (1967), 'The extended-case method and situational analysis,' in A. L. Epstein (ed.), *The Craft of Social Anthropology*, London, Tavistock.

van Velsen, J. (1969), 'Procedural informality, reconciliation, and false comparisons,' in M. Gluckman (ed.) (1969).

Vinogradoff, P. (1925), *Custom and Right*, Oslo, Instituttet für Sammenlignende Kultursforskining; ch. 2 quoted in L. Krader (ed.), *Anthropology and Early Law*, New York, Basic Books, 1966.

Weber, M. (1904–5), *The Protestant Ethic and the Spirit of Capitalism*, tr., T. Parsons and reprinted New York, Scribner, 1958.

Weber, M. (1922; 1964), *The Theory of Social and Economic Organization*, tr., A. M. Henderson and T. Parsons, London, Oxford University Press, 1947; reprinted London, Collier-Macmillan, 1964.

Weber, M. (1925; 1954), *On Law in Economy and Society*, tr., E. Shils and M. Rheinstein, New York, Simon & Schuster, 1954.

Wilson, M. (1951), *Good Company*, London, Oxford University Press for International African Institute.

Wolfe, A. (1959), 'The dynamics of the Ngombe segmentary system,' in W. R. Bascom and M. J. Herskovits (eds), *Continuity and Change in African Cultures*, University of Chicago Press.

Index

267